Social Forces in the Middle East

Papers Presented at a Conference Sponsored by the Committee on

the Near and Middle East of the Social Science Research Council

Social Forces in the Middle East

EDITED BY

Sydney Nettleton Fisher

342162

GREENWOOD PRESS, PUBLISHERS
NEW YORK   1968

The Library of Congress cataloged this book as follows:

Fisher, Sydney Nettleton, 1906–   *ed.*
    Social forces in the Middle East. ₁Papers presented at a
conference sponsored by the Committee on the Near and
Middle East of the Social Science Research Council₁ New
York, Greenwood Press, 1968 ₁ᶜ1955₁

    xvi, 282 p.   maps (part fold.)   24 cm.

    Bibliography: p. 263–274.

    1. Near East—Soc. condit.   ɪ. Social Science Research Council.
Committee on the Near and Middle East. ɪɪ. Title.

HN660.8.A8F5   1968   309.1′56   68–23289

Library of Congress   ₁3₁

Reprinted with the permission of the Cornell University
Press

Reprinted by Greenwood Press, Inc.

First Greenwood reprinting   1968
Second Greenwood reprinting   1977

Library of Congress catalog card number 68-23289

ISBN 0-8371-0074-7

Printed in the United States of America

Foreword

IT WAS my privilege to attend the meetings and to participate in the discussion of the papers presented at the conference on "The Near East: Social Dynamics and the Cultural Setting," held at Princeton, New Jersey, on October 24–25, 1952, and sponsored by the Committee on the Near and Middle East of the Social Science Research Council. It was a conference for which each paper was expressly prepared with the stated understanding that no paper was to be used for the purposes of quotation or reference without permission of the author.

As the conference progressed, however, the feeling began to grow that the papers should not perish with the end of the conference but should be published, if possible, under one cover. As a result of this general urging, the Committee and each of the authors agreed upon publication. Upon the recommendation of the Committee, the Social Science Research Council invited me to undertake the task of gathering the papers, editing them to my satisfaction as well as to that of each author, finding a publisher, and seeing the book through the press.

As a first step, it was suggested that each author, with publication in mind, should revise his paper in the light of the discussions within the conference and bring his topic up to date. Each of the contributions has gone through an editorial process, with the author agreeing to or rejecting the suggested changes in his paper. Thus, each essay, as it stands in this volume, is the responsibility of the individual author. No thought of changing the style or the content of the chapters was entertained. George G. Cameron, who moderated each meeting of the conference as the chairman of the Committee, was persuaded to write an Introduction.

After the contributions had been assembled and arranged, it appeared advantageous to have added to the volume a final chapter which might refocus the attention and thoughts of the reader upon the whole topic. There was no thought or wish that this contribution would be in any way a summary or a conclusion for the book. Professor T. Cuyler Young, Chairman of the Department of Oriental Languages and Literatures of Princeton University, was invited to write such a chapter. This choice seemed especially fitting as Professor Young, in addition to being very well qualified for such an assignment, had been prevented through illness from presenting a paper at the conference.

One of the difficult tasks in the work of editing has been keeping track of the authors in their wanderings. Students concerned with Middle Eastern affairs have always turned up in faraway places, but these contributors have been the most *"peripetetic"* scholars of all. In pursuing their studies they have used addresses from one end of the Middle East to the other.

Those who attended the conference or who have had access to the papers will observe that most of the papers have been shortened. This was done, in some instances, to accentuate the points made by the individual authors or to eliminate general discussions of their respective disciplines. Furthermore, a new title was chosen for the book because it was believed that "Dynamics" is a word that has several technical connotations, whereas "Forces" would be more readily accepted by all.

It will be noted that some writers have referred to the area as the Near East and others as the Middle East. Since these terms have obviously been used synonymously, each author was allowed to choose the more familiar term, but not to use the two interchangeably. Where the words, "West" and "Western," "East" and "Eastern," and "Oriental," refer to culture and not necessarily to geography, they have been capitalized. An attempt has been made to standardize spelling and the transliteration into English of names, places, and words of the area. A standard transliteration, however, has not necessarily been used in such names, places, and words as have come, through frequent usage over the years, to have a commonly accepted Westernized form.

Two of the essays, with the concurrence of the Committee, are already in print: Chapter I, by E. A. Speiser, "Cultural Factors in Social Dynamics in the Near East," in *The Middle East Journal*, VII (Spring, 1953); and Chapter IX, by Majid Khadduri, as "The Role of the Military in Middle East Politics," in *The American Political Science Review*, XLVII (June, 1953). Part of another essay, Chapter VIII, by Peter G. Franck, appeared, in a somewhat altered and abbreviated form, under the title, "Economic Planners in Afghanistan," in *Economic Development and Cultural Change*, I (February, 1953). The articles are included here with some changes through the courtesy of the respective publications.

The bibliography has been added to be helpful to any reader who is not familiar with the literature about the Middle East in general or in any of the several disciplines presented in this study. The bibliography is selective only and in no way should it be considered as indicating source material upon which the authors based their contributions. It is a suggestion for the reader who wishes to delve more widely into some of the topics introduced in this volume. The bibliography is the result of the joint efforts of the authors and editor; however, since the authors did not have the opportunity of reviewing the bibliography after its composition, they are relieved of any responsibility for it.

Maps I and II were prepared for this volume by Allen Hellman, Department of Geography, University of Michigan, under the supervision of Douglas D. Crary. Map III has been presented by

Peter G. Franck, under whose direction it was prepared at Haverford College. Map IV has been supplied through the courtesy of *The Middle East Journal*.

I wish to acknowledge the splendid co-operation of each of the contributors in revising and rereading manuscript several times, often on occasions when time was well occupied with numerous other affairs. The several authors will know the assistance each has given and, without my mentioning every one individually, they are herewith thanked for every favor rendered. I am grateful to Miss Molly Flynn of the United Nations Secretariat for securing the information given in the table in Chapter XIV. Above all, I am greatly indebted to George G. Cameron, without whose encouragement and confidence this volume would never have materialized.

SYDNEY NETTLETON FISHER

The Ohio State University
April, 1955

Contents

[ix]

[x]

Maps

GEORGE G. CAMERON

Introduction

THE Near or Middle East is nearer to us than we think. It witnessed the birth of civilization, served as the cradle of great religions, became the agelong nurse of literature, science, and philosophy, and is now the crossroads of conflicting political regimes. Today it is actively experimenting with Western ideas and techniques, striving to find a golden mean in its borrowing which will guarantee strength for survival and yet preserve from useless destruction old and cherished ways of life and thought. Year by year it becomes more intimately a part of Western existence, as the West is shaped by and helps to shape its being. Yet sadly one must confess that the West is insufficiently informed about the Near East and has little comprehension of its peoples, policies, and problems. One great failing is the very great inadequacy in the number of properly qualified men and women competent to provide instruction and to serve as technicians in the field.

As one means of stimulating research and of drawing attention to the increasing need for reliable information about the peoples and institutions of the Near East, the Committee on the Near and Middle East of the Social Science Research Council sponsored a conference at Princeton University on October 24–

25, 1952.[1] In attendance were representatives from universities, research organizations, national foundations, business firms, and governmental agencies. Throughout the conference the Committee sought to emphasize the forces of change presently at work, together with the strong traditional elements current in the area. At the same time the conferees were urged to examine, not what the Western world thinks about the peoples and institutions of the Near East, but the attitudes, convictions, and inclinations of the peoples themselves. Westerners all too frequently make assumptions regarding these attitudes and reactions which are completely unjustified. These in turn lead to analyses and suggested solutions of general problems which are hopelessly out of step with the past and present situation.

The participants at the conference, consequently, were encouraged to look at the contemporary scene analytically, rather than descriptively, and chiefly from the viewpoint of distinct members of various occupational groups: intellectuals, clergy, nomads, villagers, merchants, political leaders, army officers, minorities, entrepreneurs, workers, economic planners, farmers, refugees, and other immigrants. The conference focused upon what a member of each of these groups thinks, says, and does about the contemporary scene, in which significant changes in attitudes and in institutions are occurring almost daily. The ensuing discussions also revolved around the responses of each of these groups to the dynamic forces active in the region today. The general theme of the conference was "The Near East: Social Dynamics and the Cultural Setting." This volume includes the papers presented at the

[1] The members of the Committee, which was appointed by the Social Science Research Council in January, 1951, were Carleton S. Coon, University of Pennsylvania; Douglas D. Crary, University of Michigan; Peter G. Franck, American University; Richard N. Frye, Harvard University; J. C. Hurewitz, Columbia University; Majid Khadduri, The Johns Hopkins University; E. A. Speiser, University of Pennsylvania; Lewis V. Thomas, Princeton University; Bryce Wood, Social Science Research Council; George G. Cameron, chairman, University of Michigan.

A brief review of the work of the conference, written by Bryce Wood, appeared in *Social Science Research Council Items*, VII (March, 1953), 1–7; this Introduction is much indebted to that summation.

conference as revised in the light of the discussions and of events taking place since the time of the conference.

The task given the authors was admittedly difficult, and achievement may have fallen short of expectations. When the area is considered largely on its own terms—neither as a problem to others nor as an arena in which the contest between external forces may be observed—the whole picture seldom becomes visible. Yet this vantage point sharpened the more important details, which are often obscured when the area is viewed from another perspective; it also encouraged the authors of the separate topics —that is, of the individual chapters in this volume—to adopt an interdisciplinary approach and to view their hypothetical individuals in their total situations. It may be observed at this point that the authors were fully aware of the almost irresistible temptations to generalize from part to the whole and have resisted this temptation with the utmost tenacity.

The reader will note that the first chapter of this volume is, as it should be, devoted to the cultural background pertinent to the process of social change within the Near East. Obviously, social change possesses more than the two dimensions of width and breadth; it also involves depth, signifying that the roots of the contemporary crisis reach deep into the past and that people behave as they do today because they have long since been conditioned so to behave. Research into the past consequently is valid for a reason of equal merit with the sheer spirit of human inquiry, the search for origins and the unknown; the answer to the question, how far must one reach beneath a given stratum to arrive at an understanding of what is being transformed, will depend on "the length and tenacity of historic tradition that is still a living force" in the Near East itself.

Subsequent chapters view the role of the intellectual, the clergy, the nomad, and the villager in respect to the social and the technological changes with which each is confronted; examine the impact which changing political processes make on the army officers and members of the minority groups; study the individual responses of workers, merchants, entrepreneurs, and local planners within the economic setting; and bring into focus the divergent problems and reactions of the farmer in Israel and the transplanted everywhere.

Each chapter both explicitly and implicitly demonstrates with renewed clarity the inadequacy of the present state of our knowledge concerning the peoples of the Near East and illustrates specific gaps within the information already available. The meagerness and unreliability of much of the statistical information and the small number of relevant studies thus far made are factors all too clearly apparent to authors and readers alike. Yet this volume may have served its purpose well if it emphasizes anew the fact that so little is known about the social forces of the Near East.

No man can rest easy when confronted by such ignorance, for not only is the Near East nearer, but the time is also later, than we think. Knowledge, sympathetic understanding, and active cooperation are prerequisites to the elimination of tensions and the maintenance of stability, without which peace cannot come to our time.

Social Forces in the Middle East

Cultural Factors in Social

Dynamics in the Near East

In the mythology of the early twentieth century no motif was more commonly accepted than that of the Immutable East. Now, at the mid-century junction, that same East faces the reality of epochal change. The facts of today show up the error of yesterday's appraisal. Yet the earlier myth owed its acceptance to a few strands of fact that had been woven into it. There is similarly an admixture of fiction in the pattern of facts of the present. Each instance is, in part, a result of faulty evaluation which can be traced to insufficient perspective; in each, the approach has been lacking in depth. This is true of the Orient in general but is nowhere more sharply in evidence in the particular than in the Near East.

No apology should be needed for relating social forces in the Near East to the pertinent cultural background. Yet all signs would seem to point to the conclusion that the connection between the observable level of a given society and its subsurface forces is not fully appreciated. It is one of the tenets of modern pragmatism that things are not important unless their usefulness is immediately apparent. This belief, which often amounts

[1]

to an article of faith, can be seen reflected everywhere around us. In education it has led to a doctrinaire hostility toward most things past. More than one social science has little use in practice for works antedating the present century. The statesmen who strive to prepare for tomorrow help to impart a nightmarish quality to our todays because of their obtuse refusal to take our yesterdays into account.

Social processes are three-dimensional. Any cross section through the present has but two dimensions. It is flat, and so is the extreme pragmatic approach. Only a cultist kind of pragmatism can affirm that the present should cut itself loose from all tradition in order to make a success of the twentieth century.[1]

The process of social change is three-dimensional by definition. It involves a stratified medium, for such change moves from one level to the next. The question is how far down one must reach beneath a given stratum to arrive at the origin and gain an understanding of what is being transformed at long last. The answer will depend on the length and tenacity of historic tradition that is still a living force in the area involved. Because the Near East started the world on its historic course, no other part of the globe has been watched over by history to a comparable degree. Nor has tradition held anything like the same sway in any other region. The Near East, for instance, is the home of the old Eastern churches of Christendom, which still function there, through direct survivals and various offshoots, their role as a political factor having persisted in some cases to this day. There, too, one can find remnants of pre-Christian Judaism among the Aramaic-speaking Jews of Kurdistan. The superficial Christianity of the Mandaeans and the undisguised paganism of the Yazidis lead back still farther. To be sure, not all of these groups are representative of the main stream of living tradition. Nor does that tradition operate exclusively

[1] J. Glenn Gray, "Is Progressive Education a Failure?" *Commentary*, XIV (May, 1952), 110.

through religious bodies, although it is most prominent in Islam, the dominant religion of the area. The present, in any case, has deep roots in the Near East, and these must be traced through countless paths and bypaths. The region, in short, is much like a multiple palimpsest. There may be concern only with the latest inscription, but the key to its interpretation may well be hidden in the legend at the very bottom.

To carry this comparison a step farther, the immediate task is to dig down and decipher the record of the past only insofar as this can contribute to the elucidation of the present. This is not a question of recapitulating the entire cultural history of the Near East. It is on this specific issue that is found what is perhaps the major area of friction between the humanist and the social scientist. The humanist cannot give up the notion that everything which his special discipline has unearthed is vital to the total picture. The social scientist sees in the data furnished by the humanities much that is not germane to his purpose, and he proceeds thence to the erroneous conclusion that nothing of importance can be derived from that quarter. The fact of the matter would seem to be that society, which is the ultimate focus of all such studies, is not cut up into humanistic and functional segments. It is an integral body, at which the respective disciplines may nibble but which they cannot hope to fathom unless all the disciplines are brought to bear on it in harmonious co-operation. All should be means to the sole end of recapturing human progress in its totality. Yet such is obviously not the case, least of all where the Near East is concerned. Your student of the contemporary history of the area does not normally have a workable understanding of the dominant Islamic culture. The Islamist stays aloof, as a rule, from modern developments—except perhaps as a political partisan—and pays only lip service to the pre-Islamic background. And the student of the ancient Near East, while conceding that life went on after Hammurabi or Moses, will positively refuse to become involved in it after the age of Alexander. What

[3]

is thus lost in this parochial fragmentation is the sense of essential continuity between the latest manifestation of the Near Eastern experience of mankind and its meaningful explanation in the remote past.

But how can it be ascertained what cultural features of the stratified past have helped to shape a contemporary sociopolitical entity? It is plainly an interdisciplinary task since no single discipline has anything resembling it among its stated objectives. The social sciences are not geared to research in depth, and the humanities are likely to underestimate the social and political factors. What is called for is a sociocultural analysis of a whole region, strategically important and wedded to tradition, in the process of radical change; thus it might be possible to obtain a sense of the direction to which the changes are pointing. Yet it is not clear what is the nature of the basic social organism whose component parts are to be analyzed. What is the fundamental unit which has to be considered?

That unit cannot be the Near East as a whole, for that region soon proves to consist of a number of various units distinct from one another. To be sure, the Near East is the joint product of geography and history. It is articulated by people who at this particular juncture in time are responding in one way or another to a variety of social, economic, and political pressures. Because environment has given the region a vital strategic role, its peoples and its resources are the concern not only of the local states but also of the world outside. But this formulation is merely another way of describing a two-dimensional approach. It ignores the past and manages to obscure the future. Yet the geopolitical approach is about as far as diplomacy is prepared and equipped to go, and it comes close to exhausting the capabilities of political science.

Before long, however, one is bound to discover that the three states of Turkey, Iran, and Israel differ significantly among themselves, and that each is in substantial contrast with the neighboring Arab states. Evidently, therefore, the unit which must be isolated is not the same thing as a region. The reasons for the difference are just as plainly bound up with history. The distinguishing feature in each instance is the added dimension of time. To do justice to such manifestations in depth requires the services of history and anthropology.

Does this mean that it is the individual state on which the co-operating disciplines must focus? The example of the Arab world shows that the state cannot be the answer to our question. Surely, more than one Arab state has to all intents and purposes the same cultural setting. On the other hand, the concept of nation, as in "the Arab nation," will not serve either. For on closer examination the Arab states as a group fail to function as an integral unit. There are here instead several distinctive subdivisions. Looking, moreover, at "the Kurdish nation," one finds that body partitioned among Iran, Iraq, Turkey, and Syria. In none of these states are the Kurds the dominant ethnic element, and they have no independent status on the international scene. Thus neither state nor nation can be the answer.

Nor is the concept of society as synonymous with civilization really suitable for the purpose. Toynbee's Western Christendom would be roughly comparable to the Islamic Near East. It has been suggested, however—and the suggestion will be supported presently—that Turkey cannot be bracketed with Iran, that the two cannot be equated with the Arab states, and that the Arab states break up into several subdivisions. What is lacking, therefore, is a practical focus of interdisciplinary research when it comes to analyzing political entities in their significant cultural setting.

What are, then, the main characteristics of this elusive unit of sociocultural inquiry? In common with the state this is a politically significant organism of recognized international standing. Turkey or Iran, for example, fulfills these requirements. Yet each presents also other features that are not germane to the present context. To give an obvious illustration, the Kurds constitute sizable minorities in both instances, yet they have no decisive bearing on the domestic situation in either state and their voice is scarcely audible in external matters. In other words, the Kurds do not enter to any substantial degree into the group personality that makes Turkey distinct from Iran and each in turn distinct from any other state. Those group features, however, that prove to be distinctive have often been a long time in forming. Islam played a major role in shaping Turkey on the one hand and Iran on the other, but the reason that the two can be contrasted, nevertheless, is that each had already been molded in its own particular fashion long before the advent of Islam. To understand each country, therefore, and to chart its future potential, it may be necessary to recede as far back into the past as the continuous thread of distinctive group personality will carry.

In going back, however, it is important to distinguish between the essential and the incidental, the enduring and the ephemeral. The complex in question is indeed a sociopolitical organism as the end product of its total cultural career. Still, that career has been a cumulative and selective process. Over its entire course it may have involved all sorts of major changes and modifications: in religion and outlook on life, in law and government —even in language and ethnic composition. That is precisely why it cannot be readily apprehended in terms of state, nation, culture, or society as such. Each of these concepts is at once too broad for some of the present purposes and too shallow for others. What matters is the effective core within each complex under discussion—the irreducible minimum of productive features without which one such organism might not be clearly distinguished from the next in the long perspective. In short, it is not simply a question of the cultural history of Turkey, Iran, or any other state; rather it is a question of that blend of the living past and the deep-rooted present which enables each state to function in its own distinctive way. It happens that the Near East, by reason of its total history and the singular effect of its immemorial traditions, is of all the regions of the world the one best suited for such a study. It also appears to be the region that is most urgently in need of such an investigation.

The task will be greatly simplified if a term can be supplied for the concept that has just been described. The name that suggests itself is *ethneme,* on the analogy of "phoneme," [2] which in linguistics represents the minimum significant unit of sound. Just so, the ethneme would stand for the minimum distinctive political organism in its sociocultural setting. Each ethneme has its own combination of features, some constant and others variable. Environment, for instance, would have to be regarded as a constant ethnemic feature. Language is a distinctive feature in many cases, but not necessarily in all; one need only call attention to modern Switzerland or to the several linguistic strata in Asia Minor within one and the same ethnemic body. In its long historic career the Near East has been the cradle of many ethnemes. Some of these have long been extinct, e.g., the Sumerians and the Hittites. Others have been dormant for an incalculable period, notably the Kurds. In Israel, there is an instance of an ethneme that is again operative after nineteen centuries of dormancy. In any event, those ethnemes in the Near East that are now functioning reach far back into the past. Whether any new ethnemes are in the process of formation at this time there is no means of judging. For one of the ethneme's most prominent aspects is its extent in depth, and that can be appreciated only in retrospect.

Two incidental observations may be made in passing. One of these pertains to the emergent discipline of "national character" around which there has grown up a considerable body of literature within the past few years. The foregoing emphasis

[2] A better parallel in this instance would be "glosseme," or the smallest meaningful unit of linguistic communication, but "phoneme" is slightly more familiar. The important thing is that abstractions of this kind can prove instrumental in the progress of a discipline. They have clearly done so in linguistics.

on cumulative group personality might have given rise to the assumption that the proposed concept of ethneme is but another name for national character. In reality, these two concepts have certain features in common, but they differ also significantly in a number of ways. The main difference would seem to be that the psychological factor, which is dominant in the idea of national character, is only a minor feature in the ethneme. On the other hand, the accent on the formative past applies in the case of the ethneme to the historic group as a whole and not primarily to the sum of its individual members. If the ethneme turns out to be a valuable tool, it may well prove helpful in the study of national character in an incidental way.

The other observation is in the nature of a warning. It cannot be stressed too strongly that what has been said about the ethneme so far, and what will be said presently, should be construed only as program notes. The whole thing is merely stuff for transforming. The entire concept must be refined, tested, and perfected. For the present it is no more than an experiment which carries with it the promise of worth-while results.

If the ethnemic concept is to justify itself as a useful tool of interdisciplinary inquiry, one must see how it can be applied to the present subject. What is back of the ferment with which the Near East is now astir?

The logical approach to this question is through the medium of the local states. State and ethneme are often roughly comparable at first glance. It is only upon further probing that the two are found to diverge as the criterion of background is applied. For once the factor of time has been taken into account, a single ethneme may prove to have progressed through a stratified succession of states. The ideal objective would be to retrace these steps, starting with the uppermost level. In practice, however, the task is not at all simple, perhaps even out of reach. But there is a good chance that it may be possible to get down deep enough for an adequate perspective before some slip obliterates the proper course. It can be said at any rate that the Near East has left more footholds, and has spaced them over a longer stretch, than is the case with any other area.

If the Near East is viewed as a group of states, their outstanding characteristic is soon seen to be a pervasive weakness, both in internal and external matters. On the surface this weakness appears to derive primarily from external causes: the colonialism of the recent past which kept the area under outside domination in one form or another; the strategic and economic imperialism of still more recent date whereby the great natural resources of the Near East have been made the target of foreign exploitation; or, in the judgment of others, the blend of cultural and social factors that have been channeled through Zionism.

There can be little doubt that various outside forces have had an adverse effect locally. Colonialism and the Suez Canal, oil and the Palestine conflict—all these have acted as powerful irritants. Yet they are relatively superficial manifestations, symptoms rather than causes. However, for one reason or another, the diplomats' analysis of the problems of the Near East has rarely advanced beyond the notice of such extraneous factors. In fact, their diagnosis has often stopped with but one of these: Palestine, or oil, or the Suez. This is not to suggest that a more penetrating analysis would have served to obviate the present crisis altogether. Since the fundamental causes of the region's weaknesses do not stem from the outside, they have to be internal. The cure must come, therefore, from within. But a keener diagnosis might have left the outside world in a better position to know what to expect and guard against. As it is, the lid now threatens to be blown to pieces—and this in an area whose stability is essential to the world's equilibrium.

Once it is realized that the basic troubles of the Near East are rooted in the native soil, the immediate cause is not far to seek. It is the familiar chain reaction of extreme and chronic poverty on a mass scale, with the usual concomitants of malnutrition, disease, and illiteracy. Since the area is overwhelmingly agricultural, and mass poverty is a cancerous affliction, landholdings have passed in course of time from the indigent many to the successful few.[3] The vast majority of the population are consequently landless. Progress and reform are not in the immediate interest of the landlords, and the landlords have a very substantial voice in the government. The governments are weak because their mandate is from the few and for the few. They can be neither honest nor representative. Eventually, the need becomes urgent to divert the attention of the long-suffering masses from the ills within to some convenient target outside. Because of the abiding importance of the Near East, interested outsiders have always been ready to hand. They have been made to shoulder most of the blame, sometimes with good reason, but often also as mere scapegoats. In a climate such as this, it is primarily as instruments of diversion that xenophobia and obsessive nationalism spring up and prosper.

To be sure, this type of chain reaction is not restricted to the Near East any more than is mass poverty itself. It is perhaps more pronounced here than elsewhere, but it is certainly not unique. A drastic economic imbalance, moreover, is itself a symptom of something deeper. The fact has often been stressed that economic problems cannot be divorced from the total context of the given civilization. The crisis brought about by mass poverty is seriously aggravated, if not induced, by underlying social and cultural conditions. The recent history of the whole of Asia bears this out.[4] But whereas the rest of Asia has been suffering from social and cultural disintegration for a few generations, the Islamic world has been the victim of the same malady for centuries. And the Near East is overwhelmingly Islamic.

Now Islam was destined from the very beginning to become

[3] Sa'id B. Himadeh, "Economic Factors Underlying Social Problems in the Arab Middle East," *The Middle East Journal*, V (Summer, 1951), 269 ff.
[4] C. F. Hudson, "Why Asians Hate the West," *Commentary*, XIII (May, 1952), 414.

a dominant ethnemic feature, far more so than any other major religion. For it was Muhammad's conviction that his mission included the task of founding a community which should be a state as well as a church. Numerous tenets of Islam reflect the intimate blending of the spiritual and the temporal.[5] But while spiritual values often prove to be enduring, temporal policies, as the name implies, presently become outdated. By now, Islam as a spiritual experience has stood the test of time for some thirteen centuries. But it is also the state religion in a number of countries within the Muslim world. To the extent to which Islam is a state as much as a church, the effect of the system on social and political progress has been negative for a long time.

It is neither feasible nor necessary to trace here in detail the inhibitive aspects of traditional Islam in the sociopolitical life of its community through the centuries. The long-term results in general have proved harmful in precisely those fields that affect the vitality of the society as a whole. Thus the Muslim laws of succession and the institution of the *Waqf*, or Pious Foundations, have jointly contributed to the progressive fragmentation of landholdings and the critical inequality of land ownership.[6] Education in a theocratic state is of necessity slanted, limited, and reactionary. Social practices remain stagnant. And international relations are hampered by numerous injunctions that were anachronisms a thousand years ago.

The pervasive weakness of Islamic society, therefore, is due in large measure to the dominant temporal features of the underlying system. The obvious answer to the problem would be a resolute separation of church and state. This is by no means a novel conclusion. It is implicit, for instance, in the statement of a distinguished Syrian educator and statesman, Costi K. Zurayk, who has written as follows:

[5] Arthur Jeffery, "The Political Importance of Islam," *Journal of Near Eastern Studies*, I (1942), 383 ff.

[6] Himadeh, *op. cit.*, 272 ff.

When, however, it [Islam] became reduced to a set of doctrines to be taken on credence, and a code of laws and morals to be applied rigidly and blindly it turned out to be, as other religions in the same state, a burden rather than an inspiration, a paralysing shackle instead of a liberating force, the letter that killeth all real endeavor and progress.[7]

A courageous Egyptian Muslim, Khalid Muhammad Khalid, refers to the same conditions in terms of witchcraft rather than religion.[8] Yet the logical step of divorcing state from church has so far been taken by only one of the countries involved, namely, Turkey. And it is surely no mere coincidence that Turkey today is once again a progressive and dynamic state. But the rest of the Islamic community in the Near East has yet to reverse its downward trend.

It is thus apparent that the roots of the present crisis in the Near East reach deep down into the past. The surface weaknesses in the economic, political, and social fields are largely symptoms of underlying cultural ills. No lasting cure can be hoped for until the basic troubles have been attacked. Superficial reforms could achieve only ephemeral results. The best native thought in the Near East is well aware of this, in welcome contrast to outside analysis, which seldom penetrates beyond the surface manifestations. But there are formidable obstacles to the kind of reform that is urgently needed. For the opposition comes not only from the thin layer of landlords, who control the economy and have a powerful voice in the government. Resistance to reform is even greater in the religious quarters, which have arrogated unto themselves the authority over the region's cultural heritage. They can afford to be outspoken where the landlords cannot. Because they purport and are believed to have a monopoly on truth, their voice is the voice of blind fanaticism. In the much-filtered atmosphere of

[7] "The Essence of Arab Civilization," *The Middle East Journal*, III (April, 1949), 127.

[8] See the review of his book *Min Huna Nabda'* by Nicola A. Ziadeh, *The Middle East Journal*, V (Autumn, 1951), 506–508.

the Near East that voice carries far and wide, drowning out other tones. The Muslim Brotherhood (*al-Ikhwan al-Muslimun*) of Egypt and other Arab lands and the Devotees (*Fida'iyan*) of Iran may be extreme instances; yet such groups have a traditional hold on the rank and file, and their witch-doctor influence in recent developments is much too pronounced and tragic to be underestimated. The formula of the religious medicine men is particularly dangerous in that it compounds sociopolitical half-truths with age-old spiritual tenets. It is virulently antiforeign, obsessively nationalistic, and fiercely reactionary. The hopeless masses are all too ready to embrace a cure-all that bears the stamp of inspired authority. In such a climate an effective change would have to be of elemental proportions.

It follows, at any rate, that Islam is a dominant ethnemic feature in the Near East. The name itself implies submission to divine authority, and the entire history of the Islamic community points up the system as an overriding cultural factor. Accordingly, different conditions may be looked for where the influence of Islam is either negligible or has been measurably reduced. Such indeed is the case in three Near Eastern states. Israel has but a small Muslim minority; hence her sociopolitical status is markedly different from that of her neighbors. Lebanon is half-Christian, with a consequent reduction in the social imbalance from which a Syria or a Jordan is suffering. And while Turkey is overwhelmingly Muslim, her progressive career in recent years dates back exactly to the time when religion was removed officially from the sociopolitical sphere. But if this could happen in Muslim Turkey, why have not the other Muslim states of the Near East followed suit?

The question is a logical one. The answer is bound up with the further features of the various ethnemes that contribute to those differences in national group personalities that are reflected in the several states of the region. To put it differently, the Arab states and Iran have not followed the example of Turkey—at least not so far—because the circumstances have not been the same in each instance. This is, of course, a plain fact. But it is scarcely valid to account for that fact with the invariable cliché that Turkey has had its Mustafa Kemal Atatürk whereas the other states have not. The personal equation is important but it will not bear much probing in this context. A man may help to change the course of a nation only when the nation is ready for the process. Otherwise, the change would prove superficial and short-lived at best. Much that is not apparent on the surface went into the making of the Turkey of Atatürk. And since that formative background has led to results which serve to distinguish modern Turkey from other Muslim states, the factors in question would have to be either pre-Islamic or extra-Islamic. Thus ethnemic analysis, after noting the effects of Islam on the various ethnemes involved, now obliges us to go beyond the Islamic stage.

Let us dwell briefly on Iran, as distinct from both Turkey and the Arab states. Apart from geography, the outstanding differences are linguistic. Iranian has no family relationship with either Turkish or Arabic. The country has retained its pre-Islamic language, unlike Iraq, Syria, Jordan, and Egypt, all of which have become Arabized. It might be argued that Arabization succeeded where the process involved only the displacement of related Semitic languages, say Aramaic for Arabic; hence Iran was spared. Yet similar conditions obtained in Egypt, which adopted Arabic none the less. The linguistic aspect, in other words, must itself be a symptom instead of a cause. Language would seem to constitute a major ethnemic feature only when it is a vehicle for a distinctive culture.

That the distinctiveness of Iran extends indeed far beyond language is evidenced perhaps most clearly by the kind of Islam which that country has made its own. For Shi'ism, which is the sectarian stamp of Iran, shows significant differences from Orthodox Sunnism along lines that are by no means restricted to doctrinal issues. The schism, then, is basically cultural, and its roots would seem to be pre-Islamic. In other words, the distinction in this case is ethnemic. It sets Iran apart from the other Muslim states of the Near East, including Turkey, which are mainly Sunnite. Backward Yemen happens to be Shi'ite, to be sure, but that country is scarcely articulate enough to have yielded sufficient data for ethnemic analysis. There is, furthermore, a narrow Shi'ite majority in Iraq although the leading groups there are Sunnite. This may well be one of the reasons why Iraq is still ambivalent in terms of a modern state.

In pursuing significant ethnemic characteristics in the Near East it becomes evident that the period of the introduction of Islam was a very important juncture. For as a cultural influence in a political framework Islam is unmatched by any other major religion. It is a singularly powerful factor for unity and solidarity among its constituent societies. Nevertheless, the rise of Islam apparently is too late a period for the starting point of the present inquiry. For by then there had already emerged certain basic features of several societies which were to survive in a number of modern states. Those features must ultimately be the key to today's problems and tomorrow's prospects. The impact of Islam served to level them in most instances, but it could not suppress them altogether. In a region of immemorial traditions it may be necessary, it would seem, to trace the living past to its source if the mainsprings of the present are to be seen in the proper focus.

It goes without saying that Western diplomacy has not shown, and could hardly be expected to show, the least awareness of the truth of the foregoing statement. Western scholarship, however, should know better but it has shown very few signs that it does. Local elements are not quite so agnostic. Beyond the constant reminders of the past in social customs and institutions, there have been in the Near East conscious efforts to link the remote past with the present. Atatürk sought to do so by tracing the contemporary Turks first to the ancient Sumerians and later to the Hittites, with results that were far from academic so far as the effect on his country was concerned. A stridently vocal group in Iran is bent on reviving old Persian usages. Much of this activity is questionable as to soundness and purpose, yet it does reflect an inkling of a truth dimly perceived.

The Iranians behave today as they do because in some part they were conditioned that way long before the advent of Islam. The same is true of the dominant elements in Turkey, although there it is difficult to tell at this time how much of that behavior was motivated in ancient Anatolia and how much originated with the intrusive Turks. The means for making such nice distinctions are seldom available in adequate measure. If they were, it should be possible to arrive ultimately at a picture of an ethnemic personality that would bear no resemblance whatever to the facile sketches by some anthropologists— happily not representative of their discipline—who are prepared to develop a picture of the composite Japanese, American, or whatever the case may be, as readily as a composite photograph can be produced. What is known is that, say, Turkey and Iran have each responded differently to similar impulses. Whether that difference is one of kind or merely one of tempo remains to be seen. Going back to a particular juncture in their respective careers, back to the advent of Islam, their courses are roughly similar. Beyond that juncture, however, and farther back into the past, their paths draw apart. It appears that this divergence is ultimately related to the disparate contemporary behavior of these two ethnic groups, enough so to make of these groups two distinctive ethnemes.

Now when one recedes as far as the age prior to the rise of Islam, hope fails for more than the long perspective in which most details are blurred and only the broad contours are discernible. In other words, at such distance all that may reasonably be expected to be recovered are certain enduring features of the given civilization. These features, however, add up to that specific society's own way of life, a cumulative solution of the larger issues of existence and destiny which enabled the group to leave its mark on history. For present purposes, moreover, this has to be a solution which was not to be wholly discarded by the succeeding societies down to our own day. Interest, at this point, would attach to the Hittites only to the extent to which they might help to shed light on modern Turkey; to the Achaemenians as a possible clue to contemporary Iran; and so on.

Two principal sources of information are open in this connection. One is the concept of state, which represents a solution in terms of the individual's relation to society. The other is religion, which reflects both the individual's and society's integration with nature. The reason why Islam has proved to be an outstanding ethnemic feature is precisely that the system embodies the two vital aspects of church and state. This combination, however, is itself a legacy of earlier times, for the farther back one moves in the history of the Near East the harder it becomes to separate the two institutions.

In other words, Islam is a milestone in the Near East's career but in nowise the starting point of its historic traditions. By the time of its rise the people of the region had been experimenting with basic values for a very long time, singling out the time-tested solutions, and arranging them into varying patterns. Islam was largely a restatement and a special arrangement of some of these solutions. The system was successful in the main because it had long been familiar in its essentials. But where the new pattern departed sharply from the old, Islam met with proportionate resistance and required more effort to impose. A measure of uniformity was thus achieved at length, not so sweeping, however, as to obliterate all traces of the underlying differences. These differences are still apparent throughout the area in countless intimate details. An ethnemic inquiry can safely disregard most such manifestations. But it cannot ignore any evidence concerning the oldest established concepts of state. For such concepts enter intimately into each society's way of life. They are experiences that are not readily given up. In the final analysis they turn out to be the very core of the individual ethneme.

This is obviously neither the time nor the place to develop the theme.[9] It is a relatively new theme, and a vast amount of work remains to be done on it. In briefest outline, the ancient Near East bequeathed to the world two sharply contrasted systems regarding the relation of the individual to society, each embodied in its own logical concept of state. One of these was arrived at in Mesopotamia. It proceeds from certain inalienable rights of the individual, which are safeguarded by the law, and protected by the ruler, who is himself the humble servant of the law. The king's authority is further limited by the assembly which must approve all major decisions. This rule by assembly marks a substantial start toward representative government and democracy. The other solution was evolved and perfected in Egypt. Central to it is the assumption that the king is a god, beyond the reach of his subjects and a law unto himself. The resulting government is pervasively totalitarian. It is symbolized early and with singular force by the monumental fact of the pyramids.

These two solutions constitute opposing and mutually incompatible ways of life. There could be no genuine compromise between them. The rest of the Near East usually had to be either in the one camp or the other. Contrary to popular assumption and the teaching of history books, there is here a complete dichotomy. Egypt remained in virtual isolation, but the Mesopotamian way found many ardent adherents. Among these was Anatolia, whose laws and general culture in Hittite times point unmistakably to Babylonia. Syria and Palestine, likewise, owed much to Mesopotamian inspiration, although their own contributions to the distinctive civilization that was emerging are in no danger of being overlooked. Their inherent demo-

[9] A fuller statement will be found in "The Ancient Near East and Modern Philosophies of History," *Proceedings of the American Philosophical Society,* XCV (December, 1951), 583–588.

cratic tradition was to play a vital part in the ultimate development of Judaism, Christianity, and Islam. Only Iran fails to show a decided trend. Although long the cultural associate of Mesopotamia, Iran came to evolve a concept of state that did not configurate strictly either with that of her neighbor or with Egypt's.

One result in particular needs stressing in this connection. On the basic issue of a way of life, Egypt diverged sharply from the rest of the Near East throughout her long pre-Islamic history. In all the centuries since the advent of Islam, Egypt has not been able to submerge altogether this ethnemic characteristic. Her traditional apartness and her recurring stress on the unity of the Nile Valley are two of the features that cut down beneath the Islamic stratum. The relatively greater immunity of the ruler in Egypt has been another such feature. This does not mean, of course, that Egypt subsists entirely on her pre-Hellenistic legacy. The long Islamic period has been a great equalizer. Hence the pull toward Arab unity, and hence, too, the recent moves which put an end, at long last, to the abuses of which the royal house had been guilty. But the pull in the other direction is still a factor.

Another result of this examination is the distinction which it has brought out between the ethnic and the ethnemic complexes. Ethnically the Egyptians are Arabs. But by the ethnemic criterion of the traditional concept of state, Egypt requires independent listing, apart from other Arab states. On the other hand, no such differences separate Syria, Jordan, and the Sunnite Arab portion of Iraq. Since these three political entities also share other major ethnemic features—language, religion, geographic environment—they properly make up a single ethneme. Turkey shares with the Fertile Crescent the inherited feature of the concept of state, but differs from that area on other ethnemic grounds. Iran's distinctiveness expresses itself, among other ways, through Shi'ism, which proves to be a separate ethnemic feature within the larger complex of Islam.

[19]

In conclusion, it may not be amiss to apply, as a practical but strictly tentative test, the over-all results of the foregoing discussion to selected problems of the contemporary Near East.

The most revealing case by far is that of Turkey. To begin with, due regard to the cultural factor makes it necessary to center on religion as a prime ethnemic element in the region. By reason of its anachronistic tenets in the sociopolitical sphere, traditional Islam must be viewed as the underlying cause of the present ills of the Near East. Turkey has furnished support for this conclusion in that her return to a progressive course dates back to her separation of church from state under the determined leadership of Mustafa Kemal Atatürk.

It would seem to follow that the other Muslim states cannot expect a comparable improvement until each has instituted similar reforms. It is logical, therefore, to ask why they have not done so to date, profiting from the example of Muslim Turkey. This question was posed earlier in the present discussion, but no direct attempt to answer it has as yet been made. Nor is a clear-cut answer possible at this time in view of the complex nature of the problem. Some tentative suggestions, nevertheless, may be hazarded.

It is self-evident that a number of major features enter into the composition of any given ethneme. Their respective force varies from instance to instance so that the ultimate pattern is never the same. That is why each composite ethneme is a unit unto itself. In the case of Turkey, the religious factor—although far from negligible—is evidently not so pronounced as in the neighboring Muslim states, whereas other ethnemic features would appear to be correspondingly stronger. A detailed inquiry might well yield more precise results along these lines. But certain general indications are available even now.

Islam is native to the Arab world but intrusive in Turkey. Its roots are necessarily deeper and firmer in the area of its origin. Any serious interference with the system would be bound to run up against greater obstacles in the Arab states than in

Turkey. On the other hand, Turkey is heir to a democratic tradition that reaches back to remote pre-Islamic times. The reforms of Atatürk, however, were carried out, as was inevitable in the circumstances, by authoritarian methods. It is significant, therefore, that inside a generation Turkey has taken steps to correct these conditions. Have these successive changes been due to surface factors alone, or should the result be ascribed to the collective group personality that represents the Turkish ethneme? This last possibility, at any rate, should not be discarded offhand.

By the same token, the oft-voiced wish for an "Arab Atatürk" should be assessed in the light of what may be known about Arab group personality. Would Arabs respond as readily as did the Turks to the aims and methods of an Atatürk? Obviously major reforms in the system of traditional Islam can be expected to encounter considerably greater difficulties among the Arabs. As for authoritarian methods, would these, once instituted, prove more congenial to the Arab world, or less so, when compared with Turkey? It should not be forgotten that the submission which is implicit in Islam is submission to theocratic and not to strictly secular dictatorship. In any case, the answer hinges on much more than the emergence of a strong leader.

Granting, moreover, the fact of group personality and group temperament in an ethnemic sense, do the Muslim Arab states constitute a single ethneme? There are good reasons against such an assumption. Egypt is clearly a unit apart. The Arabian Peninsula can be shown to represent at least one other unit. The Muslim states of the Fertile Crescent are clearly a separate unit. This gives a minimum of three Arab ethnemes, which means that three separate lines of action can be expected in any given instance. On the issue of Islamic reform, Egypt might well pursue one course, Saudi Arabia another, and the Fertile Crescent still another. Non-Arab Iran is naturally not to be bracketed with the preceding units.

[21]

What of the problem of receptivity to communism? It goes without saying that several factors are involved. The prevailing social and economic conditions enhance the appeal of Communist cure-alls. The strong ethnemic features of religion operates in the opposite direction. In this impasse the scale could be tipped one way or another by the traditional concept of state that characterizes the respective ethnemes. On this score, Egypt would seem to be most amenable in the long run to a totalitarian solution, Iran less so, and the Fertile Crescent scarcely at all.

The issues of the Near East are, of course, not likely to be decided on a piecemeal basis. Because the fate of the region has a vital bearing on world stability, major political developments would probably take place here on a regional scale. But political questions as such are short-term problems. The fundamental issues of the Near East have centuries of incubation behind them. They require long-term solutions. It is in this connection in particular that ethnemic characteristics bid fair to play a significant part.

Events of recent weeks and months have made it abundantly plain that matters have now come to a head. The Near East is on the eve of a transition which could well be of epochal proportions. The forthcoming changes will be brought into being by the various classes and groups within the population of each state, and they will react in turn on each of the participating elements. All this calls for many detailed investigations. Yet sight should not be lost of the fact that society is not the sum of many fragmented sections. It is rather the synthesis of all of them through the entire length of its organic existence. It is a structure in depth, nowhere more so than in the Near East.

(II) CARLETON S. COON

The Nomads

NOMADS, like cowboys, are more glamorous than numerous. Except for Saudi Arabia they form a minority in every Middle Eastern country. This minority is, however, a very important one both to the nations of the Middle East and to the West. In their hands may lie the key to the immediate future of this entire region.

In the Middle East they occupy three types of terrain: deserts, Alpine meadows, and grassy steppes. Since these geographical domains are rarely in physical contact, the nomads of these three types see little of each other, and each group has its own problems. One thing they all have in common, however, is their interrelationship with farming communities and with cities, in a close symbiotic bond. Nomads need manufactured goods of metal, leather, wood, and textiles; farmers and townsmen need meat, wool, milk, and beasts of burden. Hence any influence which affects the farmer or the city man affects the nomad as well.

Unlike most farmers and the city men, the nomads, characteristically, are either independent of the central government of whatever country they inhabit or bound to it by the loosest of ties. Such a connection reaches from the head of the nomadic group in question to the pertinent government official located in the nearest settled territory. The individual nomad owes his allegiance only to his clan or tribal chief. That nomads should be organized in clans and tribes is only natural, since being virtually or completely independent they must provide the political structure of their own society. Political structure is especially needed since the nomad, by definition, migrates. Migration, in turn, depends on the seasonal availability of water and pasture, and efficient migration requires an order of march, policing, and the assignment of watering places and grazing areas.

It so happens that the territories inhabited or frequented by nomads generally lie between the settled regions. In order for traders, diplomats, pilgrims, and other travelers to go from one settled region to another, it was necessary for them to cross steppes, deserts, and mountains in the days before modern motor roads were built. Here the free nomad became a policeman not only for his own people but for others. At the price of a fee he used to guide caravans across dangerous places, protecting them the while from his rivals; without these services many travelers would have been lost to man, beast, or the weather. To do this work well he needed to be free.

Two reasons for the relative independence of nomads are clear. They live in terrain, such as mountains, deserts, and steppes, in which they are hard to catch. Being themselves the breeders of steeds, they can evade the punitive forces of old-fashioned central governments at best only equally mounted and less familiar with the terrain. Thus did the Romans led by Aelius Gallus disintegrate in the desert in their attempt at the conquest of the Yemen, while the ancestors of the Kurds rolled rocks on Xenophon and his Greeks, painfully and miraculously crossing their mountains. Their very way of life, with its healthy exercise, obedience, co-operation, leadership, struggle with nature, need of timing, feuding, and good meat and milk diet, makes them natural warriors far superior, man to man, to any brigade of poorly armed and hastily trained peasants.

As long as neither nomads nor government possessed no better means of transportation than horses and camels, and no better weapons than rifles, the balance of power between the two forces remained in a state of precarious equilibrium. Now and then the government would conquer some of the tribes and make them pay taxes and indemnities, while carrying off some of their men as hostages; this would happen when a new king, the founder of a dynasty, rose to power, cleaned house, established order in the flatlands, and whetted transportation and communication services to peak efficiency. At other times the government would become more than usually corrupt, security would totter, and services would decay. Then the nomads would ride in off their steppes and deserts and down from their mountains, to raid, to plunder, in some cases to set up new dynasties in the cities, and themselves eventually to decay.

These cycles, dependent on the common possession of identical techniques of transport, communication, and warfare, went on until new techniques were introduced, in our own century, which threw the system out of balance. Automobiles, trucks, and airplanes became the property of the government, unobtainable by most nomads because of their isolation. Thus, the very geographical fact which had set them free was now serving to enslave them. Machine guns, the peasant's compensation for poor marksmanship, nullified the painfully smuggled rifle. Bombs from above violated the most secret hideouts on the most inaccessible mountain crags. Trucks rolled across desert and steppe where camels had painfully plodded, and gangs of workmen, protected by armed soldiers, hewed roads out of the flanks of mountains. The guiding and policing business passed out of the hands of nomads. However, the European powers which had introduced these new antinomad techniques sent their agents among the tribes of desert, steppe, and mountain, spreading propaganda against the very governments they had armed and making empty promises of freedom, in a futile attempt to stem the tide of imbalance which they had themselves unwittingly caused to rise. In the lands openly ruled by Europeans, free Muslims from other lands shared the propagandizing work in both zones, those of the tame and the free, using as their vehicles the very techniques of communication, press, and radio which the Europeans had given them.

What all this has done is to set new forces in motion, to draw the lives of the nomads out of their age-old routines, and to break the ring of cycles of strength and weakness. Not all nomads have been affected the same way. What has happened to each group of them is not easy to discover. Political reporters seldom stray into nomad country, and ethnologists are rarely welcomed by governments which either cannot guarantee the scientists' safety or fear foreign meddling in a domestic issue, or both. The Syrian government, a notable exception in this instance, was offering late in 1953 every facility for studying nomads to a group of anthropologists under the auspices of the Social Science Research Council. An attempt will be made in this essay to describe what has happened to each of the major geographical and ecological nomadic groups, on the basis of personal observation, relatively reliable hearsay, and, in some lucky cases, printed documents.

The Sahara proper contains two kinds of nomads, Tuaregs and Badu.* The first were formed by the introduction of the camel, sometime after the fourth century A.D.; the Persians introduced this animal to Egypt, whence it was taken up by Berber tribes to the west. The Tuaregs were Senhajas, probably originally mountain shepherds. As they spread across the desert

* EDITOR'S NOTE: In the other contributions to this book the Anglicized forms, "beduin" and "beduins," are used rather than the direct Arabic of "Badawi" and "Badu." Here Dr. Coon is referring specifically to the Badu as a definite people, whereas in the other essays "beduins" and "Middle Eastern nomads" are more nearly synonymous.

to the borders of the Sudan, they developed a peculiarly complicated social and economic system. Some lineages became warriors, others camel breeders. The warriors, who were nobles, protected their *imghad* or serfs; the latter provided their masters with livestock, meat, and milk. Both castes employed Negro slaves and agricultural hirelings, who worked the moist upland escarpments for barley and vegetables. In addition to these castes and classes was a category of holy men, who neither fought nor were attacked and who stationed themselves with tribes and camps as teachers and peacemakers.

For their principal business, guarding caravans, the noble tribes were organized into confederations, each athwart a major trans-Saharan route. As part of this profession they also indulged in interconfederation warfare. The caravans which they guarded carried both goods and slaves, and the Tuaregs themselves acquired some of the choicest of each. As conscious as any Southern colonel of their racial purity, the nobles took black girls as concubines but not as wives; the purebred blue-eyed and hawk-nosed Tuareg women led a life of pampered privilege, bearing and training future warriors in the ideals of double-standard aristocracy. While the women wrote and read love poems in their archaic Libyan unciform script, the young men practiced dueling with six-foot swords and Homeric bucklers.

This heroic age was bound to come to an end. Having conquered both ends of the caravan routes, Algeria and the western Sudan, the French then moved out into the Sahara, fighting the Tuaregs from camels and finally conquering them. Later they brought in trucks, which now cross the Sahara over regular routes, and still later airplanes. The trans-Saharan railroad has not yet been completed, but it goes part of the way. Camel caravans are no longer the principal means of transport, for aside from the trucks much of the merchandise from the Sudan now moves northward by sea. The slave trade has been broken, if not destroyed. No longer masters of the caravan routes, the Tuareg nobles have little to do, aside from service in the French *meharist tabours*. Although the French have become their protectors, the *imghad* still feed their now powerless masters, and slaves are technically free.

What seems to have happened, and information is very poor on this subject, is that the Tuaregs have reverted to a simple camel-breeding state. Once a service activity, camel breeding has become their principal source of income, and camels are now useful chiefly as meat. The nobles, with little to do, linger on as faded aristocrats. Their women have begun to break down the color line in marriage as the nobility of their men has become meaningless, and Tuareg culture as depicted by Duveyrier, Benhazera, and L'Hote is well on the way out. Recent information from Algeria indicates that, unless something is done about it soon, the details of the old independent Tuareg culture will be forgotten before a qualified anthropologist can interview the last surviving warriors, sipping tea in their black tents. It is doubtful that Pan-Islamic propaganda will stir them, since they are not Arabs and are poor Muslims. Their ties today are increasingly with the Sudan, whence they obtain their metal tools and their clothing, including their inseparable veils, which like the American Indian war bonnet are fast becoming a last symbol of former distinction.

The other nomads of the Sahara are Arabs, whose ancestors came from their earlier desert at various times but principally in the eleventh-century migration of the Beni Hillal, Beni Soleim, and Majils. Only one tribe, the Shaamba, has ever achieved a width of territory and a degree of political power in any way comparable to that of the Tuaregs. Without a doubt they have lost their power, but what has happened to them otherwise is difficult to determine.

Up in the northwesternmost tongue of the Sahara, the Muluya River country of Morocco, are two nomadic tribes of Riffians, speaking a dialect of Zenatan Berber. They are the Beni Bu Yahyi and Metalsas. The territory of both tribes is cut by the border between French and Spanish Morocco; hence tribal authority in each case has been similarly bisected. On the Spanish side the droughts of the late forties decimated these tribes. On the French side many of their members have gone to work for French *colons*, who cultivate farms under irrigation, using both river water and that taken from artesian wells. On both sides the members of these tribes have long been engaged in smuggling, usually carrying sugar southward and cereals northward.

Arab nomads may be found in southern Tunisia, where during World War II many American soldiers saw them pasturing their sheep unconcernedly in the midst of military operations. Being simple shepherds, political changes mean little to them; all that matters is the market for wool and mutton. Over in Cyrenaica the Badu tribes, so ably described by Evans Pritchard, have been released from Italian rule and regimentation and placed once again under the leadership of their revered holy mentor, the Grand Sanussi, now King of Libya. Once more they can grow barley on slopes of their headland for export to Britain, where it is made into Scotch whiskey to bring American dollars to a faltering economy, while the intestines of their sheep form the skins of frankfurters consumed by the same people who drink the whiskey.

The nomadic inhabitants of the Arabian desert, covering parts of the territories of Saudi Arabia, the Yemen, Aden Protectorate, Israel, Syria, Iraq, Kuwait, and the two Omans, are the well-known Badu. Despite able descriptions by Musil, Dickson, and others, Badu culture is still imperfectly known. The work of the Research Branch of the Arabian American Oil Company, under the able guidance of Dr. George Rentz, is rapidly filling in the gaps.

Like the Tuaregs, the Badu are divided into tribes and clans of various grades of nobility, dependent on a combination of genealogy, martial freedom, and responsibility. Martial freedom and responsibility are in turn a function of mobility, and

[29]

mobility is a function of the species of animals bred. Cattle people cannot leave the sources of water at any season, and in Arabia they are not nomads. Shepherds are impeded by the slow movement of their charges. Only camel people have the freedom of movement that political freedom requires. Within the class of camel people are again two categories, those who habitually herd animals for others and those whose duties are primarily policing and warfare.

While the Arabian Badu of noble lineage consider themselves the most elevated and distinguished of mankind because they are free men and warriors, other noblemen live in castles, and in fact this is often the case with the heads of great nomadic tribes, who look out of their shielded windows at the agricultural work being done by their sedentary dependents below. Out in the desert at various seasons are to be found service peoples: merchants of various kinds, blacksmiths attached to camps, camel buyers, and the Sulabas, a debased group of tinkers, guides, and prostitutes. All of these service peoples habitually abstain from warfare.

In the winter the Badu go out on the open desert with their camels, which have been rigorously trained for some weeks in anticipation of this shift; there the succulent grass and cool weather make frequent recourse to water unnecessary. In the summer they go to permanent wells in the desert, in the places where agricultural communities are established, to the banks of the Euphrates, or to the oases, particularly al-Hasa and Qatif, where many of them own date gardens. Others pick dates for hire for the oasis people, many of whom are their religious opposites, Shi'ites. Meanwhile their camels get water and some grazing.

During the Turkish regime, the Badu circulated freely over their tribal territories, and only in summer when they came to settled places were they subject to the Turkish government, which levied a small tax when it could and otherwise let them alone. After World War I, British and French protectorates

were set up in Iraq, Jordan, Palestine, Lebanon, and Syria. The demarcation of boundaries within the former Turkish territory may have restricted the movement of Badu tribes a little, but not much. It was only with the independence of these states and the establishment of Israel that governments, equipped with armored cars and trucks on which Bren guns had been mounted, attempted to keep the Badu within national boundaries, many of which cut across tribal territories. Meanwhile some of the Arab states, such as Iraq and Saudi Arabia, instituted policies of settling the Badu on newly irrigated lands and turning them into farmers.

Today the Badu have lost much of the camel market, since motor vehicles are now the prime carriers in the Middle East. Export camels are raised largely for meat. Although they are still armed and still battle one another over water on occasion, the Badu have relinquished their policing duties, not only because of the rise of motorized governments, but also because of the decline of caravan travel in favor of the truck, the bus, and the airplane. Pilgrims from Iraq and Iran now go to Mecca either by plane or by bus. In Syria and Iraq tribal shaykhs now occupy high positions in the governments, and while some of their people have been settled, others continue to live as before. No longer, however, is it possible for the Shammar to raid the land between the rivers and to take over whole sections of a *liwa* (province), as they did a half-century ago. A man on a camel is no match for a truckload of soldiers with automatic rifles. In places where the Badu have settled, they still retain their tribal government; the *kaymakam* and *mutasarrif* deal directly with the shaykhs. Gradually and peacefully, a compromise situation is being reached.

In Saudi Arabia the presence of the oil company is setting a new pattern of Badu behavior. His late Majesty, Abdul Aziz ibn Saud, with all the wealth his royalties brought him, instituted wide irrigation projects, as at al-Kharj oasis, where much land has come into cultivation that had not been tilled for centuries.

All of the tribes in his territory acknowledged his suzerainty, as they now do that of his son, King Saud, and for the most part they have stopped serious fighting. Once a year the King sends his agents into tribal territory to distribute largesse, the *sadaka*, in the form of rations of rice and silver riyals.

The richest winter pasture is the cherty plain of the northern section of King Saud's territory. This is the traditional winter grazing ground of the Ruwelis, as well as of some of the Shammar and Shararat. When building the pipeline, the Arabian-American Oil Company and the Trans-Arabian Pipe Line Company were obliged to drill for water at the places where they set up their camps of workmen. These water holes were created not only at the seven regular pumping stations, but at many points between. When the construction gangs left these camps, the companies created square tanks at the artesian wells, and these tanks, maintained at Saudi government expense, contain perennial water. Those of the Badu who own no date trees now spend the summer along the TAPline, instead of going to the oases.

As the Arab towns that have sprung up or grown on this same line can serve them as trading points, there is no longer any need for the nomads to cross international boundaries. Although the market for camels as beasts of burden has fallen, the demand for meat has increased with the rise in the standard of living of the settled people. The Ruwelis raise more camels than before, not only for sale, but also for prestige. In fact, so many have they bred in response to these new sources of water that they threaten the grass. The Badu of the Rub al-Khali, such as the Al-Murra, formerly known only as names in the works of Philby, Thomas, and Thesiger, serve as guides and helpers to the exploration crews and walk in and out of the oil company offices in Dhahran as favored guests. These tiny men, each about half the size of a Ruweli, accept the giants from Texas as near-equals with the charming manners that only

a life of struggle against nature can achieve in the common (who therefore becomes uncommon) man.

The Makran is the desert country lying between the Indian Ocean and the watershed that forms the southern limit of various inland basins, notably the Dasht-i-Lut, in southeastern Iran and western Pakistan. It is inhabited by a varied collection of peoples, with some Arabs and Iranians on the coast and Persian-speaking villagers in the folds of the hills where there is enough water for them to cultivate crops. The nomads who use this desert country for camel pasture are the Baluchis, a number of tribal confederations organized much like the Badu of Arabia. The chiefs of the Baluchis own most of the Iranian villages, from which they draw tribute in cereals and among which they pasture their camels in the hot weather. Of all the Baluchis, however, the noblest are those who summer to the north of the watershed in the neighborhood of Zabol, using the permanent water of the lower Helmand River. Besides their villagers, they are served by outcaste tinkers, nurses, and entertainers called Lors, whose origin is unknown but probably similar to that of gypsies.

In the old days the Baluchis made their living by a combination of policing the caravan routes, raiding others who were doing the same, and raiding other peoples' villages for slaves, whom they sold in the Indus country and in Afghanistan. Their lightning raids, called *chapaos*, were feared as far afield as Kerman and Yazd. The Brahuis, equally noble folk of Dravidian linguistic stock and centered farther east and north, at Kalat, performed the same feats and were equally feared. Camps of Brahuis are found well into Iran.

The first step in the breakup of the power of these two peoples was taken by the British in their pacification of Indian Baluchistan and the construction of the railway from Quetta to Zahidan. Baluchis and Brahuis became enthusiastic soldiers,

guards, and policemen. In the old days the British consul at Zahidan was traditionally a friend of the Baluchis, to the discomfort of the Iranian government. With Reza Shah's consolidation of his realm the Baluchis, like other tribal peoples, were made to toe the line, and while he did not succeed in settling them as peasants, he was able to stop their raids. Brahuis, on the other hand, moved up in numbers to the villages around Mashhad, where many still live, serving as gendarmes and policemen. These services are the special prerogatives of both these peoples, who thus may be compared to the Irish in New York and Boston. However, their local power has not yet disappeared. Early in January, 1952, a *chapao* of Baluchis entered Zabol, decapitated the governor and one of his aides, and departed unscathed. They have stopped their slave raiding, apparently for good since the market has gone, but they are still to be reckoned with.

The westernmost of the nomads are found in Morocco. They summer in high pastures and migrate to the lowlands before the first flakes fall, to pasture their flocks on the grass made green by the autumnal rainfall brought from the Atlantic by the westerlies. The Middle Atlas Mountains furnish such an environment. The meadows on the saddle provide the summer forage; on the northern slope a heavy forest of cedar leads to pastures on the slopes above Meknes and Fez, while the southern side, facing the Sahara, has winter pasture in the Jebel Saghro. The Berbers who winter on the north are called Senhajas of the Shade, on account of their leafy cover, while those who go south are the Senhajas of the Sun. Notable among the former are the Zayans, Beni Mguild, and Beni Mtir; among the latter the Ait Attas and the Ait Sokhmans.

Both these groups of tribes have as their winter quarters permanent settlements which consist of walled enclosures centered around a lofty building of a type called *tighremt,* a combination

fort and granary. Some of the old people and dependents remain here during the summer to watch the grain fields and
guard the granaries, but the bulk of the population moves up
top.

So steep is the southern slope of the Atlas that the entire
tribal confederation can take but a single route on its spring and
fall migrations, and to get everyone up and down again in order
and on time requires strict discipline. For this purpose each year
the people elect a leader, whose insignia is a handful of grass
bound under his turban. The tribesmen of the Senhajas of the
Shade live in less precipitous terrain and have many paths up and
down; hence they are able to pilot their sheep over many forested
trails and have no need for a close organization. Being broken
into more numerous and smaller units, they vary their mode of
nomadism accordingly.

The people of the Shade and those of the Sun specialize in
a cash crop of wool, some of which their women weave into
thick rugs suitable for keeping them warm in their chilly tents.
These rugs find their way to the markets in Fez and Marrakesh,
and while the Arabs care little for them, they are much sought
after by Europeans.

Only elementary in the Islamic faith, twenty years ago the
Middle Atlas Senhajas were almost entirely illiterate and igno-
rant of all but the most rudimentary of prayers. Some of them
delayed circumcision until puberty or later, and religious spe-
cialists were rare among them. Of all the native peoples in North
Africa they were the least affected by Arab civilization. This
raised great hope in the minds of the French administrators
that, if once these people could be conquered, they would readily
become allies of the Europeans against the Arabs. Hence the
famous Berber *dahirs* (councils) of 1929, proclaiming the right
of the Berbers to keep their traditional form of government by
democratic council and to be judged by their ancient *qanuns*
rather than by the *Shari'ah* law, which was alien to them. The

[35]

existence of these *dahirs*, of course, raised a great clamor of protest among the city Arabs of Morocco, a clamor which has not yet died down.

Conquering the Senhajas was, however, no easy first step. The last people in Morocco to submit to French rule were the Ait Attas, who capitulated in the Jebel Saghro in 1934 after having lost most of their men. Meanwhile the Middle Atlas had been opened. Some of the tribes lost their winter pasture to French *colons*, who turned their grazing grounds into vineyards to make pinard for Frenchmen to drink at home while concentrating on finer vintages for export. Their summer pastures became fishing and skiing resorts of the French, to whom many of the former nomads now turned, in rags, to work as unskilled laborers.

An easier solution, however, was to join the Tirailleurs Marocains or the elite *goums*, and this was especially true of the Senhajas of the Sun, whose world had been smashed around their heads. These fearless and athletic warriors, led by the cream of the French army, had much to do with liberating Corsica from the Germans and distinguished themselves in Italy and France during World War II. They have lately been defending Indo-China against Communist invasion. Meanwhile, in Morocco, the nationalist struggle goes on, with the city Arabs and the French playing tug of war with the pigtails of the Senhajas, who care little for either as a people, since their loyalties are purely personal, and bloodshed their pleasure.

Probably the greatest theater of Alpine nomadism in the world is furnished by the majestic sweep of the Zagros Mountains, starting in the Turkish highlands and disappearing in the Makran, while rising to its greatest height in the land of the Bakhtiyaris, just north of the famous and troublesome oil city of Abadan. Seven separate peoples live along this arc: the Kurds, Lurs, Bakhtiyaris, Kuh Galus, Mammasanis, Khamsehs, and Qashqais. The first five speak languages and dialects of old

Persian stock and the Qashqais, a special Turkish dialect; the Khamseh tribes are divided between Turkish and Arabic speakers.

If one were to try to draw a line between the Zagros peoples who are purely pastoral and those who practice some agriculture, the task would be nigh impossible. While some of the Kurds are purely sedentary, others send their cattle and sheep to Alpine glades in summer in the care of youths and warriors, leaving the bulk of the population behind. Still others move down from summer to winter pasture en masse and back up again in the spring. Most of the Lurs are now sedentary, after their crushing defeat at the hands of Reza Shah, but a few still migrate.

While Kurds and Lurs are divided into many tribes, owing over-all leadership to no single chief, the Bakhtiyari confederation is a close unit led by a reigning family, that of Queen Seraya of Iran. As with the Ait Attas, the reason for this is simple: they have a difficult time getting all their people over the five stony passes between winter and summer pastures. Someone has to assign routes and the order of march on each, and someone also has to enforce order in the summer pasture. Both on the southern lowlands near Shustar, where they winter, and in their summer meadows the Bakhtiyari chiefs own dependent villages; in the lowlands, some are occupied by sedentary members of the confederation, others by Arabs. In the high, cold summer pasture, the villagers are Georgians and Armenians, men from the north who are able to endure the mountain winter. At both ends, the villagers keep a set of tents for the nomads while they are away. On the march they sleep in the open.

The Qashqais, too, have migration trouble and need a tight command, which is furnished by a reigning family of four brothers, with headquarters in Shiraz. It should be noted that all of these peoples winter on the far side of the mountains from Tehran, and hence are hard to reach, while in summer they

occupy inaccessible mountain fastnesses, except for the Qash-qais, who graze their animals on the open plain. Six of these seven peoples winter and summer in Iranian territory and are a local problem only. The Kurds, however, when they are no-madic, summer in Iran and winter in Iraq, or close to the border. This crossing of frontiers sometimes creates problems.

The modern world has had various effects on the Zagros peoples. Reza Shah, armed with all the trappings of the West, succeeded in conquering most of them, took away many of their animals, and burnt their tents. This unnecessary suffering also reduced their value to the nation as a source of animal materials, something that the old Cossack apparently consid-ered less important than the consolidation of his realm.

In Iraq the Kurds of various tribes revolted when the British left, and one old leader, Shaykh Ahmad, defied the whole Iraqi army at a pass before Suleimaniya, eventually fleeing to the Hazar Merd caves, then in process of excavation by that re-doubtable British archaeologist, Dr. Dorothy Garrod. Emerging from her protection, Shaykh Ahmad surrendered and was given the mild sentence of exile to Baghdad, where his son Baba Ali, a graduate of the University of California, was made Minister of Economics.

As for the Kurds of Turkey, their fate is best expressed by the pall of silence. Apparently some groups have been wiped out, others moved away, eventually to be returned as indoctrinated citizens. Still others maintain a precarious political existence. In Iran most of them managed to hold their own against the Reza Shah government until the World War II, when some were misled by the Russians into the premature formation of a Kurdish republic at Mahabad. In 1947 this was smashed and its leader, Mullah Muhammad, hanged. A refugee tribe from Iraq, the Barzanis, fled once more, this time to Soviet territory. Meanwhile the Russians keep up a continuous campaign of propaganda among the Kurds, who feel that they have grievances against Iranians, Arabs, and Turks alike.

Crushed by the armies of the present Shah's father, the Lurs live in penury and despair. The Bakhtiyaris, meanwhile, prosper, having given one of their daughters to the Shah as his queen. Educated men, the members of the Bakhtiyari reigning clan are as much at home in Tehran or Paris as in their summer pasture. Their private landing field is now open without grudge to their son-in-law, the King of Kings. Of the Kuh Galus and Mammasanis, little is known but their names. No Ph.D.'s are numbered among their ruling families, and no one writes about them in the *National Geographic*, or for that matter elsewhere. Nearly as obscure are the Khamsehs, about whom there are not even lists of tribes.

The Qashqais, however, with their four educated brothers, are very much in the news. They have built roads in their country, to truck out the stock; they have also set up their own medical and educational systems. A state within a state, they were temporarily crushed by Reza Shah but later staged a comeback of such force that they once captured a squadron of Iranian army tanks, giving them back to the government later as a present. Under the earlier rule of the present Shah their quarrel with government had died down, to be revived with the Mosaddeq crisis. Still very powerful, and related, through marriage into the Bahktiyari noble family and to the reigning queen, they should be one of the Shah's best hopes, far more in accord with his ideas than with those of either the landlord clique or the Communists, whom, like most Turks, they abhor. Owing to the education of their princes and their close organization, the Qashqais have been able to take over Western inventions on their own, and that is the secret of their present success.

The central Asiatic plain, consisting of a string of deserts ringed with steppes, crossed by rivers, and studded with oases, reaches inside Middle Eastern nations in three places: the Gurgan Plain of northern Iran just east of the southeast corner

of the Caspian; the oasis of Sarrakhs, part of which is inside the northeastern corner of Iran, and the Mazar-i-Sharif country of northern Afghanistan. In all three the dominant population is Turkoman, with Uzbegs also in the Afghan portion.

These Turkomans, descended from the Oghuz of the eleventh century, are Sunnite Muslims. Basically shepherds and horse breeders, they move out into the desert in the summer to let their animals crop the grass that comes with the midsummer rains and back into the shelter of the mountain fringes, oases, and river banks in the winter, where they can protect their animals from high winds, drifting snow, and cold. Some are sedentary, others nomadic. The distinction is largely economic, with the nomads in the wealthier category, but a close bond links the two. In fact two brothers may be divided, one nomadic and one sedentary, or a single man may live in both fashions in his lifetime, just as an American can be both a farmer and a cowboy at different times. Wherever they live, they prefer to inhabit their favorite style houses, *kibitkas* or *yurts*. These are portable round dwellings, shaped like half a globe, made of a wooden frame and covered with felt.

In the old days the Turkoman tribes were intermittently at war with each other and permanently at war with the Shi'ite Iranians to the south, whom they raided like cattle for the slave markets of Merv and the other capitals of the Turkestan khanates. As with the Baluchis, raiding and slaving were their honored occupations. With the Baluchis roaming north of Zabol and the Turkomans as far south as Qain, their raids came near to overlapping, and the whole of eastern Iran lived in terror of these twin threats before the iron peace of Reza Shah brought both to a halt. Just as the British destroyed the slave markets of the Indus, so did the Russians those of khanate capitals, leaving the Turkomans to the tamer tasks of herding, agriculture, and transport.

Today the Turkomans of the Gurgan Plain, mostly members of the Yamut tribe, are divided into the traditional sedentaries

and nomads, but they are at peace with the Iranian government. The greater threat of Russia across the barbed wire fence, keeping them from their summer pasture north of Atrek, makes them appreciate the present Iranian regime, with all its apparent ups and downs. Old men with braided beards, who once raided slaves, will now fight for the Shah, and that youthful monarch is happy to have so brave a tribe sitting on one of his most critical borders. Young Turkomans have surmounted the difficulty presented by the iron curtain and have turned to the trucking trade. Owning their own vehicles, they haul sheep, wool, hides, and "Bokhara" rugs to Gurgan, Babol, and Tehran, bringing back the manufactured products that their people need. Other young Turkomans have bought up land and installed tractors and other agricultural machinery, raising rich crops in the lee of Iran's largest and perhaps most interesting archaeological mound, Tureng Tepe. All in all, the Turkomans of the Gurgan Plain are one of the hopes of the Middle East.

The Sarrakhs Turkomans, members of the Tekke tribe, share their oasis with Arabs and Baluchis. Their present importance is purely strategic. The Turkomans and Uzbegs of the Mazar-i-Sharif country of Afghanistan have been less affected by modern culture than their brethren of Gurgan. Because of their loathing hate for the Russians, they are likely to shoot at all Europeans just to make sure that no Moskovs survive.

The moral of this essay is simple and clear. It is a plea for the preservation of nomads. Like glass, nomads are both strong and fragile. In the technological-geographical circumstances in which they arose, their strength is clear. Modern technology, in unwise hands, can destroy them, just as the breeders of hybrid corn can destroy the parent stocks from which came the succulent offspring and risk the latter's extinction in an adverse year.

The whole Middle East is suffering the pains of cultural lag. This means that while their local cultural system was surviving,

others elsewhere crept ahead of them and then gave radios to *mullahs,* just as Australian ranchers give tin cans to aborigines. The gap is much narrower, but the principle is there. How to become Western in one leap, while preserving the ancient cultural values of Islam, is a problem. In the cities it is a very serious one, as witness the perennial riots. In the villages it is also serious, and both Nasir and the Shah, to cite but two examples, are trying their best to conquer it.

But the place where Western culture can be most easily accepted and assimilated is the very place in which semi-Western governments have wished to see the local cultures destroyed —the home of the nomads—desert, alpine pasture, and steppe. The nomads of these regions understand leadership and loyalty. They are not worried about the fate of the proletariat or that of the white-collar worker. They are well fed and strong. They are used to timing events. As the oil companies in Arabia have found, they can take over the most useful aspects of our civilization without pain. One of the first concerns of the West in the Middle East is the preservation of nomads and the integration of their special qualities and values into the total picture. The West does not want to set nomads against sultan, president, or shah; that has been tried before and is one of the chief causes of anti-Western feeling in Middle Eastern countries. The West simply wants to help in any way it can to see that the people who are most immediately available are used to help the present peoples, and governments, of the Middle East. Sultan, president, and shah will benefit in the end.

The Villager

THE villager is the substance of the Near East. He is the embodiment of maps showing the distribution of population or cultivated land. He supports the worker and the merchant in the town. He pays rent and taxes, supporting his landlord and the government. He is blindly led by the politician and the army officer. Yet he is the man still to be better fed and housed, still to be educated and cured of his diseases. He is the deciding factor in the struggle between communism and the West. He is the personification of humanity in all its aspects, the raw material of race, language, religion, economy, sociology, politics —in short, he is Near Eastern civilization itself.

Of approximately eighty million people in the Near East, at least 75 percent are farmers. They and their occupation are the foundation of the national and economic life of the Near Eastern countries. From time immemorial and for various physical and cultural reasons this agricultural population has lived in villages. The villager is the peasant, the tiller of the soil. A few, however, are otherwise occupied, as brick masons, crop guards, carpenters, undertakers, and barbers—people who, on the same economic level, serve each other as well as the farmer.

But more often than not even these cultivate some land. Along the coasts of the Near Eastern seas a few villagers engage in fishing. But the vast majority of the population of the Near East is characterized by its close attachment, both literally and figuratively, to the land.

This agricultural population is very unevenly distributed. It is concentrated along the rainy and often mountainous coasts of the Caspian, Black, Aegean, and Mediterranean Seas; in the interior highlands of northern Iraq, eastern Turkey, and northwestern Iran where winter rain occurs; in the hot valleys of the exotic rivers,* i.e., the riverine oases of the Nile, the Tigris, and the Euphrates; and in the desert oases where water is obtained from the ground. Water is everywhere essential to the support of human life, but in few regions of the world, because of its relative scarcity, is it of greater significance than in the Near East. It is unfortunately available in limited areas and at limited times, a situation requiring many human adjustments. Water is the key to the economy of the Near East, the primary determinant of the distribution of population, and the chief factor in the location of villages.

A wide range of cultural conditions is represented in these areas of population density. Standards of living, degree of economic development, and political systems, as well as race and language, differ greatly from place to place. The Turks, Iranians, and Arabs are separately conditioned by their own heritages. Between, and to some extent within, these three main groups are a large number of cultural fragments whose continued existence has depended in large part upon their ability to resist assimilation, as the Kurds, Jews, Christian groups, and others. Because these peoples are minorities, and have problems, much attention has been given them.

Physically, the areas of dense population likewise show great diversity. Rainfall varies from practically zero to well over sixty

* EDITOR'S NOTE: In geography, the word "exotic" when used to describe a river means that the river rises in a humid climate and flows across an arid one.

inches a year. Temperatures range from below freezing to over 120° F. Populated altitudes reach beyond 5,000 feet. Soils include sand, swamp, clay, and alluvium. Yet several distinct environments consisting of relatively favorable combinations of the physical elements emerge which, with the necessary presence of water in some form of occurrence, are capable of supporting considerable numbers of people.

Diverse environments and different people inhabiting them create a Near Eastern complex upon which any sort of generalization is at once both difficult and misleading. A common fallacy is that conclusions based on data obtained in one part of the Near East may be applied to all the parts. Region-wide studies of the Near East, or economic plans, or foreign policy, can only be made on an interrelated area basis, as few physical or cultural elements are common to the entire region. Of the physical conditions, perhaps the climatic regime, i.e., dry summers and wet winters, but in greatly varying degree over the Near East, may be regarded as typical of the whole. Of the cultural conditions common to the entire Near East, two are paramount. These are the basic quality of the agricultural population and of Islam.

The character of the rural population exhibits a high degree of uniformity throughout the Near East, in spite of the differences in the agricultural systems of various environments, in the people, and in their types of villages. Iranians have little in common with Egyptians, except that both have similar attitudes toward agriculture, even though the practice of it is vastly different, and both are Muslims, even though the former are Shi'ites and the latter are Sunnites. The dangers of oversimplification and broad generalization, even in regard to the sedentary villager, are readily apparent. Many scholars agree

on the essential unity of this peasant group, which, sharing a common tradition of specialized occupation of the soil, extends far beyond the limits of political frontiers. One of the factors of peasant unity is the long period of occupation, from which rises a distinguishing quality:

[45]

"Le fellah est tout le contraire d'un primitif; ce serait plutôt un hyper-civilisé." Peasant life must therefore be related to a dual background of history and geography.[1]

The ancient civilizations of the Near East were founded upon agriculture. The control of water for irrigation was the measure of their political authority, and fertility insurance dominated their religion. Society developed in terms of its relationship to the land. Agriculture became a way of life, a point of view. Technique reached its optimum at an early stage and has since been merely maintained. The expansion and retreat of empires at various times in history have had little effect upon the basic agricultural pattern or the peasant's attitudes and responses to his way of life. Only during the past century has significant change taken place, the effect of the impact between East and West.

Agriculture today visibly lies at the heart of almost every aspect of Near Eastern life. Religion as practiced in the villages is concerned with the passage of the seasons, the growth process of crops, and the good or bad fortune which Allah dictates. The primary interest of the villager is still his land and his crops. They are, and always have been, his excuse for existence. Religion is a part of, and justification for, this interest. The governments have been interested in the peasant as a source of tax revenue to be used primarily to perpetuate themselves rather than to change or improve his way of life, which would be difficult even under the most favorable circumstances. Problems of the Near East may be better met when it is more generally realized that the starting point is the peasant and his agriculture.

As in many other parts of the Old World, the rural population of the Near East characteristically lives in tightly compressed villages that are essentially clusters of farm houses. This compact village is indigenous to an agricultural system in which the cultivable land is continuous and its forms of utiliza-

[1] W. B. Fisher, "Unity and Diversity in the Middle East," *Geographical Review*, XXXVII (1947), 419.

tion are more or less similar. Agglomerated settlement is most frequently an expression of the economic need for co-operation in the farming process, as in planting, tillage, harvesting, or irrigation. It is also prevalent in areas where, over a period of time, fragmentation of landholdings has taken place, resulting in scattered parcels cultivated by a particular farmer. When this situation is multiplied by the number of families in a given area, a central location in relation to the land cultivated is therefore desirable.

Combined with the mutual dependence factor is the fact that it is more efficient for the group to live en masse. Where population densities have become unusually high, as in the Nile Valley, the villages become larger, pressure within them increases, and they occur in greater frequency. Some purely agricultural villages in Egypt contain thousands of farm families. Differentiation between towns or cities and villages thus becomes a matter of function rather than of size. Where urban functions are present, as trade, industry, and administration, it may be said that a gathering of people in a consolidated mass ceases to be a village in the rather strict sense indicated above.

Until the past century agglomerated settlement best served the purposes of the villager as well as of agriculture. In areas where private ownership did not exist, there was no reason why a farmer should leave his village to live directly on the land. In fact, such a procedure would be to his disadvantage. A hundred years ago in Egypt the entire village was held responsible for the back taxes of any of its members. No farmer would willingly give up this security.

Another factor which held the village together was the need for protection. Safety in numbers and within a wall seemed to be the normal condition. This was particularly true in areas exposed to the attacks of marauding nomads or in areas occupied by minority religious groups. Protection from the elements, too, often forced people to live in clusters, as is still true in the basin areas of Upper Egypt, where safeguards from the annual

flood are necessary. The practice of collectively grazing animals owned by the members of the village on community property is also a unifying factor. Agglomerated settlement may thus be seen to be dependent upon a variety of conditions, which at the same time have developed a strong sense of social unity.

Since the beginning of the nineteenth century the influence of the West has been making considerable headway in the Near East. Its more obvious effects are apparent at the national level, chiefly in the form of organizational superstructures. Government, finance, industry, and the military have been systematically reorganized along Occidental lines in greater or lesser degree in the hope that they might function in the same way. But operationally, they are still essentially Oriental. There are any number of examples that may be used to illustrate this inconsistency, as in tax collecting, customs letting on contract, gathering statistics, land tenure, credit, nepotism, local government, importance of tribes, and the like. The degree of Western influence, of course, shows wide geographical variation, as between Turkey and the Yemen. The question here, however, is to what extent have the effects of Westernization penetrated into the agricultural community, perhaps the most fundamental of all the social and economic institutions in the Near East.

It is easy to think of agriculture and the village in the Near East as virtually changeless. The Egyptologists, for example, recognize in use today the same types of houses, crops, and tools as appear in the familiar scenes depicted on the ancient monuments. Elsewhere in the Near East connection between form and process of the present and of the past is also apparent. The extreme and widespread poverty of the peasant, with its manifold evils (to the Western mind), tends to bolster the idea of retarded civilization: that the people have existed in this depressed state for countless centuries; that they think in the same way about the same things as they always have; and

that they cannot overcome the harshness of their material existence. In many ways agriculture and the village institution have not changed very much. Yet it can hardly be supposed that economic and technical changes during the past hundred years or so have left the village unaffected or the peasant entirely unmoved.

The advent of Westernization to the Near East has given rise to a number of sequence relationships in which agriculture plays a major part and the villager its most important supporting role. As the need for economic and political advantage has developed on a national basis among many of the Near Eastern countries, so the emphasis in agricultural production has begun to shift from a subsistence economy to a commercial one. Within the past century the production of cotton, maize, sugar cane, citrus fruits, deciduous fruits, and other crops has acquired great commercial significance. Even among the traditional crops, such as wheat, dates, and garden vegetables, an increase in commercialization may be noted. New crop combinations and expanded production require new or different rotations and water supplies, more labor, more fertilizer, more land. The peasant has adapted himself to the new circumstances by growing the new crops in the old ways, by increasing his water supplies with the same techniques as he has always used, by reclaiming bits of unused land along his cultivable periphery, and by working all year instead of only part of it. Although the peasant has borne the burden of the change, and he is conscious of its implications, he has remained peculiarly disinherited from its benefits.

In the welter of Westernization many peasants have become landowners, albeit most of their holdings are infinitesimally small and their combined ownership is negligible compared to the total amount of cultivated land. Even so, ownership itself is an encouraging sign of social change. To the peasant, the land is the basis for material security; the desire to own it is deeply rooted in his philosophy of life. Partition of land by inheritance

is reducing the amount per owner to a point where it is questionable whether or not he can live on it. Purchase, mortgages, indebtedness, and expropriation are, in the order named, natural consequences. If the farmer cannot live from his own land, he will rent from another, he will become a tenant on an estate, or he will hire himself out as a day laborer. His children must work with him to earn their keep. In any case, owner, tenant, or day laborer, his way of life continues much as it always has, the unyielding and laborious existence of the tiller of the soil.

Land reclamation and irrigation schemes, both large and small, are having a profound effect upon agriculture and, by association, on the village. The extensive development of flood control, irrigation, and drainage works in the Nile Valley account for the well-known changes in the Egyptian agricultural system and the greatly increased importance of commercial crops. The same may be true in the near future for Iraq, which has a large-scale land reclamation program under way. Elsewhere projects of varying size and purpose have produced local benefits. But among the most important developments are the countless individual efforts to bring water to another *feddan*, to dig a new well, or to level a new terrace. These peasant "projects," motivated by the pressure on and desire for land, constantly attack the margins of cultivation. They account in part for the preponderance of small landholders and for the breaking down of ancient village restraints. New patterns of population distribution, revealed by the recent increase of isolated farmsteads, are coming into existence. This, too, is evidence of social and economic change.

Material items from the West are of great significance in some sections of Near Eastern society but have affected the average peasant in small ways only. Instead of homemade utensils the farmer is apt to use cheaply made glassware or metalware imported from Europe. The blue-enameled, soot-covered, "Made-in-England," metal teapot with the broken-hinged lid and the hot handle is almost universal. To the peasant the use of an

imported item as such in preference to a local craft product is of little concern, as the lid will doubtless break off the domestic teapot anyway. He has simply substituted one item for another, with little economic or functional difference to himself. He receives Western items as they are and for what they are, and uses them where they fit into his economy. It is easy for trucks to replace camels because they both accomplish the same purpose. When an airplane was seen for the first time by an Arab farmer, he was asked by an American if he did not think it was wonderful how the iron bird flew through the air. The farmer replied by asking if that was not what it was supposed to do.

Mechanical devices of Western origin are not within easy reach of the peasant, and hence may be dismissed with a few passing remarks. Of means of communication, perhaps only the radio may have any importance, as one is sometimes found bleating forth music or news in a village coffee shop. Mechanical transport in terms of direct peasant use is confined to rare instances of travel and is of indirect benefit in commodity exchange. In agriculture, tools are simple and limited; they are used with a high degree of skill and, in most instances, more effectively under existing field conditions than power-driven machinery could be, even if it were available. Motor-driven irrigation pumps are sometimes found, usually on a co-operatively owned and operated basis since the capital outlay and cost of maintenance are too great for the average individual.

From the foregoing it is apparent that some aspects of Westernization have affected agriculture but have left the peasant and the village relatively untouched. Suggestions of economic and social change on the peasant level are noted in the increase of free holders and in the tendency toward dissemination of the rural population, especially where large-scale irrigation installations have induced a change in the agricultural economy. Another manifestation of progress, possibly a derivative of Western influence, is the development of government-subsidized community projects and co-operatives. These probably represent

an effort on the part of the governments concerned to identify themselves with the national welfare and may therefore be motivated by self-interest rather than by strict humanitarianism. The ultimate success of such programs depends upon the willingness of the villagers to accept them. The peasant does not want reform from a higher authority and may regard as rank interference government attempts to initiate it. These symptoms of social and economic change are encouraging, but by themselves they are of insufficient depth or extent to indicate any marked improvement in the villager's way of life.

One of the principal causes of continued depression among the rural population of the Near East is the concentration of wealth in the hands of a few. This condition has been more or less chronic since ancient times, but with the advent of Western commercialism it has become more acute. The gulf between the rich (landowners, merchants, and the like) and the poor (the farmer) is increasing, largely because of the accelerated evolution of an economically prosperous middle class. The structure of Near Eastern society tends to sustain disequilibrium, which in part may explain the anachronism of peasant poverty. The plight of the agricultural population is not due to fatalism, lethargy, rusticity, disease, or illiteracy, which are falsely and too frequently offered in explanation; these are widespread, it is true, but are consequences of the social order, not causes of it. The farmer seems to be aware of his condition and does only what is necessary to make ends meet, which takes him fourteen hours a day, including Ramadan. It is not surprising that the peasant has not yet acquired a sense of spiritual freedom or moral dignity, or the desire to improve his lot in life. Such basic human needs will only be realized when the components of Near Eastern society, both Oriental and Occidental, become properly integrated.

The average farmer is so completely a part of the village community and the agricultural way of life that he may serve to

represent the rural population as a whole. Throughout the Near East he shares a common heritage of close proximity to the soil, perhaps his strongest conditioner. His over-all point of view toward his neighbors, his landowner, government officials, and others who come within his limited horizon is the peasant point of view and is remarkably uniform. In terms of his general attitudes and responses toward his way of life and to other Near Eastern social institutions he may truly be regarded as a sort of "collective" individual. It is in this context that he is thought of here. His manners, customs, food, houses, village structure, sanitary conditions and diseases, occupations, ethnology, psychology, and sociology are all adequately treated in the literature. It would be well, however, to know a little of what the peasant's attitudes and responses consist, if possible.

The whole body of peasant thought is pre-eminently determined by agriculture. Every aspect of the peasant's life is penetrated by it. His experience is confined to it. Even his strictly nonagricultural activities, as marriage (and hence childbirth), are timed according to agricultural activity. Only death escapes it, and is itself the only escape. Geared to the agricultural cycle, the peasant tends to regard things as recurrent; he knows that times cannot always be bad, nor can they always be good. No change from the established cycle is expected. The passage of the seasons, the sun and the rain, are mysteries and are incorporated in a large body of superstitious practices and beliefs almost approaching animism, binding the peasant to the past. He lives in the balance of nature, and neither seeks to control its forces nor those of his fellow man.

The circumscribed pattern of village life also exerts a strong influence upon the peasant's thought. The farmer's experience, on the whole, comprises a quiet, routine existence with family and neighbors in the village and the field. Except for the market which he habitually attends he knows nothing of other places. If they come to his attention at all, he probably identifies them in terms of his own village. Any departure from the normal,

and celebrations such as *Bayrama* (holiday), weddings, and funerals are normal, is a memorable occasion. Passage of time is often reckoned from it. Fires, accidents, and the collapse of a house occur with sufficient frequency as to cause only a mild ripple of excitement and are met with resignation.

The relationship between the villager and the government is typical of the attitude toward what the peasant considers to be authoritarian intrusions on his peaceful way of life. His association with the state is practically limited to taxation, assessment, conscription, or forced labor. Hence the villager regards the government with resentment and fear; his reactions to its representatives are inspired by self-preservation. The visit of the tax collector or a policeman in search of a draft evader is often met with open hostility. When government agents come into the village asking silly questions, they get silly answers. Incidentally, this is in part responsible for the well-known unreliability of Near Eastern statistical information. The peasant cannot comprehend a census, for example, purely for its own sake. An ulterior motive must lie behind it. If taxation is suspected, the enumeration is ridiculously low; but if there is a rumor of rationing, it is just as ridiculously high. Further responsibility for statistical unreliability is the indifference of the government agents themselves. They are satisfied with a mass of figures that will, in turn, satisfy their immediate superiors, preserving the jobs of both, and so on up the bureaucratic line. The handful of government officials who actually get into the villages, including census enumerators, are peculiarly unequipped to co-ordinate their activities with the peasant mentality. By position and point of view they cannot or will not reduce their work to terms the peasant can understand. The result is that the government agent in contact with the peasant serves neither the peasant nor the government.

The same sort of relationship exists between the peasant and his landowner. The peasant regards the landlord as a higher

authority, who is frequently hated. In taking a disproportion-
ately large share of the fruit of his labor, the landlord is held
responsible for his depressed condition. The peasant thinks of
the landowner as living in luxury which he provides, and he bit-
terly resents the lack of return. In this the landlord shares with
the government the antipathy of the peasant. What the peasant
receives from either is far from commensurate with what he
gives. The entire landlord-peasant relationship is a part of the
problem of land tenure. Increasing examples of land reform in
the Near East, however, and of a development of interest in
the peasant's welfare on the part of some landowners are very
encouraging.

Visits to the village of persons whose missions are beyond the
experience of the peasant and are therefore incomprehensible
are regarded as intrusions and are viewed with suspicion, skepti-
cism, and often unbelief. The public health officer, for instance,
encounters a notable lack of co-operation. In a known case,
standard procedure required a group of subjects, a group of
controls, DDT, and thoroughgoing although simplified public
lectures with exhortations explaining the project. Complete
deadlock continued until it was discovered that the village half-
wit, a few days after he had been jokingly pushed forward by
the crowd for a dusting, no longer itched. In other words, the
project was accidentally reduced to concrete terms—freedom
from itching being understandable, whereas freedom from
typhus was not. When the public service worker learns to meet
the peasant at his own level, and thus when the element of
chance, as above, is eliminated, then will progress in bridging
the gap between the peasant and those who wish to help him be
made. Those who would introduce simple Western-style benefits in health or in agriculture also must show that they are not
"really" part of the government. The successes of the Near East
Foundation in agricultural improvement and adult education
in certain villages in Iran, of the Rockefeller Foundation in

Egypt, and the agricultural development in Saudi Arabia guided by the Arabian American Oil Company adequately illustrate both points.

Among the inherent characteristics of the Near Eastern social structure is the low standard of living of the rural population. Its roots lie deep in the cultural background of the Near East, and its widespread occurrence has long been recognized and accepted as a part of the Oriental scheme of things. The depression of the peasants had no effect upon the established balance of society, it created no functional disorder, it was not important. Today, however, as a consequence of Western influence, the peasant's low standard of living has become a handicap to the development of an articulated social and economic system.

The great problem confronting the Near East today is the establishment of a co-ordinated and relatively stabilized society. There are no delusions regarding the magnitude of this task, nor the time it will take, but these are not reasons why it cannot be regarded as an ultimate objective. The problem is extraordinarily complex and involves every facet of Near Eastern culture. The solution most positively does *not* lie in Westernization, and to believe that it does is an invitation to frustration, folly, and failure. Rather it implies a mingling on a functional basis of forces from the past and the present, from the land, the environment, the peasants, the intellectuals, the state, religion, and the West. It includes self-examination and housecleaning as well as technical assistance. It requires the creation of an atmosphere in which the integrity of the individual is respected and initiative may find expression. The solution of the problem must be indigenously inspired, and foreign elements brought to bear upon it must in a sense become naturalized.

Amelioration of the peasant's depressed state in relation to the changing circumstances of the modern Near East is essen-

tial to the eventual achievement of stability. But to endeavor to accomplish this end exclusively by the application of Western principles and practices is to confess ignorance of the nature of the problem. Nothing can better illustrate the widespread misconception of the almighty power of Western technique in solving the ills of the world than the following statement made by an American government official responsible for Point Four planning: "What we are interested in is teaching the Arabs how to farm." The promiscuous imposition of Western skills and ideas upon the Near Eastern economy in what may be a perfectly sincere attempt to improve the standard of living of the peasant is to run the risk of aggravating the very condition that should be remedied. Conversely, to do nothing about it at all is to sanction the continuance of disequilibrium and to ignore the clearly recognizable demands of a changing society. Remedial action must, therefore, take cognizance of the actual needs of the Near Eastern peasant in relation to the society as a whole as well as the peasant's attitude toward it and his ability to assimilate it. His real needs may not be what Westerners think they should be. To ensure a stable order, the increase in the peasant's standard of living must be co-ordinated with the increasing tempo of the Near Eastern economy.

The mitigation of disease among the rural population of the Near East may serve as an illustration. Disease is concomitant to a low standard of living and to other depressing conditions, such as semistarvation, illiteracy, and poverty, conditions by no means peculiar to the Near East. Putting humanitarian instincts and the benefits of good will brutally aside for the moment, it is possible to envisage large-scale public health programs as detrimental to the common good. Such programs in a society lacking the economic and social capacity to absorb them can give rise to an overpopulation problem with which the society may be unable to cope. The resulting decrease in the standard of living may disrupt the entire economy. Or a specific program, as malaria control, may require the drain-

age of an area, thus removing water upon which a group of people may depend for irrigation: no water, no malaria, and no food. An analogous case could be made for literacy. A public with no economic or social opportunity to utilize its education would tend to upset the balance of society.

The title of a recent article, "Land Reform: The Key to the Development and Stability of the Arab World," [2] expresses a fundamental truth, and the thesis developed supports it. It is necessary to emphasize the relationship of land reform to the total pattern of development. Economics is only a part of the pattern. To foster the growth of this part and leave the social and political parts unnurtured is to accentuate instability. Land reform alone cannot solve the economic problems of the Near East. Total reform without it is meaningless.

The overwhelming importance of co-ordinating reform programs of all kinds with each other and especially with the total pattern of social and economic development in Near Eastern countries is readily apparent. Each venture is but a part of the combined effort to get the country going along more modern lines. Projects dealing directly with people, as education, medical aid, agricultural assistance, and others, must show immediate significance and purpose. They should be the result of the mutual desire of those who wish to help and those needing it. The difficulty lies in the establishment of rapport between the two. Other types of projects undertaken by a national government, as road construction, electrification, irrigation, or financial controls, most certainly must be involved, although they need not depend upon the people for active participation. In any case, such reform programs can be really successful only when it can be shown that they fit into the existing structure of the society, do not destroy the benefits of other programs, and are sufficiently flexible to meet changing demands. In this way a solid economic and social foundation may be established on which more completely democratic concepts may later be

[2] Afif I. Tannous, *The Middle East Journal*, V (Winter, 1951), 1–20.

built. Numerous programs heretofore undertaken, especially some of Western inception, have bogged down because they attempted to adjust the society to them. They have failed because of the lack of comprehension of their significant relevances. Isolated disciplines cannot function independently.

In his strength and sense of values the Near Eastern villager possesses the qualities which would enable him to assume his share of responsibility in co-operative development. Those qualities are evident in the peasant's ability to sustain his traditional way of life under the burden of adversity and distress. This same ability would be directed toward economic and social betterment once the weight is decreased. Co-ordinated reform programs of various sorts are a necessary means toward this end. The application of the peasant's inherent qualities toward the achievement of ultimate peace and stability consists in a sense of the transfer of the integrity of the village community to the national level. It is through the peasant that permanent gains will be made and maintained. When he is shown the way by those who understand, who care, and who belong, then a new concept of nationalism based on humanistic ideals will emerge.

The Israeli Farmer

It SHOULD be stated from the outset that it would be hard, if not impossible, to consider as one group the whole farming population of Israel. It is necessary to deal, first of all, with two distinctive types: there is the Jewish farmer—mostly a former city or town dweller and his children—who, either for national or socioideological motives or because of economic necessity, took to farming; and then there is the Arab farmer, the fellah (Muslim or Christian), who, like his counterpart in the neighboring Arab countries, is carrying on his age-old occupation. The Arab farm population is, to a great extent, homogeneous with regard to beliefs, opinions, mores, patterns of behavior, and, in particular, language and religion. It is also, like farm populations in most other countries, homogeneous in terms of occupation; the Arab fellaheen are, like most farm populations in other countries, filled "from generation to generation . . . with the children of farmers and husbandmen." Mobility among the Arab farmers—with the exception of the beduins—is slight.

With the Jewish farmer, however, it is different. He is, in the first place, a newcomer to the rural community and, in particular, a newcomer to the agricultural occupation. Not only

[60]

was his father not an agriculturist, but he himself may have switched to agriculture from some other occupation. He originates from twoscore or more European and other countries. His heterogeneity in terms of language, culture, mores, and patterns of behavior is great, although efforts are being made to create a new cultural pattern. The differences between the Jewish Israeli farmer and his Arab counterpart are so great that it is difficult to find common features. This essay, therefore, considers only the Jewish farmer.

By the end of 1951 there were, in Israel, 505,000 gainfully employed Jewish persons, of whom 70,000 were agriculturists. These Jewish farmers are by no means a unified group. Roughly, they may be divided into two general groups: the new settlers who have arrived since the establishment of the State of Israel in May, 1948; and the farmer who was by that time already settled on the land. One trait the two groups have in common is that most of them are former city dwellers [1] (except for the second, Palestine-born, generation) who changed to agriculture. But here any similarity ends.

In the pre-World War II period the trend toward agriculture stemmed either from a pioneering spirit or from the realization that a new country cannot be built up without an agricultural basis. In the scale of values which molded the Jewish settlement in Palestine-Israel, colonization, emphasizing agricultural work, came to be regarded as of the first importance.[2]

Other elements, to be sure, also went in for farming. There was the immigrant who became an agricultural worker from sheer necessity—and perhaps later an independent settler—and there were the German-Jewish immigrants of the 1930's, merchants, lawyers, physicians, who brought some money with

[1] Among the immigrants of 1949–1950 about 5 percent were agriculturists. Some of these, however, were not born agriculturists but were people who had turned to this occupation for the purpose of exercising it later in Israel.

[2] S. N. Aisenstadt, "The Sociological Structure of the Jewish Community in Palestine," *Jewish Social Studies*, X (1948), 9–10.

them and bought farms—mostly chicken, truck, and dairy farms and citrus groves—which they ran themselves. But the general spirit was dominated by the "emphasis placed on every social and economic activity" which was related, directly and unconditionally, to the establishment of the independence of the Jewish society. This refers primarily to the high evaluation of agricultural colonization and manual labor, but also to the great value assigned to every economic activity related to pioneering work that served the goal of independence—irrespective of whether or not there was direct financial and economic benefit.

Today the situation is different. The bulk of immigrants in the last five years comprised people who looked to Israel as a physical haven after being uprooted during the war, and the Oriental Jews from North Africa, the Yemen, and Iraq. Not many of these elements shared the ideologies which determined the aspirations of the former waves of immigrants. The new immigrant lacks the awareness of the functions which the immigrant must carry out in the establishment of the land as a Jewish National Home.[3] And if, of the 700,000-odd immigrants, mostly urbanites, some thousands of families went into farming, they did so principally from the necessity of making a living. Strict rationing, austerity, and food shortages also made the village [4] appear more attractive. But settling on the land hardly transformed these people into farmers. There was, and is, a considerable turnover, in part because many were unable to accustom themselves to the heart-breaking toil of a farmer. But in the main, the system of settlement, the impact of shortages in equipment, and the necessity of settling considerable numbers quickly, transformed the total settlement practice into a hasty enterprise, far from stable.

[3] A. Tartakower, "The Sociological Implications of the Present-Day Aliya," *Jewish Social Studies*, XIII (1951), 301.

[4] "Village," throughout this essay, means a rural community comprising a group of houses in which the farmers live, surrounded by agricultural land.

Even though land was plentiful after the exodus of the Arabs, there was a lack of equipment, of pipes for irrigation, of power to drive the pumps, and of water running into the new settlements. A new farmer who received his allotment of land and settled in a post-Arab, rebuilt house or in a new hut in the village soon realized that he was still far from becoming a farmer. He lacked experience, although he could compensate for this by taking practical advice from the instructors furnished by the State of Israel or by the settlement agency. But there were other, more significant, obstacles. More often than not the land was hardly prepared for new settlement. The land in the Arab villages which had been farmed extensively was sometimes exhausted and needed to be cleared of stones and fertilized in order to support a more modern form of agriculture.

Removing stones is a long and tedious process. So, too, is the process of restoring the land. Fertilizer was scarce, delivered late, or unattainable for lack of foreign exchange. Water for irrigation was sometimes cut off by power shortages, insufficient drilling, or a shortage of pipes. In many cases the settler's use of water was restricted to certain hours of the day; the flow was inadequate and sufficed for only a part of his land. Since fertilizer and equipment were not supplied, or not forthcoming in time, a new settler might buy them on the free (or black) market. The price for the produce which a settler turned in to the purchasing agency was, however, regulated. Hence at the end of the season it turned out that agricultural work did not pay the new settler even a daily wage.

What were such settlers to do? Some left the villages; others used only a part of their land, relying on outside work—road construction, factory work, and similar jobs in nearby towns and cities—for their living. Many settlers thus, during the first years, became at best part-time farmers and were connected economically and, for the most part, also socially and mentally, with the urban center. To be sure, many of them may in due course

become connected with the land and farming; in fact, some have already succeeded in doing this during the last two years. But today the new settler differs little in behavior, actions, and attitudes from the urbanite, even though he may be determined to stay on the land. Therefore, in considering the attitudes and behavior patterns of the farmer, most of these postindependence settlers should be disregarded.

At the time of the census of November 8, 1948, there were 716,678 Jews in Israel. Of these, 314,781 (44.2 percent) belonged to the labor force. Among them were 38,881 people occupied in agriculture (12.03 percent). In this study this group will be regarded as the Israeli farming population, with traits, attitudes, and sentiments representative of the Israeli farmer.

The group comprised mostly immigrants who transferred to farming from other work and to the village from urban centers. At the time of the workers' census of 1937, for instance, only 5.7 percent had been farmers before they came to Palestine—including trainees for farming prior to arrival in Palestine. In 1948 a minority, probably not more than 3,000, were these new farmers' children who had come of age and were either helping their parents or settling for themselves.

There is a difference in outlook, attitude, and behavior patterns between the first and the second (Israeli-born) generations. The first generation (immigrants who went into agriculture) came to the country for the most part with a determination to change over to this particular occupation. It was for them not a means of making a living, not even solely a result of the necessity of building up a nation. It was, rather, connected with the whole revolutionary change the Jews of the world, particularly of Europe, had undergone since the French Revolution.

Back-to-the-land ideas and the idealization of agriculture, which flourished among intellectuals in European countries in the nineteenth century as a reaction against the spreading mechanization and industrialization, also influenced Jewish intellectuals. The ideology of occupational change and of agrarian-

ization become part and parcel of the Jewish Enlightenment Movement (*Haskalah*). "Normalization" of Jewish life meant securing civil equality, adjustment to the environment in language, culture, attire, and mode of life, and also, often foremost, occupational change.

The growth of anti-Semitism brought in its wake a revival of every sort of accusation leveled against Jews. Despite the changed economic outlook, Jews were again accused of "parasitism" in exploiting the "productive" non-Jews by employing themselves in unproductive occupations. The reaction among Jews was a strengthening of the desire—mostly a theoretical one to be sure—to take up agriculture and to occupy themselves in manual work.

All these tendencies, beliefs, and sentiments were strengthened again and again in modern Zionism, which developed, among other things, as a reaction to renewed anti-Semitism. Here are the motifs of "normalization" of Jewish life, of attempts to change in response to anti-Semitic accusations, of a conscious negation of the occupational distribution in the Diaspora, and of "a desire to overcome this negation through the creation of a new society in Palestine." [5]

In negating the different forms of Jewish life in the Diaspora the aim was both to create something new, based on labor and the soil, and to return to the pre-Diaspora roots of Jewish existence. As in so many modern nationalist movements, so also in Zionism, a romantic regard for the past flourished and also a yearning to return to it—in this case to Biblical times and with it to the life in nature on the land of Israel.

Trade, peddling, and service occupations were labeled parasitic, an exploitation of the toil of others and therefore unethical (Socialist theory exercised its influence here), while agriculture was lauded and regarded as a prerequisite for any creative work and for culture generally.

For many, Zionism was based on the return of the Jew to the

[5] Aisenstadt, *op. cit.*, X, 3.

two sources of life indispensable to regeneration and growth—nature and work. "The city man must therefore go to village and field. . . . The bond between man and man, man and nature, should not be merely economic but a living bond forged in the joy of participation and creation." [6]

The exaggerated evaluation, or overevaluation, of the soil may become understandable if this element in the ideology of Zionism is taken into account. It may also seem reasonable that a people which has been far from the soil for hundreds of years, an urban element returning of its own free will to the village and meeting there with tremendous difficulties, should exaggerate the value of its action. Hence this ideology became paramount among the guiding principles of the Jewish society in Palestine, particularly among those settled on the land. It was as though all phenomena of Jewish existence in Palestine were bound up with the village.

Besides economics and spiritual life, the messianic (or revolutionary) hope of building up a new society based on absolute equality and social justice was also connected with the village. The young people, mostly intellectuals, coming from Russia and Poland at the beginning of this century and in the post-World War I years were stirred by the revolutionary movement in Russia and considerably influenced by the message of social justice which it seemed at that time to carry. It was further motivated by the all-human striving for justice, freedom, and peace which is always stronger among immigrants in a new undeveloped country. They are more inclined than people in a settled country to believe in the possibility of building up a perfect socioeconomic order by abolishing class inequality and through mutual help and co-operation. This vision of a perfect society was associated with the village, which was supposed to become the center of a self-sufficient noncapitalistic society.

[6] Reuben Wallenrod, "The Teachings of A. D. Gordon," *Jewish Social Studies*, VII (1945), 350.

Several different types of villages have been developed by the Jewish settlers. There is, to begin with, the private village (called *Moshavah*, "colony") settled by farmers who own their farms, buildings, and equipment and who engage in farming at their own risk.

But private, individual farming did not develop very extensively in Palestine. Low productivity of the land (lower even than in the neighboring Arab countries) and its high cost (one acre of land in the years 1933–1936 was worth, on an average, $128 in Palestine against $31 in the United States), together with the high cost of Jewish labor, made farming almost prohibitive on a commercial basis. Jewish farming, therefore, became a national enterprise. Land was acquired by the Jewish National Fund and rented to the farmers on a forty-nine-year lease for a small yearly sum (2 percent of its value). Most of the funds necessary for housing, machinery, and other initial investments were supplied by the Jewish Foundation Fund. The conditions for allotment of land and funds were simple: the farmer was to work the land himself without hired labor. Provisions were also made to prevent the farmer from selling or transferring his homestead to another person, thus avoiding speculation in land.

The settlers on this land, the majority of whom were young people in their early twenties, were motivated both by idealistic and practical considerations. They dreamed of a national solution for the homelessness of the Jewish people through the colonization of Palestine, and they hoped to develop there a society based on the principles of economic and social equality. They hoped to achieve their dream through collective or cooperative settlements which would be self-sufficient and thus independent of any capitalistic market.

Thus developed a second kind of village, the collective settlement (*Kvutza* or *Kibbutz*). The maxim guiding this type of settlement is: from each according to his abilities; to each ac-

cording to his needs. Everyone in such a village has the right to satisfy his economic needs without regard to earning capacity. There is no, or almost no, private property in a collective settlement. The settlers live in communal houses built, owned, and maintained collectively and eat in communal dining halls. Clothing and other necessities are provided by the village. Children are raised from their earliest years in children's houses, where they eat, sleep, and play. Schooling, too, is provided by the group. The entire income of the members—including wages from outside work—goes into the general treasury and is used in a collective way to supply the needs of the members.[7]

The other type of farming settlement is the co-operative village (*Moshav Ovdim*). As in the collective village, the land in the co-operative village does not belong to the settlers. But here the organization is based on the family principle and the individual farm. Every family forms a unit; the house, some of the tools, and the animals belong to the individual farmer, although he may owe what they are worth to the Jewish Foundation Fund. Proceeds from farming go to the individual farmer in accordance with the produce raised. His consumption and spending are again regulated only by his own will and needs. But a part of the cultivation, as well as the marketing and purchasing, is done co-operatively. There are also provisions for a great measure of mutual assistance. Should a settlement member fall sick, the other settlers usually take over the job of caring for his farm. In the same way a farmer is helped by his cosettlers in case of a disaster, although lately most of these things have been taken care of by insurance.

The percentual relation between the different forms of settlement in the preindependence period can be gauged from the figures of 1945.[8] In that year there were:

[7] C. W. Efroymson, "Collective Agriculture in Israel," *Journal of Political Economy*, February, 1950; Henrik F. Infield, *Cooperative Living in Palestine* (New York, 1948).

[8] Recent immigration and settling have changed the percentages.

	No. of farmers	Percent
Private independent settlers	7,000	34.5
In collective settlements	7,500	36.9
In co-operative settlements	5,800	28.6
Total	20,300	100.0

In addition there were some 3,700 other people occupied in agriculture—mostly agricultural workers, the majority of whom probably worked in the private settlements. Since most agricultural hired labor in Palestine-Israel is considered as being in a transitional stage, such workers may be disregarded from our considerations.

Despite the different types of villages in which the Jewish farmer lives and works, a number of features are common to them all. There is, first of all, no large landownership and no tenants in the meaning of the word in other countries. The average holding in the individual villages was, in the 1940's, about 62 dunams (15.3 acres); in the collective settlements about 68 dunams per family; and in the co-operative villages 45 dunams per farm.[9] The rise and fall of this average is generally insignificant and is a result of the type of land and crop that is being grown.

There are differences between the size of a holding of irrigated and one of nonirrigated land and between farms producing grain and those devoted to truck farming, citrus production, or chicken raising. Thus, in the old grain-producing settlements of Galilee the size of the farm may be 200 to 300 dunams (50 to 75 acres), in mixed dry farming 100 dunams (25 acres), in irrigated mixed farming 10 to 25 dunams (2½ to 6 acres), and in poultry farming as low as 1 acre (in Ramath Hashavim, for instance, a settlement of German Jewish immigrants).

Another common feature of all these types of farms was, until recently, the fact that grain cultivation played a very small

9 R. Nathan, O. Gass, and D. Creamer, *Palestine, Problem and Promise* (Washington, 1946), pp. 200 ff.

role. The low productivity of the land, plus the competition from abroad and from the Arab population with its low standard of living, made it arduous for the ordinary Jewish farmers to cultivate grain if they wanted to live on the higher standard, one somewhat nearer a European level, to which they were accustomed. The Jewish farmer, outside of the somewhat isolated Upper Galilee region, turned therefore to more profitable diversified dairy, poultry, and vegetable farming and to fruit and citrus growing. Thus, Jewish farming became concentrated mostly in the more commercialized branches, with almost total neglect of the basic production of grain.

Again the realities in Palestine, where there are no natural pastures, and the disparity between the standard of living of the Jew and his Arab fellah competitor led to further commercialization of farming. The cows and chickens had been fed concentrated food, which was mostly imported and which often cost up to 50 percent or more of the value of the produce. A great part of agriculture became, thus, a commercial enterprise, somewhat comparable with truck, dairy, and chicken farming around the New York metropolitan area.

But even so, because of competition from neighboring countries and from imports and the high prices paid for fodder, the return from agriculture was small—much smaller than in city occupations. This situation led to a constant, though fluctuating, migration to the cities, while those who remained on the land needed further compensation to counteract their economic plight. Such compensation was provided by raising agriculture still higher in the scale of values of the Jewish society. If the predominant idea was national service for the purpose of building up an independent national Jewish existence, this was considered to have been embodied in the village, particularly in collective and co-operative villages. The farmer, again particularly from these types of villages, began to be regarded as a sort of special being who, devoid of private interests, devotes his life to service, to the ideal of building up the Jewish nation in

Palestine. "The Kibbutz member became an individual to be respected and emulated by all, a symbol of the aspirations of the new Jew in Palestine. He was held up as an example to the young whose imagination was fired by his heroism and self-sacrifice." [10]

The ideals and hopes of workers in agricultural settlements, based on self-sufficiency, absolute social and economic equality, and the formation of noncapitalistic units, which the youth coming to the country hoped would materialize, may have been somewhat suited to the situation of the 1900's and 1920's. Palestine was then a country devoid of capital and capitalistic enterprises, with a comparatively small city population. Since the economy of the country was undeveloped, a great deal of economic independence could be achieved by creating semiclosed economic circles based on self-sufficiency. The settlements were mostly engaged in the cultivation of cereals and vegetables for their own consumption, attempting also to introduce their own workshops for the production of industrial goods for themselves.

But the country was undergoing a change. In the mid-1920's came a middle-class immigration from Poland, and in the 1930's a similar one from Germany and central Europe. These settlers built up cities rather than villages and engaged in industrial and commercial pursuits. Palestine, or Jewish Palestine, became drawn into the orbit of capitalistic development with the bulk of the population—80 to 85 percent—urban and mostly concentrated in three cities: Tel Aviv, Haifa, and Jerusalem. Not only did the village not influence the city as had been hoped, but the urban influence began to dominate the village. Villages situated near cities began to take on the characteristics of urban centers (Petach Tiqua near Tel Aviv, for instance). With the transformation to mixed farming all hopes of self-sufficiency and independence disappeared. The farmer, in all types of villages, began rather to produce for the urban market,

[10] S. Koenig, "Crisis in Israel's Collective Settlements," *Jewish Social Studies*, XIV (1952), 147.

and he became dependent on this market both as a producer and a consumer. Thus he had to adjust his production; in the villages market consciousness, division of labor, mechanization, efficiency, and profitability began to take the place of the former ideal and practice of production for consumption.

With this came also adjustment and change in the way of living and in social behavior. Each of these tendencies—accelerated urbanization, with villages turning into urban centers, and the encroachment of the market and profit system on the villages—has progressed far during the last two decades.

Through the development of industries, especially through the influx of new immigrants during the last six years and through the tremendous growth of the large urban centers, former villages more and more are becoming metropolitan suburbs or independent urban centers. The combined city of Tel Aviv–Jaffa harbors some 25 to 30 percent of the whole Jewish population. Some of the neighboring villages or semiagricultural settlements are being rapidly engulfed by this growing metropolitan center. The same is true of the Haifa area, with Jerusalem apparently about to follow suit. At the same time villages such as Rehovoth, Rishon Letzion, Hedera, Natanya, and Herzlia have expanded tremendously and have reached, or are about to reach, a population of 20,000 and more and are swiftly becoming urban centers (some even being incorporated). Also some of the collective villages have increased their population into thousands and are losing their agricultural character.

Another development, *accelerated* growth of a capitalistic commercialized agriculture based on a profit system and market, came with World War II. The closing of the sea lanes and the growing demand for goods by the British army in the Near East caused a steep rise in agricultural prices, a rise surpassing that of production costs. Except for citrus fruits, which suffered during the war from impossibility of exportation, Jewish agriculture was ceasing to be a deficit enterprise, maintained by Jewish

national institutions and the self-sacrifice of the settlers, and becoming a profitable venture. This served as an incentive to expand the cultivated area and encouraged efforts to increase production by better organization and methods.

These same trends continued generally during the postwar and postindependence years. Scarcity of food, rationing, black markets, the availability of land, and the importation of machinery gave the Jewish farmer a chance to expand and develop. Not only is the established village population in Israel today the only one which is well fed, but it is piling up some profits, individually or collectively, which to a great extent are reinvested in the farms.

The villages of the individual, privately owned farms, as well as the collective and co-operative ones, are assuming an air of prosperity and well being. Only the newly founded settlements in post-Arab villages or in the desertlike Negev are struggling for their existence rather than working for profit. At the same time, a shift in production is observable. The availability of land and machinery, together with the lack of foreign exchange for purchases abroad, has resulted in a return to the production of such staples as grain and fodder for cattle and poultry. With the help of newly acquired tractors this branch is beginning to play a bigger role in Israeli agriculture.

The Jewish farm population in Israel lives mostly in villages patterned on those of Europe. These villages are generally laid out with the buildings in the center, surrounded by the fields. The pattern is usually a circle, though in some cases it takes the form of a horseshoe.

This agricultural village is the farmer's home, whence he departs to work in the morning and to which he returns in the evening. Outwardly, his environment resembles that of any other rural community in many ways. He is close to nature, lives in open country, and adjusts his work and life to the changes of the climate.

[73]

The population in these villages, however, differs from the peasant population of European villages, although the settlers intended it to be "in their image."

The Israeli farmer, except for a few thousand second-generation men and women, is, as mentioned, mainly a city man who took to farming by choice or necessity. In this respect there is no difference between the private individual villages and the collective or co-operative villages. In many cases he was influenced by the Zionist ideal of return to the soil.

An idea of the make-up of Israeli farmers may be gained from examining the background of some 850 German-Jewish middle-class settlers of the 1930's:

	Percentage
Merchants and clerks	56.0
Professional men (physicians, lawyers, research workers, etc.)	34.0
Others	3.0
Agriculturists & similar workers	7.0
Total	100.0

The background of the settlers in the collective and co-operative villages was not very different. Although the percentage of professional men was much smaller, the educational status was nevertheless very high:

	Collective settlements, 1937	Workers in Moshavoth colonies, 1937
College education	5.7%	6.0%
High-school education	55.8%	36.0%
Elementary school education	34.4%	49.3%

These settlers all assumed that the new environment and changed conditions would transform the Jewish urbanite into a typical farmer with his specific characteristics, resembling the farmers in European countries. Some thought also that for this purpose one should abandon the civilized forms to which the

Jewish urbanites were accustomed and should lower the standard of education in order to attain a new specimen of a Jewish farmer, devoid of urban culture, manners, and behavior. For this purpose many settlers advocated limiting the schooling of their children to elementary school or, at most, to junior high school, with the last two years devoted more to practical matters than to academic subjects.

If, in the light of these strivings, one were to examine the characteristics of the Israeli farmer, one would find new traits in his behavior which are reminiscent of peasant populations in other countries, but that urbanism still predominated. The Jewish urbanite, turned farmer, seems to have changed his external appearance, his manner of walking, and certain facial features. The farmer also became accustomed to his work.

But there remained a difference between the first and second generations. The new settlers who became farmers by choice had a hard struggle to accustom themselves to work and life on the land. They had to learn, mostly the hard way, the mechanics of agriculture. Labor, work, accomplishment in this field, became something of an ideal to which they strove, and many even today, after years of toil, still experience the joy of accomplishment, of fulfilling a duty, or of being of service to their people.

The second generation has, for the most part, a different attitude. They differ also externally from their parents: "In height they are usually taller than their parents; broadshouldered . . . tanned, muscular and lean, with sharp and flashing glance, and slow and firm gait. They work calmly and placidly without bustle and without impulsiveness." [11] They have been reared in work and have a natural and simple attitude toward it. The youth lack the deep emotional feelings toward labor which were characteristic of the first generation. They feel that labor in itself is not a great achievement and a goal to strive for but that it is something done from practice and necessity. These char-

[11] Uri in *Darkei Hanoar* (Jerusalem, 1937), p. 196.

acteristics may resemble somewhat those of the "natural farmer," to which the older generation aspired.

"Farmers are 'escapists,'" Sinclair Lewis has said. This applies particularly to the Israeli farmer, who not only wished to escape the treadmill of the cities, but who consciously negated urban civilization with its capitalistic, competitive order. There was also something—which in theory still exists—of the attitude of a peasant who "draws his satisfaction . . . from work done well, from improvement and increase of holdings and herds, and from the knowledge of having provided for future generations." As in the case of other peasant societies "frugality and hard work were considered great virtues." Farming was conceived as a way of life, and ideas of wealth and well-being were hardly expressed "in terms of profit, capital, personal comfort or conspicuous consumption."

But the changing pattern of agricultural production, the shift from self-sufficiency and subsistence farming to commercial farming, did its share to transform these attitudes. Despite the misgivings of a few idealists and despite retention of certain older clichés, the spirit of Jewish farming in Israel today greatly resembles that of American farming: production for markets and the utilization of technical inventions with the profit motive becoming the main factor. Esteem for the intangible rewards, which are noneconomic and more in the nature of psychological compensation, is declining in favor of economic compensation.

Farming is becoming a business, with rural areas following the urban examples with regard to mannerisms, attitudes, behavior, and needs. In the collective settlements this transformation caused a change in mode of life and outlook and helped precipitate a crisis in the whole system.[12] Incidentally, these villages, as well as the co-operative settlements, were always, especially later, organizationally a far cry from the usual peasant

[12] S. Koenig, loc. cit.

type, which is simple, localistic, stable, and "governed by tradition and group centered values."

The workers' settlements, embracing a majority of the Jewish farmers, are organizationally a part of the general Federation of Labor (*Histadruth*) and the labor parties, which are of an urban nature. The farmer, unlike farm populations in many European countries, not only participates actively in the political life and reflects the tensions of the urban society, but is frequently among the leadership elite. The "attitude which established the workers' settlement as one of the highest stages in the social scale of values" in the Jewish population of Palestine [13] made the farmer seem the best human material to assume leadership in many walks of life in the Jewish community. Leaders and high officers in the labor parties, of the General Federation of Labor, of workers' economic institutions, and partially also of the government were, and are, drawn to a considerable extent from these villages. For instance, in the first *Kneset*, elected in 1949, about 25 percent of the deputies either were farmers or came from the communal settlements, whereas only 12 to 13 percent of the population were occupied in agriculture. In other words, the farmers' participation in parliament (this is true of other public offices) far exceeds their proportion in the population. From rural communities, too, a number of the people were, and still are, sent abroad on educational, propaganda, and other missions.

Hundreds, perhaps thousands, of the villagers, or their elite, live as urbanites for years, some even for decades, even though some of them choose to *show* their connection with the village life, for instance by refusing to wear a tie. Or they may do like Mr. Zisling, Minister of Agriculture in the first Israeli cabinet; on week ends he used to return to his *Kibbutz* and work there, ostensibly as a waiter in the collective dining room. But in general, their way of living, their amusements, and their needs are

[13] Aisenstadt, *op. cit.*, X, 16.

changing to fall in line with the urban pattern, modifying the former principle of austerity and simplicity. In the main, this village elite, and also a great many of the others, even while living in the villages are concerned constantly with the political parties and their affairs in the cities, participate actively in the political life, and try to influence it.

In this way the village becomes, to a certain extent, an annex of the city and its interests. The struggle between the moderate labor party, Mapai, and the leftist, pro-Communist, Mapam, found its strongest expression in the collective villages, where it led to continued quarrels, division of settlements, and the withdrawal of whole groups of members.

The physical rapprochement of the cities to the villages in the last few years, with the growth of the urban centers and the shifting of emphasis from agriculture to city pursuits, increased the city's encroachment on the farmers. If the machine came to be regarded "as the indispensable means of building up the country, of raising its economic and social status," so "machine culture" and its way of life is in the ascendance everywhere. "The increasing encroachment of the city on the minds of the *Kibbutz* youth is a topic of discussion among the leaders and thoughtful rank and file." The youth is also being influenced by other phenomena. The war of liberation, as well as the present compulsory army service, has continued to remove many of them from the villages, bringing them in contact with a different way of living and under the influence of the urban cultural pattern. This is even more true since the cultural pattern which the pioneer farmer attempted to create is still far from having formed a tradition of its own. "Folk songs and dances, experiments in the attempt to give the holidays new content, the creation of intimate bonds with the natural life of Palestine . . . all these may possibly be the first sparks of a new mode of life—but no more than sparks." [14]

Counteracting these "sparks" and modifying them are both

[14] *Ibid.*, p. 17.

the whole past of the Jewish farmer and his cultural mentality. His high educational background, his ties with European urban civilization, have remained.

It is true our people left this civilization in order to renew their lives here, but it is in their blood. Actually it serves as a spiritual background for their life on the land. . . . The background did not change. This is European; . . . there has not appeared in our lives any other positive spiritual force which is based solely on the new life in agriculture. . . . Also [this is true of] the second generation which grew up here. . . . Their spiritual life is based in that insecure, troubled, and confused world of European civilization.[15]

Probably the most pronounced expression of the urban traits of the Israeli farmer is to be found in the birth and reproduction rates of the Jewish village. Birth rates are not usually influenced by phraseologies and clichés and therefore probably best reveal any particular tendency. In contrast with almost all other countries of the world, the Jewish villages in Israel had, until recently, a birth rate lower than that of the urban population and comparable only with those of metropolitan centers. Like that of the large cities, the village population was not reproducing itself.

Thus the outlook and behavior of the Jewish farmer in Israel appear to be more urbanite than peasant. His efforts to imitate a peasant, to mold himself in that image, and to create a peasant tradition were not generally successful. Economically and socially, he is—irrespective of the organizational form of the village—dependent on the urban market for which he produces cash crops. Rural psychology in Israel, insofar as it was distinctive from urban, is now leveling off. The farmer's urbanite heritage is thus being strengthened, and it is neutralizing the attempts to create a peasant tradition. Alert, with a high educational standard, he is responsive to political, social, and technological changes. He is receptive to new agricultural meth-

15 D. Maletz, "Erkey Haamanuth Bakfar," in *Kamah*, III (1950), 393.

ods and techniques, as well as to social and intellectual trends. Mobility and changes to city occupations are not infrequent. The farmer, along with his decreasing ratio in the labor force, has also lately begun to lose, slowly but surely, the distinction of being regarded as the most important factor in building the country.

Agriculture as a national ideal is on the decline, even though (or because?) agriculturalists today are generally the only well-fed people suffering no food shortages. Pioneering (*halutziut*), service to the country, is no longer identified with agriculture alone. Industrial workers, professional soldiers, and government officials have moved up on the scale of values and are on a par with agriculturalists. This has lowered the psychological barriers to leaving the village and taking jobs in the growing urban economy or government service.

All society in Israel is now caught in the grip of social, economic, and even ethnical changes of considerable dimensions. In the midst of this whirl of transformations stands the Israeli farmer, who is undergoing a great internal and external change affecting most phases of his existence: physically, most of the older villages have been overrun by the growing urban centers; politically, a part of them—the collectives—are torn by internal strife; socially, he is losing his prestige in society; and spiritually, he is being more and more engulfed by the traits of Western civilization, to the great disadvantage of the beginnings of new patterns which it was hoped would evolve into a rural civilization. A different set of mannerisms, values, and mental defenses, urban in character, is arising.

While the Jewish agricultural population of the old vintage, the preindependence farmers, is in a stage of cultural and social change, transformations are taking place in agriculture generally. Since the establishment of the State of Israel, the number of Jewish farmers has doubled. These new farmers are of a different type, seldom motivated by idealism and the spirit of pioneering. Moreover, a majority of them are Oriental Jews, who were not

ideologically prepared for this kind of life and are motivated by personal necessity and desires. Accustomed to a low standard of living, they may more easily adjust themselves to the meager income and substandard existence of a marginal farmer.

In the spring of 1953, new tendencies were in the making. Government circles and nongovernmental bodies were sponsoring an action to induce several thousand families to leave the cities for the land. The movement "from city to village" seems actually to have had some success, perhaps because one of the driving forces was the shortage of foodstuffs in urban areas. In this shift to agriculture, both older settlers and new immigrants appear to be involved.

Since the end of 1953 new stress is being placed on agriculture, as a means both of solving the unemployment problem and of improving the balance of payments. A new Seven-Year Plan envisages doubling the number of farmers by 1960 and widening the basis of production by expanding the cultivation of grain, basic foodstuffs, and industrial crops such as cotton, groundnuts, and sugar beets. At the same time it is being suggested that dairy and chicken farming be somewhat frozen on the ground that concentration on the production of high-protein foods is a luxury that a small and poor country can ill afford. The older farmers, particularly those of the communal and co-operative settlements, however, advocate the continuation of the mixed farming system, with emphasis upon dairy and chicken farming as the main agricultural branches providing an attractive profit.

In the newer settlements, dating from after the foundation of the State of Israel, different trends have recently been observable. The majority of the settlers are apparently adjusting themselves to the new situation, although there seems to be an appreciable turnover. According to official figures, about 10 percent left their homesteads, houses, and agriculture to return to the transitional camps. It is being thought that the measure of adjustment is, to a certain extent, in reverse proportion to the proximity to a city environment. Oriental Jews

[81]

who came from a village environment and who were settled in a far-outlying region soon after their arrival in Israel, without having had a chance to live for any considerable time near a city, are showing greater stability in their agricultural pursuits. As a result of this observation new methods of settlement have recently been adopted. In the new "ship to village" settlement program, employed since the second half of 1954, immigrants—mostly from North Africa—are transferred immediately upon landing in the port of Haifa to the outlying agriculture settlements, without having a chance "to be spoiled by the city air" of Israel.

All these currents and undercurrents, coupled with the necessity of relying more on local production, may evolve some new patterns and may differentiate more the production practices, way of life, and even the attitudes of the Israeli-Jewish farmer. There may also evolve a type of marginal farmer—mostly of Oriental origin—whose income is much less than that of the other farmers.

But the main traits of the man-made farmer, of the urbanite type which is closely connected with city and city life and its values, are apparently bound to remain.

(V) THOMAS B. STAUFFER

The Industrial Worker

THE mysterious East has two veils, neither of which is easily torn aside. At most the West can come to apprehend clearly the existence and perhaps the nature of certain difficulties which prevent it from seeing the East as the West sees its own culture, or as Easterners see theirs. One of the veils over the East is the absence of information; the other is the deceptive quality of much of what passes for information. Social data, far more than financial or economic, present both of these aspects.

Statistical information is not available for most of the Middle Eastern as it is for European cultures. Where it seems to exist, it is not complete, not comprehensive, not accurate, not detailed, not timely. One must not allow an eager gratitude for what does exist, of whatever quality or authority, to obscure the fact that it is only a fragment—not a systematic sample—of what would be a desirable minimum. Only in 1950 did Syria undertake systematic employment data, or even a reasonably accurate list of factories, or of villages, these latter with estimates of the amount of arable land and the inhabitants of each. Only in 1952 did Lebanon undertake a survey of employment throughout the country. Surely employment is the

basic fact about the worker; yet in discussions of labor in Lebanon, experts' estimates of unemployment have varied by several hundred percent, depending in part on the use of a category surely pertinent in the East but unknown to Western economics—the "semiemployed"! Similarly, throughout the area quantitative social data are scanty and scattered, recent and brief, of contestable if not patently doubtful accuracy, and of very doubtful utility even for descriptive purposes. Especially in a constatation of change in any one society, sets of data which are both recent and unique present little of use.

The relative absence of the statistics is an obvious difficulty, which must be met by treating those available, like any other data, as sources of insight and of new problems, rather than as a resolution of problems or as a true measure of phenomena. But phenomena themselves are elusive, and Western categories are subtly transformed in Eastern contexts. Let no one think that a Middle Eastern family is a social or economic unit comparable to an urban American one, or that no forces are at work in the labor market in Lebanon which are not comparably active in Detroit. The motives and satisfactions of workers in two societies may be only very vaguely comparable, and any attempt to reduce the data of the two systems to comparable tables may cast more shadow than light, introducing obscurities of method into our understanding, when there are none in our subject. It will be necessary in several connections to return to this theme, that Eastern and Western social phenomena are not commensurable simply or in a single set of scientific notions; perhaps more truly, that Eastern trends are not simply intelligible through the categories of Western society. The length of Dr. Mosaddeq's political survival in Iran, in the face of the persistent and unanimous chorus of Western fiscal experts who predicted his early ruin, should caution Western students against too Procrustean a view of the standards of their own intellectual and social disciplines.

The public news value, in Western society, of the revolu-

tions in Egypt and Iran, has very largely to do with the relations of these countries to the West. But it is noteworthy that though both these governments exploit xenophobic nationalism as a short-run support, their permanent institutional programs, the most fundamental changes they have contemplated, relate to the life of the peasants—elements even more remote from the Western ideal and Western influences than are the workers. The active movers in these revolutions are groups easy for Westerners to single out—the military, the intellectuals, the press, and the religious leaders, all somewhat aware of or responsive to Western influence, if only by dislike. It may be that the xenophobia, at least so far as it has acute manifestations, even violent ones, is peculiarly the property of urban elements, including at least the leaders of the workers. But the inertia whose movement or resistance will determine their success and its permanence is, as they recognize, that of peasant society.

The true worker of the Middle East is the peasant—socially a villager, economically a farmer—the most fundamental, the most universal, perhaps the most permanent feature of the Middle Eastern world. He and his family are seven or eight out of every ten people; the figure varies as the nomads are or are not lumped with the sedentary rural groups. The peasant's labor is the substance of the society; his thoughts its soul. It is not meant here to discuss "the villager," but only to set "the worker" in his true and tiny proportion.

"The worker" in the Middle East is an ambiguous term, even in the sphere of manufactures. This ambiguity embodies the contrasting forces of native tradition and foreign innovation. All intelligible discussion depends on keeping the various senses of "worker" distinct and examining separately the application of various categories of our thought to each. The workers in artisan trades are the largest group in the society, apart from the peasants. They supply the bulk of its consumption of manufactures. They are as old as the society itself. The workers in large-scale or highly mechanized industry, though locally nu-

merous in places, are a small and a very new group. For the most
part they are still without characteristic new social attitudes of
their own, however much the customary patterns of thought
and behavior may have been distorted by their new circumstances. These groups, therefore, artisans and factory workers,
though economically they may be lumped together as their
products are, must be considered separately for the most part.

Insofar as there are urban or specialized concentrations of
factory workers, they are not the great sources of recruitment
for other social forces, the armies or the religious movements
such as the Muslim Brotherhood, and in this respect they stand
apart from the mass of society.

Authoritative figures for Egypt, for 1951, record 1,033,321
workers in industry, 623,207 in commerce, and 576,000 in
services, trades, and professions; this leaves nearly 6,000,000 agricultural workers out of 8,000,000 employed persons in a population of about 21,000,000. Equally recent or accurate figures
for other countries are not available, but Egypt is not the least
industrialized country of the area. "Workers" apart from agriculture, by these figures, are about 7.5 percent of the population; of these workers, the majority are artisans. The artisans
carry on the traditional hand manufactures, in shops with very
little or no mechanical power and few employees. (Under both
Syrian and Egyptian law, establishments are listed as factories
or artisan shops by taking account of both these factors, the
number of employees being set at ten.) Factory workers are a
larger and more important group than artisans are in a few
places, though it is noteworthy that many of these places are
new as centers of economic activity or population. This is true
not only in the oil industry and the countries in which it is
important but, for instance, in regard to the new industries in
Egypt. The textile mills at Mehalla el-Kubra have concentrated
18,000 workers and their families in a district formerly rural.

The general labor force—the total of those willing and able
to enter the labor market under existing social and economic

standards—of the area is hard to calculate. Housewives, for instance, are not in the labor market, no matter how hard they work. In America, the present labor force is about 40 percent of the population; in some countries of Europe it approaches 45 percent. The figures given for Egypt show a labor force of 26 percent, but the 1947 census showed just over 35 percent of the population employed. Even allowing for the radically different age distribution of the Egyptian population as compared with the American, and for the omission, as seems to be the case, of government employment, this figure must appear very low to anyone who has seen the women and children working in the fields. Probably these figures show only heads of families engaged in agriculture.

The separate and important status of artisan organization appears primarily in the labor laws of Syria, which provide for employee, worker, and mixed or artisan associations, in which nominal master and nominal employee are joined in matters of economic interest or concerning the solidarity of the whole industry. And in most towns of Syria these mixed associations or workers associations, which are in fact associations of small entrepreneurs, are far more important and effective than the unions of industrial trades. So also in Lebanon, the taxi drivers, for instance, are organized as a "labor union," but their problems are those of small entrepreneurs—licensing, fuel rationing, operation of foreign competitors, and the like.

In the Middle East artisan activity does not connote a high degree of skill or refinement. Partly, this reflects the material and spiritual stagnation and poverty of the region in recent times; partly, the effort to compete with mass-produced factory-made goods, largely imported. There are also specific historical causes such as the devastations of Tamerlane and his deportation to Bokhara of the masters of the guilds of Damascus and other capitals.

But this low technical level does not mean a disintegrated social structure. New wares and new trades have followed old

patterns, and in Damascus the garage *suk* and the bicycle mender's *suk* have found a place beside trades long established.

Artisan activities are, of course, dispersed through all the settlements, and in other ways, too, they are not remote from the rest of the society. Such new techniques as have shown themselves in the artisan economy have not provoked new ideas or new patterns of organization. The artisan has always been and still is an established part of the scene, well integrated with the traditional organization and not in any large measure either a source of disintegration or a channel of cultural or ideological innovation.

To distinguish the artisan from the factory worker, and to find the artisan well integrated in the historic society, is not to say that the factory worker is a dislocated element. There may be areas, such as the Arabian oil fields, where the new economy has constituted a new society, but in the old settled areas the mentality of the factory worker is still very close to that of the village society. This is also very largely true of the commercial workers. Industry is new, and a minor factor in the social economy. Therefore, in terms neither of skill nor of social attitudes does the factory worker, on the whole, have a new outlook on life.

The principal fact affecting his status is the nature of the labor market. It is not large, well differentiated, and exacting as it is in established industrial regions. There is not an abundance of alternative *industrial* employments; the alternatives are often one or a few factories, idleness, or agriculture. Contrast, for instance, the opportunities of an oil worker, semiskilled, in Texas with those of his confrere in Saudi Arabia. There is a converse, too, of course; the absence of a developed labor supply for any given enterprise. Industry does not recruit from a "labor market" but from the undifferentiated society.

This fact, combined with the novelty of industry, keeps in the factory worker many of the attitudes of the nonindustrial society; he remains a villager, a member of the traditional so-

ciety. Industrial employment is not yet a way of life, and the mobility of labor between jobs and between kinds of employment, is extremely high. The textile mills of Mehalla in Egypt had for a time a turnover of about 300 percent, whereas an American firm would find 25 percent very high.

Consider what such a rate of change means in terms of the worker's closeness to his origins rather than to his employment. Think of the difficulties in developing a program of social welfare in such a transient population. At Mehalla and elsewhere it was found that even in purchasing consumer goods, the worker, recently a villager, tended or preferred to deal with his village or his relatives rather than in a market at the place of employment. Again at Mehalla, village society was reconstituted around the new jobs, with the factory taking the place of the arable land as the productive focus of activity. But new patterns and values did not emerge; the old ways were adapted, but all essentials were preserved.

The origin of the factory worker is close to traditional social structures; so is the method of his recruitment. In Beirut, to hire an office boy one does not put an ad in the paper but informs the head clerk of the opportunity. When all his relatives have had the refusal of the job, the second clerk's relatives have their turn, and so on until status and blood ties, or even village ties, have been exhausted. This is not an inefficient method where indigenous skills are sought. A willing worker with good social security behind him has been recruited, and he will have guidance and discipline even apart from the job, because his sponsor's prestige is at stake. In its negative aspects, the system is nepotism; but that is only the corrupt form of an enormous and adaptable solidarity of *persons*, not of merely functional ties.

In Saudi Arabia the Aramco personnel staff has observed the same phenomena in the recruitment of whole classes of labor. Although efforts were made to introduce personnel testing and placement methods in the hiring of local peoples, these had to

[89]

cede in practice, in large measure, to custom and pre-existing social ties. These gave rise to something very like the caste system in India, though without its prejudicial and invidious aspects. Partly by accident, partly by preference, certain kinds of work at Aramco came at first to be done by recruits from certain tribal and regional groups—these in the mess, those in the garages. Later recruitment had to adapt to these facts, so that each segment of Aramco life tended to draw on a separate segment of Arabian life. This, again, was not in itself inefficient, except as it led to friction with Western methods and standards.

Attempts to improve or alter the social system of the Middle East by legislation on Western models have shown the vitality of the historic structure and the inapplicability of foreign ideas not less clearly than the organic accompaniments to changes in the economy which have been noted. Repeatedly, laws based on foreign ideas have been ineffectual and sometimes even harmful. This is due in large part to the absence of statistical, fiscal, and administrative preparation by the governments concerned. The laws themselves have often been skillfully prepared with aid from the International Labor Organization.

A draft of a social security law in Lebanon began with a series of proposed benefit entitlements, modeled after Western developments and assuming an increasingly atomized society with individuals, or at most small parent-and-child families, in direct contact with state administrations. One of the criticisms made of the law was that if unemployment benefits, which the law intended to introduce at a late stage, were put in the first stage, the "extended family" structure would provide most of the other benefits intended, such as widows' and childrens' benefits, old age pensions, and the like. Similarly, an elaborately prepared social security law for Egypt, promulgated in May, 1950, was altered to take account of the extended ramifications of the family in *"Shari'ah"* law, as well as of the predominance of the peasants in the economic life of the country. (The draft of this

Lebanese law had many interesting results; among other things it provided a battleground for French and British administrative influences. It also united labor, management, the foreign companies, the unions, and the Communists in opposition to ill-considered changes in the pre-existing social laws, a situation in which the initiative, discipline, and resources of the Communists gave them some tactical advantages.)

Other well-meaning laws on foreign models have had harmful effects. Most laws governing the welfare of workers and apprentices are limited to factories, establishments employing more than ten or some small set number of persons. But the additional burden of costs, resulting from expansion, is a sufficient deterrent to prevent many enterprises in the artisan class from expanding. Thus additional workers are not employed, and those already working do not benefit from the welfare laws. The small artisan master has not and cannot obtain the capital to finance these changes, and the law gives him no relief.

With respect to the worker in society, therefore, there are few indications of radically new patterns or attitudes. To a visitor who had not been in the Middle East since the present industrial beginnings, there would be real surprises—the factories and their machines, not the factory workers. In the *suks* it would be the bicycle that would startle him, not the bicycle mechanic. The factory workers and the more numerous artisans taken together are still a very minor group in an old solid society of peasant villages.

In the discussion of the worker in the society, there have been presented lines of inquiry which might document the suggested theses that neither the spontaneous social accompaniments of industrial development nor attempts at planned intervention in social matters have brought to the workers or the society as a whole the full benefits of foreign social techniques. Western social standards have not been approximated, and phenomena analogous in detail to the industrial society of the

West have not been produced. Future planned social development for industrial workers must be adapted to both the positive and negative factors stated: the vitality of the peasant village—the primary community centered on local production—as a social unit and the limitations of government capabilities of action.

Planning can best deal broadly with large natural wholes and all the factors at work in them—an island like Cyprus, or a Nile Valley, or the Biqa' of Lebanon. But *execution* can well deal—especially where the resources to be employed are limited —one at a time with natural or social units within these larger wholes. Most work can be carried out by local authorities in small units such as a subwatershed or a village with its fields and other lands. At this level the social unit and the unit of production and economic life generally coincide. Important experiments at the Port Company at Beirut, and those in Egypt already referred to, indicate that the village model may be adapted to a social development of industrial life and the small primary community recreated around the factory. Such development may and should be done within the framework of balanced general plans for larger social divisions. At Mehalla in Egypt, although large numbers of workers had to be accommodated in a place remote from any city—far too many for a single village on a traditional scale—the problem is being met by the multiplying of new villages, not by building a new city for the accommodation of a mass of desocialized individual workers.

Within these small production-centered social units a balanced program of basic social developments is possible. Schemes which proceed one village at a time within a general plan make the most effective use of the rarest resource in the area, trained personnel. By their small scale and concreteness, most of the administrative problems of large undertakings are avoided. Local activity for local benefit and under the eye of the local population has also repeatedly been able to tap local resources in labor and money which the national fiscal systems had left untouched;

in addition, increased local welfare and local activity are sources of new wealth to the society as a whole.

Further, being balanced social units with immediate sources of wealth in their structure, these villages are able to provide an important "social income" of communal services often not generally available. Mere cash payments to individuals would not produce these services, and under the old habits and the old circumstances would be dissipated in luxury and vice, or by rising prices. The establishment of consumer co-operatives by the Anglo-Iranian Oil Company in Iran is said to have been a model of intelligent action of this sort.

All these experiences tend to show that a labor force stabilized around a new productive center can be brought not only to higher social standards but to higher economic productivity as well.

The notion that new developments in production should be accompanied by social development must be extended in two ways. It should apply to agricultural as well as industrial development; it should compensate for the disruptive effects of such developments as the relocation of labor by providing a positive program for the smaller society immediately dependent on the given project.

Where, as in Egypt and Iran, there are nation-wide schemes for such developments, the principle is not altered, but only the rate of progress and the number of village units affected at one time. The realization of such plans does not depend on their desirability or on policy decisions but on the available resources, especially personnel for the local units. The essence of these plans is that within each local production unit—peasant village or factory village—a balanced program should be carried out independently of other like units, with a maximum role for local resources and initiative. The basic social pattern is maintained; the techniques at its disposal are improved. In time, as resources, especially of personnel, become available, all units within the over-all plan are affected; but in the interim resources

available at any given time are not ineffectually dispersed or given aspects of village life altered without regard to complementary factors.

The worker, including the agricultural worker, is the great resource of the economy of the Middle East, although this concept is much misunderstood. Labor is ill paid and is, therefore, thought to be cheap. However, in terms of productivity it is very costly in both production and administration. The low wages and abject living standards of these workers do not make it advantageous to employ them. The skill of the individual workers and the stability of the labor force are so low as to make labor cost per unit of capital or per unit of output very high. It is questionable whether, given these labor standards, capital investment in manufacturing, from sources outside the region, can be justified in terms of return to the world economy.

These faults, however, are by no means intrinsic or necessary. Trained Middle Eastern workers can work as well as any others, but social patterns conducive to high productivity do not exist, and the recruitment and training of a stable skilled labor force is a major difficulty. This is an important way in which individual private enterprises, such as the oil companies, can directly contribute real goods to the surrounding economies, though they have not on the whole done so willingly or on a scale commensurate with their opportunities. It is significant of the casual assumptions about labor in these societies that the famous Seven-Year Plan for Iran had no labor chapter and no estimate of the amount, kind, or quality of man power that would be required from time to time, either for the plan as a whole or for the individual projects. It should be noted that the shortage of qualified foremanship and supervisory skill is even greater than the shortages of mechanical skills.

A further mistake about labor in the economy is the belief that the workers lead a life of toil. True, the methods used are often toilsome, since labor is cheaper than machinery, but partial unemployment is a permanent feature of the economy—

not the temporary total unemployment of an individual which the West knows, but the state where almost everyone works only part of a normal work year. This wasted man power, estimated for Greece and for Egypt at one-third of the potential annual man-days of the country, is the great idle resource of the area and could be its salvation. In a sense an underdeveloped country is not one with a backward technology nor one with material resources unexploited, but one which does not offer its people productive full employment. If this idle man power were put to work, as it has been in some places, in the formation of locally financed, real social capital—roads, terracing, land reclamation and improvement—the demands for foreign capital made by these areas would be greatly reduced. Moreover, the funds obtained would be used more effectively and the whole level of production and exchange considerably raised. The example of Haifa, though it does not relate primarily to unemployment, is illuminating. With no important capital outlay for new machinery, a reorganization of the labor force of the port increased its goods-handling capacity an estimated 50 percent, with a related fall in unit costs of handling goods. Similar results were reported from Port Sudan.

In the Soviet states this principle of the formation of real capital by the expenditure of labor otherwise unused locally, instead of primarily by the transfer of existing capital from other sectors of the economy, seems to be enforced by violence, through slave labor and conscription. Repellent as these outrages may be, there seems to be no denying their *economic* effects, and in free countries similar *economic* effects could be obtained if idle man power were put to work by the methods and incentives of free societies. But there must be proper organization to prevent the disruption of existing production. In the Middle East, for example, road building need not be done exclusively by fancy and expensive foreign machinery; certainly, it should be done not by man power taken away from agricultural operations but by surplus labor and in the slack season.

[95]

The worker in the economy is also a consumer, but at a subsistence level. Until there is a developed internal market for manufactured consumer goods, industry must remain extractive or concerned with export processing. But labor is not now efficient or productive enough to earn a high living standard. Moreover, experience has shown that "higher standards" do not necessarily mean higher material standards which would expand the internal market. Greek workers, for instance, want to meet their present modest material requirements, or perhaps very slightly higher ones, in less time and with less effort. What they want is leisure for the highly institutionalized enjoyment of what seems to us very modest comforts indeed and a vigorous family and social life. Such a scale of values does not in the short run offer the expanding internal market which would justify consumer manufactures in these countries.

The impact of foreign influences on the worker in the economy has been primarily as an element in a technology. It has not been on him as a member of a system of social values and ideals. Overt communism has not been an effective force in the Middle East. While Soviet Communist imperialism is thought to seek to foment and exploit unrest, such communism as does exist is almost entirely a phenomenon of the white-collar classes, the diploma-proletariat. With few exceptions communism is not important among the workers, urban or rural, and does not deal directly with their immediate concerns. To the extent that they do appear overtly, Communist ideas and other forms of Soviet influence labor under a double disability of cultural and national foreignness. Some Communist successes have occurred, however, in groups with cultural or racial ties with the Soviet Union, such as the Orthodox church groups and the Armenians.

None of the Communist agencies has put forth agrarian programs like those of Egypt and Iran. The strategy of communism has been taken from Stalin's early writings on colonial questions —an exploitation of nationalist sentiment rather than an ad-

vocacy of specific reforms. The essential Marxist principle of a society of industrial workers is in every sense foreign to the circumstances and ideas of the contemporary Middle East.

The exception to all this has been the apparent strength of the Communist Tudeh in Iran. It should, however, be considered that the ineffectiveness of the Tudeh in the present crisis reflects its true strength and that its apparent strength arose from sources other than disciplined militancy in the interest of Communist ideas or of the Soviet state. The first of these sources is the xenophobic nationalism, now an issue on the part of the government, which reinforces its pre-emption by a working arrangement with Islamic activism. The second is that the nucleus of the Tudeh, reportedly, is largely railroad workers, who in all societies are from the nature of their employment among the first groups of workers to have extensive and effective organization. But the railroads are not vital to the economy or interior strategy of Iran, so that much discussion of Tudeh, as of other factors in Iran, seems to have been based on misapprehensions.

In Lebanon, also, there is a militant and cohesive Communist minority among the labor unions. At present, however, they do not control any important sector of the economy; they were ousted from the public utilities union in 1950. The majority of the unions are under soundly non-Communist leadership. Future developments will strengthen this pattern in Lebanon and in other countries if they enable the unions to serve the immediate welfare of their members.

The peculiar social institutions of the West most closely associated with industry and industrial workers, labor unions, are recognized in principle in all the principal Middle Eastern states but are not important or effective in the life either of the workers or of the large society. No matter what improvements they may be capable of undergoing, there is little prospect of their becoming effective as long as the Middle East is very little industrialized and unemployment is persistent.

It is worthy of note that some progress is made with industry-centered welfare schemes run by industrial management. Except for those in Egypt, almost all are run by foreign enterprises, and in Lebanon in 1950 there were no industrial welfare schemes by native management at all.

In brief, it is to be concluded that Western influence, insofar as it has been constructive, has been as a morally neutral technology rather than as a system of social and ideal values. This thesis is more especially true regarding industrial workers, inasmuch as they are not a markedly distinct class. Whether or not, in these countries as in the West, they will emerge as a class more distinct than they are at present remains to be seen. It is also uncertain whether or not such a distinct class would be receptive to Western cultural influences; might it not be, like the peasants who are to benefit by the land reform which the West applauds, a class in which the peculiar ideals of the traditional culture are especially firmly rooted? Such developments are "democratic," not in the sense that they make these countries like the Western democracies, but in that they make their institutions freely and truly representative of their own people.

The social forces of the Middle East will not, or at least ought not, to seek to result in any radical or fundamental transformation of the historic society, its structure or function, or its peculiar social values and ideas. Rather the forces at work in further healthy development, whether those within the society itself or those which intelligent good-will may bring to bear from outside, must not seek changes of social principles but the perfecting of a permanent and inviolable individuality, not something which diligent inquiry or hard work can render entirely intelligible to the West, or like the West or its society, but an essential and sacred mystery.

(VI) DALTON POTTER

The Bazaar Merchant

WHENEVER cultural forces are mentioned by social scientists today, you can be sure that social change is the problem which stimulates their interest and gives rise to their inquiry. Initially, this interest prompts the description of the factors affecting the members of a society, then leads to an examination of the consequences of sets of influences in conjunction with antecedent patterns of behavior. In this essay the bazaar will be examined to see how the acquisition, exchange, and use of the material goods govern the tempo and direction of social change.

Without begging the question of why some elements from an alien culture are assimilated more easily than others, it is assumed that goods which fit already established cultural requirements are accepted, and cultural influences, especially in the realm of material culture, from sources external to a society find access to an indigenous cultural pattern by supplanting or supplementing existing traits. Only rarely are new traits and patterns adopted without adaptation and always through reinterpretation into the local cultural idiom.

The role of the bazaar merchant in introducing new goods into Middle Eastern culture is revealed in great part by the special distributions of patterns of market activity and types

of goods in the bazaar itself. The bazaar is, in a statistical sense, a "representative sample" of the total society in which the desires and needs, the preferences and susceptibilities, in sum, the internalized aspects of the material culture and the value systems arising therefrom are displayed and are subjected to new stimuli in a dynamic social situation.

An attempt will be made in this study to describe the salient features of the bazaar and to call attention to those which illustrate the mechanisms by which alien cultural traits are assimilated.

The first section outlines the basic anatomy of an idealized bazaar. Most of the information on which this paper is based pertains to Beirut and Damascus. The bazaars of Istanbul, Konya, Kayseri, Aleppo, Baghdad, and Amman were investigated, but little evidence was found running contrary to the patterns in the two cities studied extensively. The bazaar is, in each case, modified from an idealized pattern by city planning, land contours, and historical accident.

The second section deals with the personnel of the bazaar. Primary emphasis is placed on the bazaar merchant and his pivotal role in the interrelationships that make up the institution of the market.

Although the bazaar is a typical Middle Eastern institution and the basic pattern can best be analyzed in the context of Middle Eastern society and culture, several ideas derived from general theoretical problems are important. These have a bearing on the dynamics of any retail market. The relations that exist between types of goods, prices, turnover, and the concentration of shops are clearly illustrated in the bazaar and have important consequences for the merchant.

The most important factor considered, however, is that of cross-cultural influences. There has long been an active trade between the Western centers of trade and manufacture and the Middle Eastern markets, but the types of goods in the bazaars have tended predominantly to satisfy indigenous tastes,

and their acceptance has been conditioned by local tradition. With the increasing adoption of Western culture traits we find the bazaars supplying goods to different cultural contexts: the traditional Middle Eastern life of the rural population and the semi-Westernized life of the city dwellers. The consequences of this phenomenon are significant for the merchant. Since he becomes the mediator for the alien culture traits, the concern with the retail merchant of the bazaar lies in the nexus of social forces in which he plays his role.

The social organization of the Middle East has been based, from its earliest days, on the two economic activities of agriculture and trade. Each has given rise to different subcultures that are mutually interdependent within the society as a whole. Each constitutes a complete social structure. The interdependence is focused in the twofold function of the merchant. For the urban population he buys and redistributes the agricultural products of the rural workers. He is almost the only member of the urban pattern who has contact with the rural economy. For the rural population he collects the vast range of goods that are indispensable to the rather specialized rural economy. He plays, therefore, a crucial role as the mediator of the multiplicity of forces for change in the Middle East, because his is the one function that intersects the ways of life of all other members of the society.

The bazaar is the one typically secular institution in the Middle East. The market dynamics are such that religious factors have little impact on the social structure. It might be shown, to be sure, that the character of certain religious sects predisposes them to trade, but in the Middle East the fact that many of the religious minorities are found in urban trading centers is probably a result of the fact that such sects tend to arise in the cross currents of cultures to be found in the cities and that trade is the one activity open to them. It is noteworthy that the influence of the dominant religious doctrine is attenuated in the cities and particularly so in the markets. Here

is an area of life peculiarly crucial for the society but with a dynamic of its own distinctive enough for the norms of the larger society to impinge only as tangentially as the contact that the customers have with the merchant. Yet the bazaar is a characteristically Middle Eastern institution.

It is, indeed, extraordinary that no one has sufficiently noticed the bazaar to remark upon the fact that the principal *raison d'être* of the large cities in the Arab world is the chain of markets from one end of the Middle East to the other. Each market is linked with the others by bus and truck, as in the past by caravan. Unlike the great trading centers of the Western world that deal in capital and producer's goods, the principal types of merchandise in the Middle East are food, wearing apparel, household goods, and luxuries such as candy, perfume, and jewelry. The larger markets have a dual function. They are collecting points for produce, from near and far, supplying the needs of the local inhabitants, and they are wholesale centers for the constellation of smaller markets in the region. That the kinds of goods and the organization of the market and its characteristic personnel are remarkably similar from Istanbul to Baghdad to Jerusalem testifies to the constancy of the role the market plays in the life of society.

The characteristic pattern of the cities of the Middle East is roughly circular. Originally a fortified central core, usually on a hill, the city afforded protection not only to the inhabitants, the storehouses, and the center of social power, but to the basic industry. The work shops, the bazaars, and the caravansaries were almost invariably within the fortified structure and usually located near the central governmental buildings.

To the casual observer the bazaar of Middle Eastern cities is characterized by the variety of goods displayed for sale. Unlike the typical American shopping center or European market place, the bazaar offers good to all class levels of the society and to all ethnic minorities. It is not a special place where strange and exotic goods are offered to the local people but

rather the characteristic retail institution of the culture area. Considered in this light, the bazaar is not merely the dim, aromatic, stone-vaulted corridor lined with little stalls that, because of their novelty, typify this part of Middle Eastern cities to the traveler, but the whole market area of the town is an integrated economic and sociological complex.

The bazaar of Beirut was selected for extensive examination, partly because it was more accessible than Damascus or Baghdad but chiefly because it displayed in a highly developed form the extended ramifications of the market area that are found in more rudimentary forms in Aleppo, Jerusalem, or Kayseri.

The market area of Beirut occupies a roughly star-shaped area in the center of town. The market spreads out from the base of the crest of the hill on which the fortress and central government offices are built. The roads from Damascus, Tripoli, and Sidon end in the main square that borders the bazaars on the east.

The Place des Canons is the focal point for communications with other cities. The taxis and busses that run into the hill towns and environs of Beirut start there. At the north end of the square are the busses and taxis for Tripoli and northern villages; at the south end for Damascus and the Biqa'. The bus drivers have several supplementary capacities. They are the agents of the bus line. They also act as agents for small farmers in the villages and deliver small consignments of fresh food to merchants in the towns through which they pass. They are the messengers who carry news of relatives and gossip of the outside world from village to village. They are perhaps the modern equivalent of the caravan driver, who was the unofficial medium of communication between all parts of society. They bring news of prices and goods from the bazaars of town to the remote villages.

The layout of the bazaars in Beirut does not completely follow an organic pattern since the city planners of the French administration cut boulevards through what was once an ir-

regular pattern of narrow streets and arcades. But these improvements have only affected the peripheral areas and have
not changed the central bazaar sections. These still have the
physical characteristics typical of bazaars throughout the Middle East. The passageways are narrow and cobblestoned, with
a central open drain and the buildings built over the street
frequently meeting to form a masonry roof over the thor-
oughfare. The jewelry bazaar is usually the only section of
the market completely shut off from the rest by walls and
gates.

A generalized picture of the marketing facilities in a Middle
Eastern city can be sketched from differences in the types of
goods for sale, in the degree to which those goods represent
daily needs of customers, in their perishability and the rate
of turnover, and in the permanence and safety of the shops.
The bazaar area represents the result of the interaction of the
drives or demands arising out of these differences. Each of these
elements in the basic skeleton of forces that constitute the
bazaar changes in a characteristic way from the center of the
bazaar to the outskirts of the city.

Taken one at a time, these factors illustrate the complex basis
for the bazaar as an institution. The types of goods vary in
the extent to which they are used in the indigenous and traditional culture of the area and in the extent to which they are
expended in use. In the bazaar area proper, goods, although
they may be made in Manchester, Marseilles, or Mainz, are
offered for use in the traditional idiom. The needs of the
household include fresh foods, wearing apparel, preserves, household equipment, and hardware. The last two types and jewelry
are the goods bought least frequently. The difference in the
perishability of goods puts pressure on the merchants either
to increase their turnover or to provide for safe storage of valuable nonperishable goods. In actuality, the pattern of these differences in the bazaar is by no means as regular as described,
and the sale of perishable and semiperishable goods by peddlers

interpenetrates areas of the market dominated by other factors.

Nevertheless, Beirut and many Middle Eastern cities can be divided into four concentric zones starting at the center. The first zone nearest the fortified core of the city is the most stable and characterized by the shops of merchants of nonperishable goods whose capital investment is high and whose rate of turnover is low. The second zone is characterized by merchants dealing in semiperishable goods and items of everyday use. The rate of turnover is higher but the capital investment is less than in zone one. The third zone is characterized by clothing merchants and, in the open spaces, by the variety of perishable goods. The merchants do not all have permanent shops but may set up portable stalls or merely spread their wares on the ground.

The first three zones comprise the bazaar proper. It is a recognizable complex of shops, passageways, and open spaces, distinctly differentiated from the rest of the city by the high tempo of social interaction. The bazaar is distinguished from other shopping areas by the fact that the narrow passages or streets lined with shops or stalls are not accessible to traffic other than pedestrian. In Damascus some thoroughfares cross the bazaar area and the shops on either side of those streets are almost as isolated as if they were on either side of the open market spaces in the Kayseri or Beirut bazaars.

The fourth marketing zone of the city is characterized by small shops at principal street intersections and by peddlers. The variety of goods available to the customer decreases with the distance from the center of the bazaar, and the retailers in the fourth zone are either highly specialized merchants of foreign goods or dependent on localized demand in the neighborhood.

The central bazaar zones one, two, and three provide all the basic essentials for the traditional Middle Eastern style of life and cater primarily to the settled urban families in the nearby

neighborhoods. An internalized disposition toward a maximum of expenditure of effort in order to minimize capital investment is expressed in the shopping pattern for daily requirements. The most perishable items of food are, of course, bought every day on a trip to the market, but odd household items such as spices, nails, or string are also bought only in the quantity needed for immediate use; even preserves, oil, flour, olives, and dried fruit are bought a small amount at a time.

The market changes character as the distance from the center increases. The first most important change is the appearance of assimilated Western goods. The goods in this category are dry goods for sewing women's dresses in European patterns and style and men's ready-made suits; they are found in zone three. In Beirut this section of the market is more pronouncedly Western than in Damascus or Aleppo in that the patterns of cloth and the cut of men's suits are closer to European styles than to the typically Middle Eastern styles.

The Western shopping section in zone four on the outskirts of the bazaar proper offers the full range of goods that complement a completely Western life style: American, British, and French kitchen equipment, optical goods, radios, electrical appliances, and imported canned goods. The fresh fruit and vegetable markets, the meat and cheese shops are equipped and operated along European and American lines. The selection of fresh foods caters to Western cooking. The household equipment and decorations are appropriate to Western styles of furnishing, entertaining, and household management. Some, but not all, of the Western goods are offered for use in the local tradition. It is not unusual, for instance, to find an electric refrigerator occupying a prominent place in the dining room of a semi-Westernized Middle Easterner whose house is furnished, staffed, and run on characteristically traditional lines. The Western food-storage space is assimilated as a prerogative of the master or mistress of the house, not as an item of kitchen equipment, for the master never and the mistress seldom goes

into the kitchen. The wealthy beduin may well select his portable radio from the fluorescent-lit, chrome-decorated display room of the local General Electric or RCA agent in the Western shopping section of town.

The shops in this area do not follow the bazaar pattern of sectional differentiation by shops of particular specializations. The food shops are not all in a row. The electrical shops are not concentrated on one street. This lack of spacial differentiation is partly a reflection of the relatively recent establishment of this shopping area. Partly, it is an indication that the control, formerly exercised by the traditional merchant guilds, over the number and location of shops is lacking. More than these it testifies to the fact that a merchant of one type of goods does not depend on an amorphous demand on the part of a mass of consumers for goods of a limited range in a cultural reference. Each merchant is rather a technical specialist drawing his customers, in competition with other shops of similar type, by the special selection he has available and the individualized attention he gives to the problems of each customer.

The degree to which Western goods are concentrated in the areas just surrounding the bazaar proper is an indication that the process of assimilation of Western goods has not taken place in terms of the local styles for the customers of the principal market of the city. This is particularly significant since one would expect to find Western goods in zone one with goods of similar economic character: high overhead, high markup, and low turnover. There are several possible explanations for the fact that Western goods are not scattered throughout the bazaar in the same proportion as they are used in the culture. The principal reasons are the aversion on the part of the Westernized Arab to shopping in the bazaar and the slow rate at which the bazaar merchants assimilate Western values.

Assimilation of Western goods into the marketing area of the Middle Eastern city has proceeded under a twofold handicap. The value adhering to Western goods increases their

[107]

salability. As an example, excellent locally designed and hand-built electric fans are stamped with marks to indicate European or American manufacture—but as far as the average merchant is concerned the speculative nature of offering goods in a cross-cultural transaction so increases the risks that they are greater than he cares to undertake. The conservative merchant believes that foreign goods, such as plumbing fixtures, however valuable for conspicuous consumption or as status-increasing accouterments, are overpriced in comparison with serviceable and familiar products indigenous to the culture. The high initial cost and intrinsic or exchange value of foreign goods, even when used, put them in a price range with goods normally bought for security, such as jewelry. These awkward characteristics of cross-cultural trade are, of course, not mitigated by the additional handicap of currency fluctuation and the difficulties inherent in importing goods.

Each area of the market is characterized by different types of customers and merchants. The principal aspect of the change is the emphasis on the necessities of life, as far as the traditional style of life is concerned. The farther from the center of the bazaar the greater the emphasis on goods not essential to daily life and the increase of indigenous luxuries. The customers' inclination to spend money for personal satisfaction increases with the distance from the center and sets the social tone of each section of the bazaar.

In the center of the bazaars the customers fall into two types: the local household women shoppers and the visiting shopper from outside the city. The household shoppers come to market every day for the daily needs of the family. They are the older women of typically Middle Eastern homes. They know individual merchants and spend some time surveying the quality and prices of the foods in season. The visiting shoppers are mostly men in town for a day, drifting through the bazaar and enjoying the crowd.

In the peripheral areas of the bazaar the customers are a

much less homogeneous group, but there are fewer poorly dressed women shopping for daily needs and many more men and women in Western dress more or less drifting through the bazaars, shopping for cloth, trinkets, or some item of household equipment. The activity in this area is greatest in the afternoon and early evening when the office workers are on their way home. The fresh food stalls in the peripheral open market spaces are most active at this time. They display vegetables and fruits in a higher price range and of a broader selection than those of the open markets in the morning. The beduin women selling freshly gathered herbs, whose jute sacks were spread out in the morning market near the center of the bazaar, move to the active afternoon areas at noon and pack up for the day at about six o'clock.

In the European shopping area a tenth of the customers at most are in the traditional Middle Eastern dress of the urban middle class, and the rural types are very rarely seen. The semi-Westernized city dwellers, while dominant in numbers, are no longer the only representatives of the Western style of life. Women in the latest Paris fashions frequent the beauty salons or shop for luxuries, and men in suits tailored in Continental traditions order apertifs in the cafés or tea in the patisseries. In the type of customers from zone to zone of the bazaar may sometimes be seen the differential exposure and acceptance of Western values and life styles of members of a single well-to-do household. The servants or frequently the dependent relatives shop and seek recreation in the old bazaar areas; the head of the household does business in the offices and takes his leisure in restaurants and coffee shops of the peripheral areas of the bazaar; his wife shops for dress goods in the same semi-Westernized milieu; but his sons and daughters, whose assimilation of a Western style of life is almost complete, chafe at the home atmosphere and seek expression of their emancipation in the shops, cafés, or night clubs of the Westernized section of town.

The merchants of the bazaar are of two general types: the chandler and the entrepreneur. The fundamental distinction between the two lies in their approach to their social roles. Without oversimplifying, they are in contrast one to another: the active entrepreneur and the passive chandler.

They represent the basic dichotomy of the participants in Middle Eastern economic life. The difference is clearly drawn in the goals toward which human effort is directed. Although both types of merchant may exist within the frame of reference of traditional life styles, the chandler's effort is based on his inheritance of the shop, its stock of goods or his craft specialty, and his social status. His effort is directed to maintaining the continuity of his function and social role, while the entrepreneur's effort is expended on the turnover of goods and the minimization of invested capital. Each performs his retail function by dividing among his customers for their individual needs the bulk goods available in the wholesale markets.

The chandler also inherits a relatively stable clientele. His job is to stock the kinds of goods, in quantities sufficient to take care of normal demand, that the social and cultural group from which his customers are drawn will need. His shop is a storehouse for a large number of households, all of whom will sooner or later need some of the useful items in his store. He may act as adviser on repair problems, but most of the time his knowledge and skills are the same as his customers' and the range of his goods reflects the same range of experience with goods as his customers'. He seldom has demands made on him that he cannot fulfill because his customers' ken is the same as his. On the other hand, no effort on his part can increase the rate of turnover of his goods. He does not suggest to his customers that they attempt to usurp his function and buy some item that they may at some unforeseen moment need. He is not a hawker of wares, and his prices are relatively stable. Bargaining is minimized. He is securely engaged in being sure that he has on hand

what his customers will certainly need from time to time. His stock selection is as stable as basic cultural skills.

The merchants in this category are:

The household suppliers
String, nails, chains, charms, glue, paint, brushes, washers, dyes, lye, plaster, wax, sponges, solder, hammers, locks, saws, needles, hinges, mousetraps.

The preserves storekeepers
Pickles, olives, oil, cheese, dates, grain, flour, soap, seeds, coffee, herbs, dried fish.

The wood merchants
Chairs, boxes, stools, caskets, brushes, mallets, bowls, ladles, sticks, rollers.

Others (each purveying a speciality dependent on the material rather than the use of the goods)
Tinsmiths, coppersmiths, gold- and silversmiths, rope merchants, pottery dealers, and the sweets, nuts, and biscuit merchants.

The entrepreneur predominates in the periphera of the bazaar area. In contrast to the chandler, the entrepreneur, as he engages in a more profitable but less stable business, is more and more subject to the pressures of a consumer's market. He buys in the wholesale market each day what he expects to sell. His markup is small but his investment is seldom tied up for more than one day. In the central sections of the bazaar he does not participate, except to a limited extent, in modifying the tastes of his customers. He is under economic pressure to select what the shopping public will buy during a shopping day. He remains active as long as customers are in the market, and he buys just enough goods so that by the end of the day all will be sold even though the rate of profit for his effort drops on any individual sale to almost nothing in the last hours of the day. The difference between making a profit or losing money is in the selling of the last 10 percent of his produce.

The luxury fruit dealers and the cloth and clothes merchants

have longer buying and selling cycles than the fresh food merchants. The same lot of fruit may be sold over a period of several days. A bolt of cloth may last several months. The range of goods that must be stocked to attract customers is larger. The pressure is always strong to sell to every customer some piece of merchandise. Since his overhead is relatively low and the unit price is low, he can manipulate his markup over a wide range depending on the customer's desire and the volume of business activity. He must, moreover, be sensitive to changes in customers' demands and can take an active part in forming the tastes of the public by making certain types of goods more attractive in price or in quality.

In the Western shopping area the merchant representing the same principle as the chandler is the dominant one but for a somewhat different reason. Whereas the traditional chandler's business continually depends on his maintaining the respect and confidence of his clientele, the Westernized merchant caters to the upper economic levels of society and depends for his success on establishing his position as a solid authority on the proper accouterments of a Western style of life. The identification of the semi-Westernized Middle Easterner as *nouveau riche* depends less on his practice of conspicuous consumption, which is an indigenous culture trait, than on his eagerness to know and adopt what he believes to be the proper aspects of Western life. The shops in the Western style, brightly lit and spacious, offer a wide range of goods of many different types. The merchant's overhead is high and his rate of turnover is low in proportion to the size of his stocks, but his profits more than compensate. He must be thoroughly familiar with the desires and style of life of his customers and actively contributes to the formation of their tastes.

In many cases the merchant acts as the agent of a manufacturer who absorbs the overhead and merely pays the merchant a commission on what is sold. His involvement in the processes of taste and value formation are only slightly less immediate

but no less irrevocable than that of the independent merchant. It is only as a result of an extension of the Western style of life that opportunities for his increasing the demand for his company's goods will develop.

The market behavior of the customers and merchants varies, but in different degrees, from the center of the old bazaar to the Western shopping area and constitutes the interactive pattern of participation in the market. Shopping, bargaining, hawking of wares, and advertising are the responses to the social pressures in the changing structure of the institution.

The shopping behavior, whether an active survey of the available goods in the market or an idle scanning of the array of offerings in shops and advertisements, is the initial step by the customer in participation in the market. The customer is exposing himself to goods of various types. In the old bazaar areas the dominant shopping pattern is active surveying of the quality and prices of goods that are required for daily consumption. This is somewhat modified by the establishment of a regular pattern of buying. The regularization of these patterns means that an almost permanent relationship may be established between the customer and a particular merchant which involves unquestioned acceptance of their mutual interdependence and a ritualization of the periodic transaction. This type of regularization of shopping also occurs in the Western market area where there is an equal degree of Westernization between customer and merchant. In the intermediate sections of the market the customers are predominantly engaged in active shopping. The type of shopping that differentiates the Western market area from all the rest is a passive scanning of the goods available. It reflects the distinctively Western characteristic of consuming as a constant preoccupation that can, in shopping, be vicariously satisfied.

Bargaining, so often thought the dominant characteristic of the Middle Eastern bazaar, is essentially a claim by the consumer that he knows the market as well as the merchant and

that the price quoted does not represent an accurate appraisal of current supply and demand in the sense that economic theory uses the terms. However, in the old bazaar area where transactions tend to become ritualized, bargaining is also ritualized or disappears altogether, and in the Western market area, where the prices are largely based on world conditions and therefore on supply and demand beyond the appraisal abilities of the customer, bargaining may be reduced to a minimum. In the intermediate areas energetic and continual bargaining takes place. It becomes a necessary preliminary to any transaction, so that both customer and merchant in a sense reassure one another that the other has performed a difficult social task satisfactorily.

The crying or hawking of wares by merchants in Middle Eastern cities is not universal and develops as a result of economic pressures. It is not a distinguishing behavior of either merchant type. Although in the bazaar proper it is most characteristic of the entrepreneur, the dealer in perishable goods particularly resorts to this method of attracting attention.

Two forms of hawking are common. The most usual is the repeated shouting of "Fish!" "Oranges!" "Tomatoes!" However, the vendors frequently call only the price. This tends to standardize the price of a given item and almost completely eliminates bargaining at the level of the individual customer. However, sometimes late in the evening two adjacent hawkers may be calling different prices for similar goods. Eventually, the caller of the higher price reduces his bid, to the cheers of his competitors.

Peddlers, by definition, seek their customers, but their activity is not purely random. They follow the same route day after day. One peddler sold fish in the winter and spring and tangerines during the hot season. As extensive a ritualized relation is developed between the peddler and his clients as between the chandler and his customers. The crying of wares by peddlers follows the theory on which much Western ad-

vertising is based: keep your name (and special wares) in the public eye. In the bazaar hawking is not part of the behavior of the chandler but rather of the entrepreneur. It is particularly characteristic of the areas of the market where perishable goods are the principal commodity.

Advertising, if defined as the use of mass media of communication for the purpose of conveying to potential customers the existence and virtues of a merchant's wares, is exploited in most of its various techniques in semi-Westernized contexts throughout the Middle East. The scale on which advertising is conducted does not compare, of course, with American levels but is more nearly that of Europe.

Advertising depends on and tends to encourage a large turnover of goods. Consequently, in a system of extensive subdivision of the market into many independent merchants selling unbranded goods, advertising offers little advantage. In the traditional Middle Eastern context, it is beyond the ken of the merchant to spend money, a part of his profit, on each item to sell more items. There is a sense of the saturated market. The fierce competition among the entrepreneurs arises from their sense of the low level of consumption at which saturation will occur.

In conclusion, the role played by bazaar merchants in the pattern of Middle Eastern society's response to Western goods has been shown to be circumscribed by social, psychological, and economic factors, all of which interact to limit his ability to introduce into the society goods and patterns of life that are foreign to the indigenous culture. Much of the meaning of a foreign culture is conveyed to the customers in the market by the foreign goods available there. The merchants who offer those goods are unconscious exponents of the new patterns of life which are emerging from the amalgam.

The Entrepreneur Class

THE title of this essay is untranslatable. As an economist pointed out, "enterpriser" sounds too dashing and "undertaker" somewhat sinister. It is also vague, and thus allows for some leeway. It has been chosen in order to focus attention on the main topic, the industrialist class, shifting whenever necessary to such fields as finance, commerce, or even, in one or two cases, the professions. First, the growth of the entrepreneur class in the principal Middle Eastern countries will be rapidly traced and then the main features will be sketched.*

A long historical glance brings out a very significant fact: at its height Islamic civilization was highly commercial. Islam has been described as the one major religion to have been founded by a successful businessman. The Meccan aristocracy, which first opposed, then rallied to and finally took over from Muhammad and his followers, was a trading aristocracy. Unlike agriculture, which was looked down upon by all self-respecting Arabs, and unlike the crafts, which were left to the subject populations, trade was both highly esteemed and widely

* The author of this essay is a member of the Department of Economics of the United Nations. The views expressed in it, however, are entirely personal and do not necessarily reflect those of the United Nations or any other organization.

practiced by the very "best people." The impression of intense commercial activity gained from reading *The Arabian Nights*, is confirmed by more sober accounts. Thus the Iranian traveler Nasir-i-Khusraw in his *Safar Namah* relates that practically all transactions in eleventh-century Basra were settled by cheques, not cash. Indeed, one of the most striking differences between Muslim and Western feudalism is the extent to which the former was based on a monetary economy and used monetary reckonings for its normal transactions. Another important difference for some centuries was the high development of the crafts in the Middle East.

In the twelfth to the fourteenth centuries Islam passed through a terrible crisis, being assailed first by the Crusaders and then by the still more devastating Mongols and Tatars. Islamic society survived under the Mamluks, but at the crippling cost of militarization and the debasement of its economic and cultural life. The diversion of the trade routes completed the ruin of the Middle East.

At this stage, however, a new factor of economic development began to make itself felt with increasing force. It is significant that, in its heyday, Islamic commercial activity was directed eastward and southward—to India, Indonesia, Africa, and for a short while even China—not westward to Europe. This may perhaps be explained by the poverty of Europe and the wars and piracy which rendered the Mediterranean insecure. At any rate, when trade relations did begin, it was the Europeans who initiated them: first the Amalfians, Genoese, and Venetians, then the Portuguese, French, and British. By the beginning of the eighteenth century the Middle East had been drawn into the network of European trade, supplying such products as silk, cotton, and coffee and receiving in return manufactured goods. A certain amount of transit trade also continued, Egypt re-exporting the products of Africa and Constantinople those of the Caucasus.

The important thing to notice about this trade is that it

was carried on by European companies and merchants established in Istanbul, Aleppo, Isfahan, and Cairo. As far as is known, there were no important Middle Eastern merchants. They lacked the liquid capital, the enterprise, or the security afforded by the Capitulations. But in the course of the eighteenth century, perhaps because of increasing anarchy in the Ottoman empire, European merchants began pulling out of Egypt and Syria. Trade, however, did not cease; at first their place was taken by Aleppo Jews, who became the consular representatives of some European states, established branches in Italy, and handled a large proportion of the foreign trade of Egypt and Syria. In turn, these Jews began to be replaced by Syrian Christians. When Bonaparte established a Council in Cairo, the Christian Syrian community was deemed sufficiently important—as well as pro-French—to have five representatives on it.

A parallel development occurred in Greece. In the course of the eighteenth century Greek shipping and commerce expanded considerably, and when, during the Revolutionary and Napoleonic wars, British and French ships and merchants withdrew from the eastern Mediterranean, their place was generally taken by Greeks. Prosperous merchant colonies were established in Odessa, Venice, and other Adriatic seaports. Incidentally, these colonies played an important part in organizing and financing the Greek Revolution.

Greece and Lebanon and Syria are interesting because they furnish the earliest Middle Eastern examples of the spontaneous emergence of an industrial class.

In Greece the development of shipping and trade, especially after 1830, led to the emergence, on the islands and in those parts of Asia Minor lying on the Black Sea–Mediterranean route, of handicrafts related to shipping. The introduction of steam led to the need for fuelling stations and ancillary industries. At the same time the development of agriculture stimulated the making of simple tools and crude chemical fertilizers.

But the real stimulus to Greek industry was the influx of refugees from Asia Minor, following World War I. A few of the refugees had a little money, which they used to establish small-scale industries. (Incidentally, the same phenomenon is observable today in Jordan.) Most of them were destitute, but they included skilled weavers, carpet makers, and other craftsmen. The vast majority settled in the cities. The International Loan granted to Greece was used to build houses, instead of to resettle the refugees on the land, as had been its original purpose. The result was the development of textile, food-processing, and other industries. When the depression struck in the 1930's, the government helped industry by means of import quotas, tariffs, and foreign exchange control, leading to considerable further development. Some of these industries have now become sufficiently efficient to be competitive, but most still depend heavily on protection. In recent years shippers have not shown much interest in industry, preferring to reinvest their profits in their own line of business.

It may, therefore, be said that Greek industry evolved spontaneously from the handicraft to the manufacturing stage.

Lebanon's economic evolution has run roughly parallel to that of Greece, except that the mainspring of activity has been not shipping but entrepôt trade and emigration. Early in the nineteenth century Beirut began to establish itself as the foreign trade channel of Lebanon, Syria, Palestine, northern Arabia and Iraq, and southern Anatolia. A prosperous class of Lebanese Christian merchants grew, with close contacts with Europe. At the same time French capital began to interest itself in the country, developing its silk resources and building ports, railways, and public utilities.

The breakup of the Ottoman empire was a heavy blow to the Beirut merchants. They lost their Anatolian market and much of the Iraqi market as well, while Haifa replaced Beirut as the port of Palestine and Transjordan. This was, however, offset partly by the growth of the Syrian and Lebanese markets,

partly by the rapid development of tourism, and partly by the development of a money market.[1] As present Beirut is by far the most important financial center in the Middle East, and the Lebanese merchants have been making good use of their wits in foreign exchange transactions. A good example is the gold trade. Gold is bought in Mexico with United States dollars, sent by plane to the Persian Gulf, shipped on little sailing boats which navigate the Indian Ocean, smuggled into India (and until recently into China), and sold for rupees. The rupees are then transferred to Saudi Arabia, where they are exchanged for sovereigns, which are then used to buy dollars, and so the cycle is complete. Other modern *Arabian Nights* stories are told, for instance, about the Lebanese merchant who financed a copper deal between Spain and the Soviet Union, and of another who, learning of a purchase by an American merchant of Iraqi wool, interposed himself between the two offering the American a slightly lower price in dollars and the Iraqi a slightly higher price in dinars, thus concluding the transaction to the satisfaction of everyone except the Iraqi Exchange Control.

These various activities provided one source of liquid capital for the development of industry. Another came from the emigrants who, ever since the 1860's and more particularly since the 1880's, have been leaving Lebanon for Egypt, the New World, Australia, and, as readers of Graham Greene's novels know, West Africa. Today there are probably as many people of Lebanese descent living outside the country as within it, and the story goes that a Lebanese upon being asked what was the population of his village replied: "Thirty thousand abroad, and ten thousand at home, for purposes of reproduction." Many of these emigrants have done exceedingly well for themselves, the outstanding example being those in Brazil, where Syrians and Lebanese own no less than five hundred large industrial enterprises, including some of the largest textile plants in the

[1] More recently, the development of the Persian Gulf oil fields has had very favorable repercussions on the Lebanese economy.

world. Thus emigration provided another source of capital in the form of both remittances and transfer of funds.

In the late 1920's some of this capital began to be invested in local industry. The Mandatory authorities directed most French investments into monopolies, such as ports, electricity, water, tobacco, and the like and used their influence to block Lebanese investments in those fields. Some foreign capital also went into the cement industry. But for the rest, most of the businesses were founded by Lebanese capital contributed either by emigrants who had made money, such as Arida, or by merchants, generally importers like Assaili and Tamer. During the 1930's there was further development, but many enterprises were in a precarious state when the war provided them with a shot in the arm. There comes to mind only two firms of any consequence which were not established by either traders or emigrants but grew from the handicraft to the factory stage, a biscuit factory and a jam factory.

Syria's development has differed from that of Lebanon in two important respects. In the first place, it started much later, and so far has made less headway. Secondly, whereas in Lebanon the Christian merchants have kept the lead they won in the nineteenth century, in Syria Muslims have tended to catch up with and overtake them. The example of my maternal family aptly illustrates the evolution of many Damascene Christians. Toward the beginning of the nineteenth century my great-great-grandfather owned a textile workshop. His profits enabled his son to engage, in the middle of the nineteenth century, in large-scale trade with Egypt and other countries. That, however, was the end of any business ability in the family: my grandfather and his brother, equipped like so many Christians with a French education which gave them a start over their Muslim contemporaries, went into the professions and the civil service, while their sons have tended to concentrate on the professions. Of course, many Christians are still prominent in business, but the Muslims have shown considerable ability and are taking

over an ever larger share. And when it comes to modern industry, the Muslims are playing a predominant part.

Except for some French and Belgian capital in railways and
public utilities—most of which have now been nationalized—
there has been practically no foreign capital investment in
Syria. Industrialization has been achieved entirely with local
funds, a small start in the prewar period being followed by
greater development after the war. Three main groups may be
distinguished. First, the so-called Khumasieh group of Damascus, which has established spinning, dyeing, vegetable oil, and
soap factories and taken over the Damascus cement plant. It
consists entirely of Muslim merchants, most of whom worked
in the import trade. Secondly, there is the Sahnawi group, also
of Damascus, which has set up glass, sugar, alcohol, vegetable
oil, glucose, starch, and dyeing factories. Its president, and some
of its members, are Christians, but the majority are Muslims;
almost all of the group consists of traders, practically all being
importers or representatives of foreign firms. Lastly, there are
various Aleppo industrialists: Mudarris, owner of a large textile
plant and notable as the only example of a Syrian landowner
who has taken a real interest in industry; Hariri, also a textile
manufacturer; and Shabarek who has just set up a cement
factory. Both of the latter are traders.

Whereas Greece, Lebanon, and Syria provide examples of
the spontaneous and slow growth of a business class, in Israel
there has been a completely different phenomenon—the trans-
plantation of a highly developed group of entrepreneurs from
Europe. Because of the very diverse origins, both social and national, of the Jewish immigrants into Palestine and Israel, it
is difficult to give a clear-cut picture of the background of the
industrialists. Broadly speaking, it may be said that the entrepreneurs in Israel established firms either in the industry in which
they had previously been employed (as owners, managers,
technicians, artisans, or workers) or else in an industry in which
their country of origin excelled. As examples of the latter tend-

ency, there are the German Jews who founded the chemical industry, the British Jews who set up metalworks, and the American Jews who established the precision instruments industry.

Examples of the former tendency are numerous and diverse. Thus the textile industry was founded by Polish owners of textile factories in Lodz; the chemical and pharmaceutical industry by German chemists, doctors, or merchants dealing in chemical products; the engineering industry by engineers, sometimes in partnership with former importers; and the diamond industry by Belgian diamond cutters who took advantage of the opportunity created by the cessation of Belgian and Dutch exports and the availability of African diamonds to establish in Palestine a new industry based on a different division of labor. An interesting development is that of printing, carried out by east European Jews who combined a high educational level and a knowledge of several of the many languages current in Israel with experience as printers in Europe.

As in other Middle Eastern countries, but to a lesser extent, there has been a tendency for importers of an article to start producing it; examples are paper, leather, and some textile products. Another trend, which has its counterpart in Lebanon, though the differences are more important than the similarity, is the creation of big enterprises by businessmen who gained their experience abroad, for example the potash, cement, and electricity works, all founded by Russian Jews—Novomeysky, a mining engineer; Lifshitz, the owner of oil wells; and Rutenberg, a politician. A tendency which has gone much farther than in other Middle Eastern countries is the establishment of branches of foreign firms to manufacture such things as Kaiser-Frazer cars, Philco refrigerators, Philips bulbs, Firestone tires. This has been facilitated by the existence of a large supply of skilled technicians and workmen, the opportunity for export provided by Israel's large import surplus and dollar gifts and loans, and the close contacts between Israeli and foreign busi-

nessmen. Finally, there is a phenomenon unique to Israel, namely, that of corporations formed by Jews living abroad which raise funds abroad for investment in Israel, e.g., the South Africa Palestine Company, the Palestine Economic Corporation, which is American, and the Palestine Corporation, which is British.

So far the private sector of industry, which accounts for over four-fifths of the whole, has been considered. The rest is owned by the *Histadruth*, whose managers are either former engineers or administrators who have made their way up the ladder of the trade unions or *Kibbutzim*. A high percentage of these men came from Poland or Russia, while the technicians are mainly from Germany and western Europe.

Egypt's economic history differs profoundly from that of the other Middle Eastern countries because of the fact that it was developed much earlier and that that development was achieved by the investment of vast foreign capital and the influx of a large foreign community. Hence Egypt's entrepreneur class, when it came into being, had to wrest its place from foreign rivals. Apart from a largely foreign-owned public debt of £E 94 million, much of which had been spent on productive works, foreign investments in 1914 amounted to £E 92 million. At that date the foreign community numbered 150,000, out of a total population of 12,000,000, and that figure does not include Europeans or Levantines of Egyptian nationality. Up to World War I these foreigners completely dominated Egypt's financial and commercial life, as well as whatever little industrial activity there was, and even controlled petty trade. As Lord Cromer put it in his *Report* for 1905: "Bootmending, as well as boot-making, is almost entirely in the hands of Greeks and Armenians. The drapery trade is controlled by Jews, Syrians and Europeans, the tailoring trade by Jews."

Such an unnatural state of affairs could not last indefinitely, and as early as 1879, when the Egyptian press began to enjoy some freedom of expression, a first attempt was made to remedy

it by laying the foundations for a native bourgeoisie. Under the leadership of two Lebanese journalists, Adib Ishaq and Amin Shimayyel, a group of prominent Egyptians, including Sultan Pasha and Omar Lutfi Pasha, drew up a prospectus for the creation of a national bank which should buy up and redeem the public debt. In this prospectus they pointed out that the only way open before underdeveloped Oriental countries desirous of getting rich was trade and industry, which required large amounts of capital that only banks, drawing on the savings of the public, could provide. The sponsors disposed of objections based on the Qur'anic prohibition of usury by different arguments and quotations from an impressive number of authorities.

The moment chosen was, however, most unpropitious, and nothing more was heard of a national bank until 1911, in which year the Egyptian congress recommended the institution of such a bank while a young employee named Talat Harb—later to achieve fame as founder and president of Banque Misr—brought out a book entitled *Egypt's Economic Remedy; or, The Project of a Bank for Egyptians.* This was Harb's fourth book; the other three are worth mentioning as shedding some light on his personality. In 1899 he had opposed Qasim Amin's call for the emancipation of women, a somewhat amusing matter in the light of the fact that his own factories were, in later years, to employ thousands of women workers. In 1905 he had written a history of Arab and Muslim states, in which he showed himself, as always, an orthodox and devout Muslim. In 1910 he had forcefully and cogently argued against the renewal of the charter of the Suez Canal Company, unless accompanied by much more favorable terms including the employment of Egyptian directors and personnel.

In his book on banking he stressed the need for a "really Egyptian bank, alongside the existing foreign banks," which would help and encourage Egyptians to enter various fields of economic activity and give "Egypt a voice in its own money

[125]

market and defend its interests just as other banks defend those of their countries." At the same time he assured foreigners that an Egyptian bank would not reduce their business, since there was plenty of room for all. He expressed his confidence in the business ability of Egyptians and the availability of Egyptian funds for his scheme.

No immediate results came from this book, but in 1916 Harb was charged by the government Committee on Industry, which formed a landmark in Egypt's economic history, with studying means to develop the country's industry. Basing his arguments on Germany's experience, he urged the creation of a bank which would finance industrial development. By 1920 many prominent Egyptians had come to believe that political independence needed to be consolidated by economic independence, and 126 shareholders subscribed £E 80,000 for the creation of Harb's Banque Misr. By 1927 the capital had been raised to £E 1,000,000. In the meantime the bank began to found affiliated companies in the following fields: 1922, printing; 1924, cotton ginning; 1925, transport and navigation; 1925, cinema; 1926, sugar-cane growing; 1927, silk weaving, cotton spinning and weaving, fisheries, and linen; 1930, cotton exporting; 1932, airways and sale of Egyptian products; 1934, insurance, maritime shipping, tourism, and tanning and leather work; 1938, spinning and weaving of fine cotton goods, mines and quarries, and vegetable oils. The combined capital of these companies amounted to about £E 3,500,000 and their reserves to £E 1,500,000. An affiliated bank was also opened in Beirut and a branch in Hejaz.

There is no doubt that Talat Harb succeeded in his primary aim—that of setting up purely Egyptian businesses, keeping their books in Arabic, and training a body of men in the various economic and financial branches. There is equally no doubt that his enterprises suffered from overextension, neglect of the rules of sound banking (such as not borrowing on short term and lending on long term), favoritism, mismanagement, and in a

few cases downright dishonesty. The outbreak of war in 1939 caused a run on Banque Misr which was staved off only with government help. A thorough reorganization was then carried out and, thanks to the war boom, the situation of the Misr group is now basically sound. After the war they added to their long list a large rayon plant.

In addition to Banque Misr, the 1930 tariff played a large part in stimulating Egyptian industry. Under its shadow many enterprises sprang up, some owned by Egyptians, others by foreign residents. World War II brought more industries into being, mostly Egyptian. As in other Arab countries, most of the Egyptian industrialists have sprung from the trading class.

Perhaps the best index of the progress achieved is the percentage of the total capital of corporations registered in Egypt which is owned by Egyptians. Whereas in 1933 the percentage of share and bond capital originally subscribed by Egyptians was only 9 percent of the total, it had risen by 1948 to 39 percent. A breakdown by subperiods shows that in 1934–1939 Egyptians contributed 47 percent of new capital subscriptions or increase of capital of existing companies; in 1940–1945 the proportion was 66 percent; and in 1946–1948 it was 84 percent. It should be remembered, moreover, that a substantial amount of share and bond capital originally subscribed by foreigners changed hands and is now held by Egyptians.

Another way of measuring the progress made in Egyptianizing business is to study the *Annuaire des Sociétés Anonymes* (1951), which, of course, covers finance and commerce, where Egyptians are less well represented, as well as industry. Out of a total of 1,406 names which can be identified with any degree of certainty, 31 percent are Egyptian Muslims, 4 percent Copts, 17 percent Jews, 12 percent Syrians or Lebanese, 9 percent Greeks or Armenians, and 31 percent Europeans. The proportion of Muslims and Copts is still very low, but some thirty years before it was almost nil.

If Egypt provides an example of a native business class which

gradually pushed its way mainly by its own efforts, Turkey furnishes an example of a business class which was brought into being mainly by state action. This took two forms: elimination of foreign elements and encouragement of natives.

Until the end of the nineteenth century practically all business was in the hands of Europeans or Greeks, Armenians, and Jews. The railways, banks, public utilities, and mines were foreign owned and staffed by foreigners or members of the minority groups. Foreign trade was also in the hands of Armenians, Greeks, or Jews, and these groups supplied practically all of Turkey's professional class. Thus almost all pharmacists were Armenians, and there was much rejoicing and considerable publicity accompanying the graduation of the first genuinely Turkish pharmacist. The only nonagricultural economic activity of any consequence which was in Turkish hands was internal trade.

Gradually at first and then much more quickly, things began to change with the disappearance of the Armenian and Greek minorities. Many foreigners, and all the members of the minority groups, thought that the country's economy would never survive such an amputation, but, as usual, foreigners both overestimated the technical difficulties of running anything and underestimated the resilience and resourcefulness of a people determined to make things work.[2] At first Mustafa Kemal expected private Turkish businessmen to step into the breach, but their response was disappointing for the simple reason that there were so few of them.

In these circumstances the government decided it had to do things itself and launched its policy of the state-owned and state-run enterprises. Following the Central Bank and the İş Bank, a purely Turkish commercial bank, came the Sümer and Eti banks, which founded and managed a large variety of industrial and mining enterprises. At the same time foreign-owned

---

[2] A strikingly similar phenomenon was the exodus of Jewish businessmen from Iraq in 1950 and 1951; here, too, foreigners expected a disruption of the Iraqi economy, which did not occur.

railways and practically all mines were nationalized, and coastal shipping, heretofore largely in Greek hands, was reserved for Turks. It was hoped that eventually some of the state-owned enterprises could be sold to private ownership, but this has been a slow and exceedingly difficult step to arrange.

In order to attract capable young men into the government-owned banks and enterprises, much higher salary scales than those prevailing in the civil service were offered. This had the desired result, and with training and education abroad a group of competent managers was formed. Under Inönü a move was made to bring these salaries in line with those of the civil service; as a result many of the most capable employees left for private business. A reversal to the old policy is now taking place.

In the meantime private business was growing, as a result of the country's general development. A good illustration is provided by the career of Vehbi Koç, one of Turkey's leading magnates. As a very young man he came with his father, on a donkey, to Ankara in quest of work. In view of a building boom at the time, he was advised to cart tiles, which he did so successfully that he is now one of the country's richest merchants. Recently, in partnership with foreign capital he founded a large factory for making electric bulbs. Some other merchants have established other industries, such as textiles and cement, while in the south a few landlords set up ginning machines and flour mills to process local produce. Nevertheless, the state still plays a leading part, owning about 30 percent of all industry and having a monopoly of heavy industry and most branches of mining.

It is in commerce, finance, and, above all, the professions that the Turks have taken over from the minority groups. A rapid glance at the shops in Ankara failed to detect a single non-Turkish name. In Istanbul, which handles two-thirds of the country's foreign trade, although there are many shops which are owned by Greeks, Armenians, Jews, or Levantines, the Turks are taking over an ever-increasing share. Once more they

have been helped by a government measure, the *Varlik Vergisi* or Capital Levy of 1942, which fell heavily on minority groups, many of whose members were ruined. The *Varlik Vergisi* undoubtedly played an important part in the Turkification of economic life by enabling Turks to buy up, at very low prices, the businesses and property of other groups.

Lastly, a few words about Iran, about which there is even less information than about the other countries. British capital has developed the oil industry and banking. As in Turkey, members of minority groups have played an important part, the Jews in foreign trade and the Armenians in foreign trade and some handicrafts such as silverwork and furniture making. Neither of these groups, however, has figured at all prominently in industry. Also as in Turkey but to a lesser extent, much of the country's industry has been founded and is operated by the state, which secured the necessary funds by a monopoly of foreign trade and heavy taxes on consumption. The rest has been created mainly by Iranian merchants, mostly exporters or importers, many of whom were enriched by the inflation caused by heavy government investment. Quite a number of Iranians have made their fortunes in trade in India and the Far East. Of these, however, very few have invested in Iran, and even where there has been investment, as in the case of the shipowner Namazi who has been a great benefactor to his native city of Shiraz, it has been on a small scale. It is difficult to think of a single factory which has been founded by an Iranian landlord.

Following this historical account of the development of the industrial classes in different countries, some general statements regarding their origin, character, desires, and influence may not be out of place. In order to create modern industries in the set of circumstances prevailing in the Middle East, four conditions were necessary: capital; business ability and initiative; technical competence; and political prestige and power. Broadly speaking, the first two have been supplied by the

merchant class; the third by foreign technicians and foremen; the last by a few politicians who took an interest in industry, such as Sidqi and Hafez Afifi in Egypt and Khaled al-Azm and Faris al-Khuri in Syria. An alternative form has been the creation of industries by the state.

The bulk of Middle Eastern manufacturers has come from the merchant class; indeed, many have continued to practice trade while engaging in industry. A few examples can be shown of landlords setting up industries, and a still smaller number of craftsmen have expanded their business to the size of a modern factory. The vast majority of industrial enterprises have been founded by traders or financiers, generally merchants engaged in foreign trade, for it was the latter class, alone, which had the liquid capital necessary for such an undertaking. This, of course, refers to the pioneers, who first created new enterprises. Once established, industrial firms have attracted an ever-widening circle of investors, who have been encouraged to buy shares by dividends which are high compared to the low rates of interest paid by banks and the almost equally low returns on land bought at inflated values. Thus, in Egypt, successful doctors, lawyers, engineers, politicians, and civil servants have been drawn into industry as shareholders, directors, or administrators, and landlords have taken a rapidly increasing interest in investing in, and even founding, industrial enterprises.[3]

The merchants supplied not only capital but business ability, though not precisely the kind required by industry. To be more precise, they have plenty of entrepreneurial ability but little knowledge of plant management. It takes years to make a Middle Eastern merchant realize that a factory is neither a car, which runs perfectly well if the right buttons are pushed, nor a shop, which an able man can manage with the help of a

[3] It may be stated, parenthetically, that developments in nineteenth-century Russia and other parts of eastern Europe were basically similar. When they were not established by the state, by foreign capital, or by resident Germans or Jews, industries were created by local merchants. At a later stage, landowners and other classes began to take an interest in industrial development.

couple of clerks. They expect immediate and substantial profits and are disappointed when they find that this is not forthcoming. They pinch pennies and stint the technicians on the funds required for experimentation. They grudge these technicians their high salaries, which they cannot help comparing with those paid to their clerks. The following remark by a Syrian industrialist, though perhaps not typical, is worth considering: "I have a clerk who knows perfect English and French, keeps books and makes excellent coffee; I pay him £S 300 a month. Why do you ask for 700 for a technician?" They fail to understand how much has to be done before local raw materials become suitable for processing, local workmen are broken in, and the machines have the "bugs" taken out of them. They try to manage everything themselves and do not appreciate the need for delegation. Above all, they are reluctant to reinvest, preferring to distribute profits.

Technical obstacles have been overcome with the help of foreign engineers and foremen. In general, Middle Eastern workmen have shown intelligence and a remarkable capacity for learning, but good foremen are still scarce and local technicians are not always able to apply in a practical concrete way the lessons that they learned at school. It is still a subject for complaint that the educated Middle Easterner, be he Arab, Iranian, or Turk, is reluctant to dirty his hands, but encouraging progress is being made in this direction. The shortage of managers is more serious, and a long time will have to elapse before it can be overcome.

It would be most unfair to stress all of the shortcomings of the Middle Eastern entrepreneurs without indicating the adverse economic, social and political factors with which they have to contend. Thus, while the inflation of the last fifteen years has undoubtedly stimulated business, the constant depreciation of currencies since World War I has also strengthened the already ingrained habit of taking the short view and requiring immediate returns. Again, whereas the foreign entrepreneurs were

completely protected by the Capitulations, local businessmen have to take the rough with the smooth in their relations with the government—and there is plenty of rough. Thus the International Bank for Reconstruction and Development in its report, *The Economy of Turkey*, states that "private producers in general have grown increasingly apprehensive of expanding state operations and the possibility of expropriation," and urges "prompt elimination of government practices which give public enterprises advantages over their private competitors." Similar conditions prevail in Iran. In the other countries there is no competition from state-owned factories, and the danger of expropriation of native, as distinct from foreign, concerns has been negligible, but there is plenty of administrative red tape, heavy handedness, and excessive preoccupation with fiscal considerations, which have not created an ideal climate for private enterprise.

So much for the origin and character of the industrialists. Now a few words regarding their desires and influence. Naturally, they all clamor for protection, and in the main their wishes have been met; less has been done, however, to help them in other, more fruitful, directions. Thus, surprisingly enough in view of the abundance of oil, fuel costs are often very considerable because of transport costs, the high price charged by the oil companies, or high excise duties. Inadequate transport facilities hamper industry almost everywhere. Industrial credit, in most countries, is unorganized, and industrialists are forced to borrow on short term, at high rates, from ordinary commercial banks. A Lebanese industrialist has related that he had to pay nine percent on such loans; moreover, the fact that he could not pay in cash compelled him to offer higher prices to his suppliers. He estimated the combined charges at 15 percent of his capital, a figure which cut deeply into his profit margin. This deficiency has been remedied in Israel, and is being remedied in Egypt and Turkey by the recently founded industrial banks, but not in the other countries. Repair facilities are very inadequate

and constitute a heavy burden on industrialists, who often have to fly in a spare part from Europe or the United States; they also often have to fly in a technician to repair the machine, a fact which has resulted in some Czechs, sent by Skoda, refusing to return and choosing freedom in Syria. And technical education is almost nonexistent, except in the more advanced countries, i.e., Israel, Turkey, Egypt, or where it is undertaken by the oil companies.

One more point remains to be noticed in this context—the desire of many industrialists for some form of economic union among the Arab states. Most Egyptian, Syrian, and Lebanese manufacturers realize that such a union would broaden their market and enable them to produce on a larger scale and more efficiently. Naturally, some vested interests oppose such a measure, which would expose them to competition, and, unless steps for union are taken soon, with the passage of years such centrifugal forces may gain in importance.

Lastly, a few words regarding the relations between industrialists and other classes. Needless to say, there have been many clashes with labor concerning wages and conditions of work. As elsewhere, employers have tried to keep wages as low as possible and, except in Israel whose *Histadruth* is the most powerful body of its kind in the world, the unions have not been in a position to offer much resistance. In Turkey, however, state enterprises have offered excellent conditions to their workers, as have several Egyptian firms, notably the Misr textile mills.

Opposition between industrialists and farmers has begun to be manifest. Perhaps the best place to study this is Egypt, where the process has gone farthest. First, there is taxation, over which, since the 1930's, a closely fought contest has been taking place. The landed interests scored several points in quick succession, such as the imposition of prohibitive duties on imports of wheat, the levying of an income tax on commercial and industrial prof-

its but not on land rents, and, during the war, the raising of the rate of that tax and the imposition of an excess profits tax.

After the war, however, the industrialists had their innings and managed to repeal the excess profits tax, to remodel the tariff to suit their interests, to raise the rate of the land tax, to subject income from land to the general income tax, and, above all, to pass an agrarian reform law. They were also instrumental in the fixing of a minimum agricultural wage and the enactment of compulsory secondary education. These achievements are the more remarkable in view of their slight representation in parliament compared to that of the landlords. So far, however, they have not been able to repeal the measure compelling them to use expensive high-grade Egyptian cotton in their textile factories—an economic absurdity, equivalent to using mahogany for kitchen tables—nor have they succeeded in their primary objective, the raising of the level of the Egyptian peasant.

In Syria, where industry is still embryonic, the beginnings of a conflict can be discerned. The vegetable oil refineries would like to export cottonseed cake, but the landlords prevent this in order to feed their livestock; conversely, the landlords prefer to export maize, which the starch factories require. Industrialists also complain of the labor law, which is very generous to workmen and which was passed by a parliament in which they were practically unrepresented; needless to say, it does not cover agricultural labor.

In Lebanon agriculture plays a very subordinate part in the economy as its contribution to the national income is far less than those of industry and construction combined. Here the clash is between manufacturers on the one hand and merchants and financiers on the other. Thus importers favor a low tariff while financiers are opposed to the setting up, with foreign help, of an industrial bank on the Turkish model.[4]

[4] In 1954 the Industrial, Agricultural, and Real Estate Bank was founded; its capital is to be provided by both the government and private enterprise.

But a final word of warning is necessary regarding these conflicts. It must not be forgotten that, unlike European society, and perhaps even more than American, Middle Eastern society is fluid. There is not yet any counterpart to the great industrial and commercial families of the West. Moreover, many industrialists and merchants mark their advent to affluence by the purchase of land. This is usually done for noneconomic reasons, such as prestige, or as a long-term investment, but it nevertheless does help to create a certain community of interests between them and the landowners. Still more important is their common fear of a social revolution, the prospect of which restrains the industrialists from pressing the landowners too hard. The same dilemma faced the German bourgeoisie in 1848 and the Russian bourgeoisie before the Revolution; E. H. Carr's comment on these situations seems to be applicable to the Middle East:

That they were weak was undeniable. But a more significant cause of their hesitancy was that they were already conscious of the growing menace to themselves of an eventual proletarian revolution. One reason why history so rarely repeats itself is that the dramatis personae at the second performance have prior knowledge of the *denouement*.[5]

But precisely because of the greater knowledge and awareness today, it may well be that the Middle Eastern bourgeoisie, with help from abroad, will be able to steer clear of the reefs which wrecked the ships of so many of its predecessors.

[5] *The Bolshevik Revolution* (London, 1950), I, 42.

Economic Planners

THE province of this study is the exploration of certain aspects of the mental metabolism which appear to have influenced recent government and business decisions in several Middle East countries in the domain of economic planning. To relate attitudes and decisions of individuals and groups to the impersonal problems of planning should contribute to an understanding of persistently recurring pitfalls in certain Middle East countries. However, the problems of economic planning in any country are not neatly isolated from other economic affairs and from social and political problems.*

Because of personal experiences the focus of this study is upon economic planning in Afghanistan, with the expectation that analogies or contrasts with other Middle East countries can be established as the general problems are discussed and developed.

Perhaps the fundamental stimulus to planning economic development is the persistence of a miserable affliction. In the midst of abundant but idle resources, be it unreclaimed land,

* EDITOR'S NOTE: The essay, in part, is based on unpublished reports of the Morrison-Knudsen Company and the Export-Import Bank.

underutilized man power or untouched subsoil riches, masses of people live on a bare subsistence standard and have little if any voice in the shaping of the economic process of which they are a part. Well known are such basic causes as a dearth of capital, the lack of foreign exchange, and a famine of trained personnel, government administrators, engineers, agronomists, and teachers. Less known or less understood is the lack of the complementary resources required to exploit water for irrigation and power, or minerals for processing and export, or raw cotton and oil crops for industry. Among these missing complementary resources are not only physical ones, but managerial talent, which is almost completely absent.

The paramount function of this missing managerial activity (which for want of any better term might be labeled *planning*) is to enable the government officials and private businessmen of these countries to translate the potential economic wealth into concrete achievement and thus reverse the deteriorating trend. People in positions of authority and influence in Middle Eastern governments and businesses are fully aware of this problem. Most of those involved in, or anxious to take a hand in, straightening the erratic course of official economic policy have recognized that economic emancipation is linked: (1) with a determination of priorities essential in an environment of limited natural, financial, and administrative resources; (2) with stability and continuity of effort at the legislative and executive level where long-term investments are involved; and (3) with offering foreign technicians, financiers, and contractors solid, realistic, and wide administrative services without which harmonious and productive international co-operation cannot work.

There are many illustrations of this awareness. An economist from Lebanon was the chairman of a group which suggested measures by which underdeveloped countries might free themselves from the strangling grip of economic underdevelopment

and constantly fluctuating official policy. Reports prepared by the Turkish government exhibit an acute realization of the conflict between a large military expenditure program, a tight budget, limited voluntary savings, and the need for large investments in industry and agriculture. In the domain of private industrial investment, the Industrial Bank of Egypt has complained that many applications for funds were inadequately prepared, while some were "fantastic" and most not ready for financing. Important has been the Bank's recognition of the high priority that the recasting of technical education deserves if industry is to gain a sound economic footing. Furthermore, the Bank warned that the gap between industry's need for people trained in the use of machinery and power and the training provided in schools was widening. Finally, to revert to the Afghan case, there is the statement of the Minister of National Economy, in 1949, defending an application for credit from the United States Export-Import Bank:

My Government believes that the projects submitted represent the closest approximation to a minimum and necessary program of public and private investment that could be designed.
What convinces me of the soundness of the proposed projects, taken together, is their economic interdependence.

What then is behind the seeming paradox of awareness and incompetence?

There has certainly been enough planning in the Middle East, enough honest attempts to arrest the disastrous waste of energy which is reflected in the number and volume of blueprints for national development programs and for individual projects in addition to the finished and half-finished structures. Shortcomings of planning in the Middle East are of two types. One arises from inadequacies or misjudgments in the *blueprinting* stage which are due to misconceptions about the economics of mobilizing resources and about methods or procedures for

economic development. The other stems from more inadequacies and really serious difficulties (serious, because costly) in the *implementing stage* of planning.

One of the most vexing issues in the Middle East is the lack of real purchasing power. This lack so restricts the market for an increased supply of industrial and agricultural products that it discourages both private and public investment from the outset. Even the most illiterate readily recognize the enormous technical opportunities which come with the replacement of primitive methods of production. Technically speaking, it is easy to convince observers of modern plants or farms how large is the physical productivity of one dollar invested in capital equipment compared with investment in real estate. Unfortunately, the observer almost inevitably takes this to mean that installation of more and better equipment anywhere will increase income.

This narrow and misleading approach was followed by Syria when she established a glass factory in Damascus and soon found that the market for its output was too small. A similar error was made by Turkey when she industrialized certain fringes of the economy, realizing much later that the returns are disappointing on a single investment project, or even a group of projects, which do not affect the purchasing power of the larger segments of the economy. Several avenues of escape have been tried. For years Lebanon has pressed for preferential tariff systems or free-trade areas in order to create adequate markets for large-scale industries. At Havana in 1947–1948, during the fiery discussions about the commercial policy provisions of the Charter for the International Trade Organization, all Middle Eastern delegations lined up behind Lebanon to make such trading areas acceptable to the other major trading powers.

Such an answer to the problem, however, mistakes mobility within countries or between countries for wealth. If by legislation or government order trading areas, previously blocked from

each other, could become one and *pari passu* rich enough to buy the products of new industry or mechanized agriculture, the problems would be solved.

Another answer to the problem, popular in the Middle East, has been to subsidize the new plants or branches of industrial or agricultural production in the vague hope that experience and the training of workers will eventually put them on a sound economic basis. This hope is only justified if the subsidy is tied to a simultaneous increase in productivity in other segments of the national economy.

It is not too difficult to see why this misconception is so common in countries whose methods of production are appallingly primitive but whose cultural heritage includes science and other achievements without which modern technology would have been impossible. If one adds to this the continuous contact with modern technology since the Western industrialized nations have taken an interest in the resources of the area and tapped them with modern devices, one may understand why there is something emotional and physically attractive in modern production patterns. Another factor may have been the West's own preoccupation with engineering problems, which were translated into encouraging and facilitating education in engineering. In short, then, behind this first and fatal misconception is the engineering approach to investment in development projects.

Significantly, the Minister of Public Works who first introduced Afghan economic development plans to American financial institutions and his successor in that function, the Minister of National Economy, when presenting Afghanistan's case to the Export-Import Bank did not fall victim to this fallacy as the reference above appears to demonstrate. The first application for credit in February, 1949, requested foreign aid for five years in eight private projects, costing $49,000,000, and eight public projects, costing $69,000,000, each of them in different branches of the economy and geographical regions of the coun-

try. An American economist, after studying these plans, reported that the "projects are fairly well planned out, both those for the near future as well as those for the long run. They have been sensibly chosen and are precisely those which seem to be called for at this stage in Afghan development."

But, as foreign aid became available for only one public project, centering upon the utilization of soil and water in a rather narrowly confined region of one valley and as the private investment projects in new transportation, textile, cement, sugar, soap, and hydroelectric power were allowed to lag behind, all the dangers of pushing ahead with a relatively large investment, $28,000,000, in one isolated economic area alone began to hover over that project.

These dangers appeared avoidable only if some of the other projects could have been aggressively pushed. But here a second danger looms.

This is the danger of overinvestment—the undertaking of development activities which, though they do not by themselves produce anything consumable for a certain period of time, nevertheless consume existing resources. Not only have the "investment" workers to be given tools and equipment and materials but they have to be fed and clad, perhaps more so than before, when they were underemployed and shared the meager yield of their nomad or peasant families' farms. The additional resources required must be met either by complementary domestic savings or capital imports. Neither source of capital is plentiful in the Middle East. Hence an aggregate of development projects that meets the requirement of concurrent investment in several directions may be in excess of the financial resources. Moreover, it may be in excess of the physical and managerial resources, in terms of personnel, available to the country.

The most obvious case of such overreaching development was the Seven-Year Plan in Iran. The administrative organization

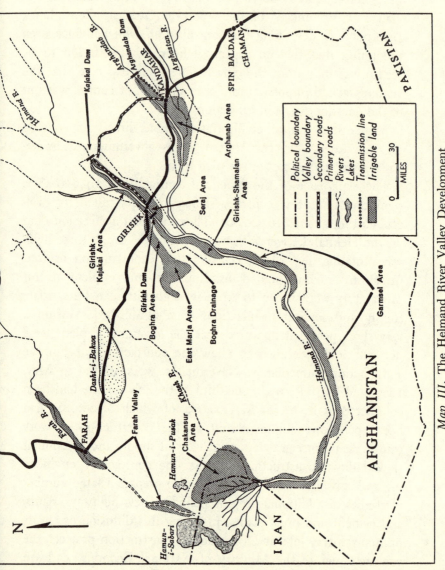

Map III. The Helmand River Valley Development

required to carry out what the *Majlis* and the American engineers felt ought to be carried out was painfully immense. A glance at Volume V of the report of Overseas Consultants, Incorporated, describing that organization, will convince even the uninitiated that to expect such an administration to be set up was folly from the outset, unless one expected that the Iranians would import it from abroad. This, of course, was out of the question for political reasons.

Afghanistan is another illustration, more directly of concern to Americans, since the United States government is underwriting part of the cost of the plan there.

The experience of the American contractor in 1946–1948 is significant. The first contract, signed in 1946, called for projects costing about $16,000,000. They included a diversion dam on the Helmand River with 90 kilometers of canal, three highways totaling 445 kilometers, and the reconstruction of four irrigation structures and dams. Engineers and implements for preparatory work began to arrive in Afghanistan in June, 1946; supply and service organizations were established. Within a very short period it appeared that the government plans were not sufficiently detailed to allow the contractor to begin the construction immediately. Nevertheless, work started in May, 1947, and by June, 1948, one-third of the job volume had been completed at a cost of $11,000,000, of which $4,000,000 had been spent on equipment and on the construction of work camps. As unforeseen delays in delivery of supply and equipment slowed down construction progress, the contractors' engineering and survey crews were appointed to prepare a large number of studies of additional projects including new highways, dams, and cement and brick plants. Justifying this diffusion of efforts on many survey jobs and a few actual construction projects, the contractor wrote the Ministry of National Economy early in 1949:

It has been necessary to prepare studies on many projects in order for the Government to determine a sound program. In addition to the

eight original projects included in the original contract, there have been added 25 additional engineering studies and some other small construction work.

The construction work included a Kabul customs house, machine shops, a hospital, the royal mausoleum, and the king's apartments.

In spite of the failure of the work to reach the predetermined goal, the government had to incur the predetermined expense. While a portion of these expenditures was actually wasted, a very sizable portion reflected the high overhead construction costs of which the governmental planners were obviously quite unaware. It is plain that the contractor, as well as the government, had been tempted by the volume which the original Five-Year Plan had held out to each. But neither the technical preparation nor the financial resources were available to support that volume.

The first indication that the planners in the Ministry of National Economy had overreached themselves came when the Plan failed to be approved by the cabinet and parliament. Although there were political and personal factors involved, an annual exchange burden of $16,000,000 for a period of five years, to be followed by a new five-year investment period, appeared beyond the country's capacity, even if all the controls over imports and consumption demanded by the Ministry of National Economy could have been enforced. In addition, the government had obtained only $21,000,000 in foreign credit and not the $55,000,000 it sought. Even after being cut down, the Plan still overtaxed the facilities available.

The experience after 1949 was no different. As construction of basic irrigation installations approached completion, the Afghan government was reminded of the assurances it had given that it would create a commission with full authority to ensure proper administration of the Plan. Not until April, 1952, however, was a commission set up to help carry out an important part of the Plan. Even if the cabinet had been able to

overcome some of the political and technical hurdles, it would not have been able to locate enough administrators to handle the commission's job as originally envisaged.

A concrete illustration concerned the settlement of the nomads in the Helmand Valley. The Afghan government had declared:

The resettlement plan will be put into operation when the irrigation projects . . . are completed. The Government will undertake to build roads, schools, arrange for public health facilities, but will leave the work of building houses, subsidiary water channels to the settlers themselves.

But no formal allocations or budgets were made in 1950 or 1951. Although the area required exceptionally careful staking out of the homesteads and preparing of the land because of differences in soil quality and the abundance of third-class land, no official provision had been made for preparatory work. No technical service had been started when the first settlers started squatting along the new irrigation canal.

New inadequacies developed when by 1951 over 4,000 acres had been developed and put under cultivation. This had been accomplished by machine operations in order to save time—a gain in time which might have meant a gain in production and income for settlers had plans for settlement reached the appropriate stage. Instead, a good portion of the newly prepared land was leased out to large landowners. Furthermore, the use of water was not controlled. Unattended ditches and distribution laterals became flooded or filled with sand.

At one point, someone had blocked a culvert in a sub-lateral: . . . water in the sub-lateral had consequently risen and washed out a road. . . . Farmers were blocking laterals to get unnecessarily high water levels. Too much water was being used; at one place the ground water level has risen 5 or 6 meters and is now less than 2 meters from the ground surface. Water is standing in some drainage ditches. . . . Farmers have taken it on themselves to develop new lands, appropriat-

ing water from the canal and building new ditches without permission. Locks on turnout gates have been broken or stolen.[1]

Typical settlement difficulties soon emerged. Afghan farmers had learned in thousands of years' experience that soil and crops differ radically in water needs. But with the need for allocating the newly available water among as many as eleven crops over a twelve-month period, a new educational process was necessary. By the spring of 1951 only incidental help had been rendered the farmers on diversified irrigation cropping. No qualified Afghan agriculturalist had been brought officially in contact with the project. This may have resulted from the fact that, when the promoter of the Helmand project had left that immediate political scene, subordinates belonging to opposing political factions showed a natural tendency not to be caught supporting, or even acting in connection with, the former minister's program. What opinions United Nations experts voiced privately were unfavorable. Questioning the agronomic justification of the whole project, they were dismayed over the lack of adequate preparation by the government and refused to take responsibility for technical assistance in the Valley, lest the stigma of the scheme's failure smear other United Nations efforts.

The lack of understanding of soil management problems was further revealed when farm sizes were determined by the government. The government assumed that a family of five could be supported on twelve and one-half acres of average land. According to the contractors' data, a family needed at least twelve acres of first-class land and twenty-five acres of other land, the latter being defined as "land that couldn't produce wheat, cotton, or sugar beets without special treatment." Moreover, the large number of applicants for land induced the government to reduce the average farm size for settlers to between ten and seven acres.

[1] Memorandum from American contractor to Afghan government, February 1, 1952.

This partial picture seems to indicate that a number of the defects surrounding the scheme might have been avoided if the aid administered by the government had been greater and of a different nature. The local personnel for handling the problems in the first settlement area never consisted of more than five government officials, who had to devote their time to such a large number of miscellaneous tasks that little time was left for the actual settlement.

It is obvious that the Afghans, who had received all the technological and financial aid they thought necessary, were unable to forecast the amount of human ingenuity needed to carry the organizational burden called for by the occupational and social adjustments in the settlement plans. None of the difficulties encountered could be considered insurmountable. But they required trained personnel, which was not available in adequate quantities.

The sad aspect of this was that the arrangement with the contractor to build the canals and roads on the first 16,000 acres was greatly delayed. By April, 1952, only 8,000 acres had been furnished with laterals, distribution canals, and farm ditches, although 15,000 applications for land were stuck in red tape between two ministries. Only 125 settlers were on their land, with 375 more waiting—just squatting while the land allocated to them was farmed by large lessee landowners, pending the disentanglement of the red tape. Some 60,000 more acres which could be irrigated, at least during the spring season, were awaiting the outcome of contract negotiations. All this time the government was unable to find or decide on personnel capable of and willing to shoulder the administrative responsibility for land classification, contract work, settlement, and cultivation.

Clearly the administrative capacity of the government was inadequate to accommodate the achievements of the construction phase. How far behind the government's administrative resources were became evident from the number and scope

of supplemental contracts signed with the American construction firm. It assumed responsibility for the purchase of farm machinery, highway maintenance, new stream-gauging installations, aerial and economic surveys of the downstream reaches of the Helmand River, the reconstruction and repair of canals and dikes, the operation and maintenance of the canal and water-distribution system in the Valley, and the training of crews to handle these jobs in the future.

Moreover, the government was warned of the cost entailed by inadequate planning and administration. It was pointed out that the only way to protect the Afghans against the waste of maintaining the organization and equipment in idleness was to recommend new construction projects or to cut back personnel not easily replaced. The vicious circle, however, in this pressure for more work is all too clear: construction projects require studies of economic feasibility, cost estimates, and engineering work which must be sufficiently ahead of the construction crew's progress. Without these surveys none of the prerequisites could be met, and the government had to absorb some idleness costs.

The preceding remarks seem to point to a causal connection between arrested economic development, however favored by foreign financial aid and personnel, and incompetent government. At the same time it can be argued that underdeveloped government is a result of economic debility. Nonetheless, governmental weakness and economic stagnation in Afghanistan and most other Middle Eastern countries form two parts of an iron ring, each supporting the other and together strangling the development plans of the countries concerned.

The instability and inadequacy of the administration seem to arise from several causes. In Afghanistan, as in several of the Arab countries, political power conflicts within the governing groups and between the governing group and the opposition are immediately transmitted to technical personnel at the

intermediate level. The vagaries which accompanied the preparation of the Afghan Five-Year Plan in 1949/50 may serve as an illustration.

There was in the first place the personality of the Minister responsible for the plans, a man who grew from rags to riches at the trade crossroads of central Asia, established his country's first commercial bank, and held the financial strings over the country's only industrial plants. Though not related by marriage or blood to the ruling clan, his business acumen, diplomatic talents, and autocratic ways paved his way into the post of Ministry of National Economy at a time following the world depression when the country needed business leadership. Not endowed with any predilection for statistical detail, his decisions on allocating financial resources among the country's private and public segments were based on guesses which he could justly claim had in the past been crowned by commercial success. In addition, where choices for the use of resources were limited, the tolerable margin of error in statistical information was, happily for him, fairly wide. There was also a uniqueness about his staff. He was ably assisted by an under-secretary whose devoted government service was fortified by his contacts with education and life in France, Germany, Italy, and the United States. His handicap, however, was that, without practical experience in making economic decisions and assuming the responsibility for them, his concept of economic relationships and his development plans were rarely separated from emotional and nationalistic wrappings. A second aide was a mature vice-president of the textile plant who had been trained in business organization and methods in Germany. He lacked the vision and imagination that the other two had in abundance.

The strength of this group rested in the personal influence of the minister himself. In dealing with his ambitions and proposals, one had to be aware of the unusual concentration of economic power represented by him and his aides and at the

same time of the narrowness of its political base. Despite his control over the Ministries of Public Works, Mines and Transportation, and Agriculture, the Central Bank, and the much larger commercial bank, he was never able to sell his Five-Year Plan to the Council of Ministers. One of the major reasons for this defeat, as well as for the corollary delay in ratifying the credit agreement with the United States government, was the conflict between the minister and the prime minister. Not only were the drain on foreign exchange and the high cost of the American contractors' operations ascribed to his policies, but a large body of traders and intelligentsia took a dislike to his private business methods. When the parliamentarians were not satisfied with the explanations, he found himself virtually without political support. He resigned and with him faded the dynamics of a getting-things-done attitude.

It took almost half a year for his younger associates and the new appointees to pick up the strings and obtain Cabinet action on some of the projects of the Five-Year Plan and parliamentary approval of the American credit and the new contract with the American construction firm. However, no governmental action was taken on the industrial portions of the Five-Year Plan. Instead, the former Minister of National Economy, resuming his activity as president of the commercial bank, assigned German firms to the textile expansion and hydroelectric power projects, which he was able to push because of his unique control over a large part of the country's foreign exchange earnings. Thus a development plan, which in 1949 appeared reasonably cohesive and balanced, fell victim to paralyzing political conflicts. It is quite possible that, in conceiving this plan, the minister had underestimated the degree to which his programs would have encroached on the economic power of his political opponents or, if he did understand these ramifications, he underestimated the resistance.

One of the causes of administrative incompetence is clearly political instability and the inevitable corollary, frequent changes

in personnel. The administration of technical assignments need not be affected by political changes at the top provided there is a body of experienced senior and junior civil servants who can operate the administrative machine. Such government servants have been slow in appearing, and such as have emerged have been able to do so in spite rather than because of official policy. In fact, there is no policy to train, "in service" or otherwise, a civil service system. On the contrary, many trained at great cost abroad are wasted on minor jobs after their return.

Another weakness is the lack of fruitful co-operation with the people's representatives. In most Muslim countries the concept of a class of officials serving the state rather than their own interests is only just emerging. Official duties have been in the hands of favorites and friends of the ruler. Throughout the area there have been centuries of corruption based on the view that everything within the domain of government could be bought.

Having been so long indifferent, if not opposed, to government intervention, the masses of the people still seem to be dominated by a passive contempt, if not active animosity, toward the state, especially when co-operation with a parliamentary body has failed to materialize. The effort to unify divergent factions and tribes is still a hard struggle. In respect to economic planning, the significant aspect of this struggle is that the ruling power is more frequently than not in alliance with feudal landowners, many of whom double up as influential traders. They inevitably direct public programs toward limited ends. The result is likely to be a governmental policy shifting irregularly from planned economy to laissez-faire and back again. An alliance between a business middle class and the state is generally still impossible because the former does not yet exist on a large enough scale. Where it does, it struggles against indifference and hostility toward expanding industrial activity. In Egypt as late as 1951, the Chambers of Industries complained that the government departments still regarded industrial plans as *"établissements nuisibles."* Where the state authority is as-

sociated with a monarchic or other vested interest, intervention in economic activities by the state tends to become a
tool by which the ends of that clique are furthered.

Evidence on how far even those with reasonably adequate
experience still have to go may be gathered from the planned
structure and power of the new Development Commission for
the Helmand Valley. Its departments of engineering, financing,
planning, settlement, education, agricultural extension, industry, and power were to have absolute power over all regular
government activity in the Valley, even to the point where
the local governor was to align himself with the policy of the
Commission. The new organization would supersede the established agencies. But the possibility of conflict with the groups
entrenched in the regular Ministries was not recognized.

A more fundamental cause for governmental weakness in
the economic realm is the rather vacillating attitude toward
the role of government in business. There are four aspects to
this problem that need to be emphasized.

1. As many have observed, private investment in the Middle East has a distinct mercantile odor about it. Much of the
original wealth that went into textile plants in Turkey or
Afghanistan stemmed from profitable trading operations, and
many of the present shareholders are at the same time active
in trade, domestic or foreign, or both. The limited market for
manufactured products and the persistently high profit in real
estate investments have kept weak the propensity to invest in
industry. High profits have, indeed, been earned because the
manufactured products were able to substitute for imports so
that a new market did not have to be created, because investors
were able to reap the scarcity profit that lack of skilled entrepreneurial services frequently creates, or because inadequate provision for capital replacement and high inventory revaluation
(under persistently inflationary conditions) have added illusory
profits to actual profits. In the Middle East a 20 percent margin is generally the goal at which investors are shooting. Wher-

ever such a margin can be expected and where investors have confidence in the business management and its marketing practices, investment in industry has attracted not only the trader but also the thrifty farmer and small town merchant. One should not be surprised at the initiative taken by the large landowning families in the Adana region in promoting industry and power projects in their part of Turkey. But what is more significant is the enthusiasm their plans evoked among the small farmers in the region. The willingness of this private group to underwrite the large local cost of the Seyhan River power and irrigation project reportedly caused the International Bank to reverse its earlier opposition to the undertaking and to advance $25,000,000 to finance it.

A fundamental part of the character and psychology of the Middle Eastern entrepreneur has been the monopolistic position he frequently enjoys. Whether under the umbrella of a government license, charter, or government restriction on imports or under the protection of a less artificial monopoly over funds, marketing outlets, and foreign exchange resources, he rarely is exposed to the competitive pressures of the oligopolistic or traditional type familiar to an American entrepreneur.

The operation of free capital accumulation and investment in response to market incentives owes its existence to the power and size of a class of citizens endowed with specific virtues such as managerial know-how and technological skill in ever-recombining productive factors. As in Europe in the seventeenth and eighteenth centuries, this class, though growing in the Middle East, has a hard time struggling for recognition, let alone participation in the affairs of state. As long as it is juxtaposed to well-entrenched economic and social groups, it cannot be counted on to rescue the Middle East from the stationary equilibrium of underdevelopment.

2. Another aspect of the vacillating nature of the state's relation to private investment is that the state authorities have not as yet evolved a clear, let alone consistent, idea of how to fill

the vacuum left by impotent or politically weak private enterprise. Only the diehard advocates of free enterprise at any cost ignore the fact that in other than developed capitalistic types of society the forces that have to perform certain indispensable economic functions may have to be organized deliberately through a form involving central instead of individualistic direction and demanding public instead of private financing. But this recognition, apparently widely shared in Middle Eastern countries, certainly in Turkey, Iran, and Afghanistan, and to lesser degrees in Iraq and Syria, is no guarantee that economic stagnation will be successfully overcome. It is commonly overlooked among state enterprise advocates that turning over economic progress to state bodies merely alters the administrative form, not the economic nature, of the solutions. Unfortunately for progress, however, the economic solutions carried out by these bodies so far have shown ineptitude and serious miscalculations. Turkey may serve as an illustration.

The investment activities of the Sümer Bank and the Eti Bank, the major economic enterprises of the government, though controlled by a General Economic Commission provided by law, have no relation to the Ministry of Finance and are financed under their own budgets. Their capital was originally provided by the government and is added to by the public borrowing power the banks enjoy. But neither has paid any interest on the investment funds, and depreciation funds set aside by the individual plants are retained by the banks for reinvestment. Plants operating at a loss were financed by those earning profits, and reinvestment was channeled to areas where profit prospects were good regardless of the benefit of such investment to the economy as a whole. In addition, some enterprise managers were able to push new investment merely as a means of strengthening their personal influence. Thus certain advantages of central control fell by the wayside as responsibility for operations was merged with responsibility

for growth. Operational decisions, however, as to the procurement of raw materials and marketing of products have frequently been handled by the head offices of the banks. This preoccupation with operational detail may explain why many investment decisions have been made by the banks without consideration of the merits of the new projects in relation to the needs of other segments of the economy. One of the more conspicuous results has been the serious neglect of investment in agriculture, at least until recently, thus leaving virtually unchanged the Turkish farmer's purchasing power.

One has the impression that state enterprises, in Turkey and Iran in particular, tend to be put between two chairs. They are permitted to enjoy all the financial rewards of private initiative but are protected against all the risks associated with it. The result is that they do not prepare their managers for eventual independence from public tutelage nor do they help the state push forward a diversified and balanced program of economic growth.

The question of the administrative form of economic growth is still hotly debated, particularly in countries where neither alternative discussed here has had a chance to show its mettle.

From the experience with state control of investments in Afghanistan an insight into similar shortcomings may be gained. It was considered possible, at least by the planners in the Ministry of National Economy, that the investment function in regard to new projects, such as a cement mill or hydroelectric power projects, could be left in part to private hands—the *shirkats* (joint-stock companies)—with the major stockholder the commercial bank, if some deliberate co-ordination through "joint boards" on which the *shirkats* would be represented was assured. Apparently, it was thought that all that was necessary was to make the funds available to buy the tools and other implements of production.

There was no recognition that investment in the form of workers needs a continuing flow of capital in the form of sub-

sistence. This, in real terms, some other class of the population has to supply. If the workers were to be drawn from the overcrowded eastern valleys or from the nomadic tribes, the transfer of the subsistence funds that supported them in their previous occupation would not automatically occur. On the contrary, it had to be expected that the peasants or nomads remaining behind would consume the subsistence set free, and not save it. They would have to be taxed to mobilize this fund, or requisitioning would have to be instituted, or some other complementary source of savings would have to be tapped. Whatever the source, it was clear that some measure, enforced by the state and the state only, would have to be taken to mobilize the resources necessary to keep the new "investment" workers going. This seemingly natural function for the state was not recognized. The same blindness was noticed in financing public capital projects. The result was that the government and other investing agencies found themselves consistently short of funds to pay for wages, and other local expenditures. It was possible to make the government see, however, the impact of large investment activities on imports of consumable things and the need for larger allocation of exchange to cover them.

3. A further aspect of public investment activities is the misinvestment that frequently accompanies it. The early dissipated efforts in Afghanistan, due to inadequate preparation, have been mentioned above. A more tragic misinvestment in this early phase was authorization for the establishment of lavishly furnished supply camps and workshops by the contractor when it could have been ascertained that they would be economical only if the contractor could count on an annual construction business totaling $10,000,000. The scale of the investment in the overhead facilities should have been geared to a much smaller volume of business. More significant yet for the international ramifications of transferring advanced technology was the realization that perhaps the capital-intensive nature of the contractor's technology itself should have been analyzed. In

Afghanistan as well as in many other parts of the Middle East, American contractors are blamed for excessive costs as compared with European charges. At least in Afghanistan this was due to the difference in the proportions in which labor and capital were combined, rather than in absolute expense. For the American contractor, labor is the high-cost factor, so that laborsaving construction equipment is welcome because of its relatively low cost. But in Europe, and even more so in the Middle East, labor is available at a relatively low rate, while the acquisition of machinery is hampered by high local capital cost and foreign exchange shortages. This difference is not off-set by differences in labor efficiency, as it might be in the highly skilled industrial trades.

The result of the transfer of an American contractor and his construction method to a labor-intensive economic environment must inevitably be a clash with the prevailing concepts of waste and economy. An Afghan worker would think nothing of walking for hours to retrieve a bag of sand that had fallen off a truck. To recover the lost bag is wasteful to the American and yet a natural economy to the Afghans. The American technology appears far more expensive than the European or Asiatic technology applied to the same job over the same period only if the element of time is disregarded. But the American method appears in a different light if time is measured in terms of value lost—like the opportunity lost in the Helmand Valley to produce better crops in a given year. Consideration must be taken not only of the value of the annual income produced by a quickly completed construction project, but also of the economic and social instability caused by slow construction methods in a country in which the bulk of the population lives at the bare subsistence margin in the midst of great potential resources. But then again, time is not measured that way in the area. Hence it is difficult to say whether the whole arrangement with the American contractor by which he was free to

transfer American "standard" engineering and construction technology to Afghanistan was a misinvestment. But the point that should be made is that the Afghan Public Works Ministry which initiated the contract never recognized this economic problem.

Most cases of misinvestment, or unbalanced investment, on the part of Middle Eastern governments concern neglect either of projects complementary to other projects already under way, whether private or public, or of projects creating social or public overhead facilities whose benefits are common to many different lines of production. Roads, power plants, ports, public storage, and water supply facilities are typical. They create external economies to enterprises producing commodities for sale and thus possibly determine the profitability of any one of them. For example, the new $8,000,000 Arghandab Dam in Afghanistan may increase grape and deciduous fruit production in the next several seasons. If refrigeration, transportation, storage facilities, and better farm-to-market roads do not follow quickly, the dam will prove to be at least a premature investment, if not a misinvestment. Similarly, if Turkey does not speed up its grain storage construction, its recent intensive expenditures on farm implements and extension services will prove to be a waste of effort. A contributing factor in the confusion about public investments in the Middle East has been and still is the vacillating policy of international financial agencies toward them, particularly toward investments in social overhead facilities. As they do not liquidate themselves as such, but merely contribute to the return of other "productive" enterprises, they have been less attractive than the latter. Several governments have misunderstood this as a sign of lack of economic value in general.

4. A final point in regard to the difficulties of working out a stable relationship between public and private investment is the unstable flow of public investment. A good example of

recent date is Egypt's Public Works Budget for 1950/51. Instead of spending £E 59,000,000 on new works as authorized by the Chamber of Deputies, the actual expenditure reached barely £E 39,000,000.

But the narrow base of the fiscal revenues in the Middle East forbids one to ascribe fluctuating outlays solely to fluctuating minds. If the United States' domestic investment drops, there is at least the comfort that the decisions which determine the volume of that investment are made within the boundaries of the country. That is not the case with most of the Middle Eastern countries. Investment decisions by public or private bodies are to a large extent determined by the value of exports to industrialized countries. These in turn depend upon fluctuating demands upon which the limited political and economic influence of the exporting countries has little bearing. With a recession in the industrialized countries, demand for industrial and agricultural raw materials frequently drops drastically, and people in the Middle East suffer restrictions on income if not unemployment. The consequent stoppage of government revenues affects other economic branches adversely. Thus much of the activating force behind those fiscal vacillations resides outside the Middle East.

It is hard to put a common denominator under the various aspects of inadequate planning. To say that they reveal inadequacies in economic conceptuology and in government is not enough. To blame economic debility and underdevelopment on poverty is misleading. As an educator has observed:

They are not too poor. What they mistake for poverty is merely an error in dealing with first resources first. The greatest resource they have, the resource without which they fumble the development of lesser resources, is their own people. For each of the hardworking Afghan boys being given the rudiments of literacy, there are 15 or 20 others being given no education.[2]

[2] Harold W. Benjamin, UNESCO National Commission News, January, 1950.

Unless the level of understanding among the presently illiterate is raised and the best use made of those already highly trained, much of the worry about instability and economic stagnation in the Middle East will be present for a long time. These steps can be taken by the Middle Eastern governments themselves. Farsighted and dynamic leadership, with proper support from without, is the prerequisite.

(IX) MAJID KHADDURI

The Army Officer: His Role

in Middle Eastern Politics

DURING the past seven years several Middle Eastern countries have experienced governmental changes in which the army took an active part. In Syria and Egypt the army deliberately intervened to overthrow discredited regimes and to depose the heads of state. In Lebanon and Iraq the heads of state, themselves alarmed by an intense struggle among rival political parties, invited the army to intervene to maintain order. In Lebanon the army refused to crush the opposition, acting only as a caretaker; in Iraq the army agreed to support authority against disorder, and the effect of its intervention cannot yet be foreseen.*

This control of government by the military is indicative both of serious defects in democratic processes in the Middle East and of the eagerness with which Middle Eastern leaders seek high political office. In Western democratic countries tradi-

* EDITOR's NOTE: Events which have occurred since the first publication of this essay in June, 1953 (events such as the fall of the Shishakli regime, the split among the military in Egypt, and the trends toward concentration of power in the hands of the military) seem to substantiate the conclusions Dr. Khadduri has advanced in this paper.

[162]

tions have developed which tend to keep the army isolated from domestic politics, although military advice has often been sought on foreign policy and persons whose careers have been in the military service are not infrequently elected, or appointed, to high political positions. This is quite a different matter, however, from the military's choosing to occupy high political office through the weapons of its own profession.

There is an almost nostalgic longing in the Middle East, common to all political groups, for a "strong" regime which will tolerate neither multiplicity of political parties nor anarchy of ideas. This is due in pàrt to the failure of democracy to provide agreement on fundamentals. Beyond this, however, the forces set in motion since World War I have artificially speeded up the process of Westernization beyond the ability of the people to adapt the imported ideas to their social needs. Such abstract concepts as sovereignty, self-determination, and democracy were thrust upon the people of the Middle East without their having been prepared for them. If the Western powers, in taking an active part in the reorganization of the Middle East after World War I, had known the Eastern countries better and had had a greater appreciation of the historical process that was going on, the Eastern peoples might have been given an opportunity to adapt Western political concepts and institutions more slowly and would probably have developed their own form or forms of democracy to fit their needs and aspirations. It did not help that the Middle Eastern leaders who cooperated with the Western powers never tried to reconcile Western concepts and institutions with existing institutions so as to avoid conflict with religious and conservative groups. As a result, democracy from its very inception failed to command general respect, and when adequate reforms were not achieved, democracy had to bear the blame. Opposition to democracy came from the right (religious) as well as from the left (Socialist and Communist) parties and groupings; and when neither side could muster sufficient support to achieve

[163]

power, the army intervened to carry out a moderate program of reform by force.

For centuries Islam provided for the believers a way of life, the validity and perfection of which no pious Muslim ever questioned. As a divine system, Islam set up the principle that authority belongs to Allah; but the caliph, though enthroned by the people to enforce Allah's law, was not constitutionally responsible to the electorate. However, the caliph and his subjects were both bound by the divine law, the violation of which would make them equally liable to punishment. Such a theory of the state, placing ultimate responsibility in Allah, is not inherently democratic. However, since Islam is regarded as the embodiment of Allah's will and justice, its believers derive satisfaction from the moral conviction that their political system, though authoritarian in nature, could not possibly be matched by any other system. Further, Islam is regarded as immune from foreign encroachment or attack, for, as the power of Islam is Allah's power, no other community could successfully launch an attack on it: failure would certainly be on the side of the infidels, since success could not be divorced from Islam.

The pious Muslim, witnessing the change of Islam under the impact of Western ideas and institutions, is undergoing a moral crisis. Not only is he shocked that Islam should be divorced from the caliphate and the divine law replaced by secular legislation, but also that the West should be encroaching upon Islam with impunity. The challenge of Westernization has been responded to differently by the various shades of opinion. The agnostic new generation, attracted by the positivistic philosophy of the West, advocated a complete break with the past and the adoption of Western secular institutions. Following World War I when democracy had become fashionable, the new generation accepted democracy without trying to adapt it to existing conditions. The learned doctors of the divine law, supported by the older generation, objected to the introduction of Western insti-

tutions because of their incompatibility with Islamic institutions. Apart from the slogan "Go back to Islam," however, they had little to offer in the way of a constructive program of reform which might have combined the best of Islam and Western institutions. Thus the conflict that ensued was between two extreme schools; the new denounced the old as incompatible with modern life, and the old, witnessing a sudden break with the past, emptied the vials of its wrath upon those in authority for permitting this change.

Nor was the experiment of the new generation with democracy a happy one. For no sooner had democracy begun to operate, with its complicated procedural problems of electioneering and parliamentary debates (to say nothing of the endless quarrels that developed among rival parties and politicians), than the people began to learn how scandalously its processes could be misused by unscrupulous leaders. To the old school, democracy failed to command the respect or allegiance of the people in the same way as Allah's law had done in the past. The activistic character of democratic politics appeared too vulgar and too worldly in the eyes of pious Muslims, who have habitually revered the awe-inspiring traditional institutions. Further, democracy as practiced in the West seemed to emphasize liberty, not equality. But to peoples who for centuries have been accustomed to authoritarian regimes, liberty could not possibly be as much appreciated as equality, since it permitted the enrichment of the few at the expense of exploited masses.

What rendered the situation more difficult was, of course, the absence of any significant middle class with interests intermediate to those of the few rich or of the many poor. Such a middle class would have championed democracy against autocracy and feudalism as did the middle classes of western Europe. But a sudden rise of the middle class is hardly to be looked for in predominantly agricultural countries where feudalism has persisted for a long time. In such countries the freedom permitted under democracy only rendered competition more acute, and

the desperate masses, bent on improving their economic condition, were bound to fall under the influence of radical ideas. The people of the Middle East, not unnaturally, judged democracy by the results achieved rather than by its theoretical soundness. The judgment to which they have come is that they have been deceived by those in authority and that democracy has failed them.

During the latter part of the nineteenth century, a good start in Islamic reforms was made by a number of enlightened teachers such as Jamal-al-Din al-Afghani and Muhammad 'Abduh, who saw no harm to Islam if the believers borrowed Western ideas and concepts. Muhammad 'Abduh offered a formula of reform which advocated the "modernization," not the "secularization," of Islam. Although he was opposed at the outset by the Azhar University of Cairo, 'Abduh's approach gradually gained the support of Muslim opinion, and the Azhar graduates were eventually dominated by the 'Abduh school.[1] After the introduction of democracy, however, the Azhar, without carrying the constructive reforms of 'Abduh forward, supported the existing regime and hence could no longer attract liberal Muslims; these preferred to go to the Westernized schools and thus lost touch with Islamic learning. As a result, there is no moderate Muslim reformer such as 'Abduh who can offer a reform program combining the best of Islam and Western civilization.

This situation gave an opening to lay religious leaders, who revived the traditional religious zeal combined with intense nationalism. The Muslim Brotherhood (*al-Ikhwan al-Muslimun*) may be cited as probably the best expression of this lay religious revival. Contemporary critics still differ on the significance of the Brotherhood's contribution to the modernization of Islam. While it is true that Western technological inventions have been readily accepted, the Brotherhood could hardly be credited with having improved on 'Abduh's contribution in the realm of

[1] See Charles C. Adams, *Islam and Modernism in Egypt* (London, 1933); and H. A. R. Gibb, *Modern Trends in Islam* (Chicago, 1947).

nonmaterial values. One could even discern in the Brotherhood
a falling away from 'Abduh's religious toleration by arousing
religious fanaticism mixed with nationalism. Moreover, since
the Brotherhood derived popular support by its opposition
to the existing regime, it was critical of democracy. Lacking
the constructive approach of 'Abduh, it was unwilling to attempt the reconciliation of democracy with Islam and instead
advocated the re-establishment of theocracy. Shaykh Hasan
al-Banna, leader of the Brotherhood, came very near to achieving
power during the Palestine war, but he came out into the open
too soon and clashed with the ruling oligarchy. He was criticized for having resorted to violence and terrorism, and the
government used this as an excuse (after he was treacherously
assassinated) to close the headquarters of his organization. The
Egyptian government could not completely suppress the movement, which was temporarily permitted under the regime of the
Revolutionary Command Council to resume its activities, but
the movement suffered seriously from the blunders committed
by its leaders.[2]

Even if the Brotherhood had achieved power (with the consequence that similar moves might have been attempted in
Syria and Iraq), it is unlikely that its members would have enjoyed a long term of office. The Brotherhood's program was
too Calvinistic in spirit to be tolerated for any length of time.
The re-establishment of a theocracy, regarding all other states
as un-Godly and inferior, would have been incompatible with
the new international order. Furthermore, the theocratic emphasis on the solidarity of the faith and the strict enforcement
of the divine law, an emphasis which disregarded the medieval
methods by which these objectives might be achieved, would
have been strenuously opposed. The Brotherhood and other
religious movements overlooked the fact that in a modern
society, under the impact of a world-wide trend to regard re-

[2] For a discussion of the Muslim Brotherhood, see J. Heyworth-Dunne, *Religious and Political Trends in Modern Egypt* (Washington, 1950).

ligion as a matter of individual conscience, no such solidarity is achievable.[3]

It has become a popular slogan, repeated again and again by Muslim as well as Western publicists, that the one power which is equipped to serve as a barrier to communism in the Middle East is Islam. On purely doctrinal grounds Islam, probably more than any other religion, is hard to reconcile with communism. As a system which evaluates all values of life in terms of a divine juridico-theological code, it is opposed to dialectical materialism and, of course, to atheism. To the pious Muslim, communism appears to reduce life to a mere mechanical process, stressing earthly rather than spiritual values. Further, Islam recognizes the institution of private property and free enterprise, and the divine law regulates all kinds of possession and disposal of property, including its transmission to the owner's children and the near kin by inheritance. Even the rights of the state to own or to dispose of property are limited by the divine law during both war and peace.

Yet there are a few Muslim thinkers, witnessing the present plight of the poor and their exploitation by the landlords, who argue that Islam is equally opposed to the great disparity between rich and poor. They cite traditions to the effect that the Prophet Muhammad often expressed his aversion to poverty. From early Islam the doctors of law and theology often have advised the caliphs to pay proper attention to the poor, since the law required the distribution of alms among them. Modern Muslim thinkers, regarding Islam as an ideal system of social justice, argue that Islam is inherently opposed to exploitation and poverty and that it is the duty of the community to regulate its economic life on an equitable basis. "Social justice," said one of them, "is like the *jihad* [holy war], a collective duty upon all Muslims," i.e., its enforcement is required by the law; if it is not fulfilled, all the Muslim community, including those

[3] See Herbert Butterfield, *History and Human Relations* (London, 1951), p. 132.

in authority, fall in error and become liable to punishment.[4] But these modern Muslim thinkers had little influence on the ruling oligarchy or the Azhar, who seemed to be satisfied that the oft-quoted sacred citations and the sermons given in the Friday prayers in support of property rights and capitalism, would provide moral strength against poverty and unemployment.

Such attitudes quickly gave an opening for the rise of militant leftist groups who either argued that Islam could be reconciled with socialism or tried to turn their faces completely against Islam in favor of communism. The moderately leftist groups maintain that Islam is not opposed to socialism, arguing that the early Islamic creed, divorced from later accretions, was in accord with socialist ideas. Their socialism is based on the Islamic principle of equality, which recognizes no differences in society on the basis of wealth. No social or economic distinctions, they maintain, were imposed by Allah upon the believers; although, as revealed in the *Qur'an*, He "created you of male and female, and made you races and tribes," He recognized no differences among people save on the basis of "piety" and "Godfearing." [5] The socialists cited as evidence for their argument the case of a companion of the Prophet Muhammad, Abu-Dhar al-Ghifari (whom they regard as the first Muslim socialist), who criticized the caliph for his departure from Muhammad's puritanical life by acquiring wealth and ignoring the interests of the masses.

Communists, deriving their ideas from the teachings of Marx and Lenin, repudiate almost all national and religious institutions as the bulwark of the reactionary classes. The Middle East extremists, who argue with Marx that religion is the opium of the people, attack Islam and its teaching with an antireligious religiosity. Their program, advocating a complete reorganiza-

---

[4] Muhammad al-Ghazzali, *Islam and Socialist Programs* (Cairo, 1951), pp. 35–37.

[5] XLIX, 12–13 (Palmer's translation).

tion of society based on the doctrine of world communism, is probably the most constructive (as well as destructive in its sweeping denunciation of existing conditions) so far offered to any Middle East group in opposition to the ruling class. Its appeal to the masses and malcontents, who have not grasped the most elementary principles of communism, is due to the persuasive ability of the local leaders, who present communism as the panacea for all social ills. The discipline and solidarity displayed by the Communists (though they often quarrel on procedural matters) and their tenacity in fighting repression have rendered their work effective and enhanced their prestige among the masses. However, despite their outcry against exploitation, graft, and corruption, they still have a long way to go before they can claim active support from all the masses. Except perhaps for those who are regular members of secret Communist parties (all Middle East countries, except Israel, have either refused to permit, or have suppressed, Communist organizations), most of their followers may be classed as sympathizers who probably have certain mental reservations about the doctrine. Communism's opposition to religion and its disdain for other mores, to say nothing of its affiliation with a foreign power, are but a few of the factors which still make many hesitate to accept in toto the Communist creed. If, however, these sympathizers were forced to choose between the existing regimes and communism, it is not unlikely that their choice would fall on communism.

The failure of any of these platforms to gain full support from the masses, as well as the vulnerability of the democratic regimes, made the people look elsewhere for leadership—toward the army.

The interest of the Middle Eastern countries in building up strong armed forces probably goes back to antiquity when the power of the monarch was dependent on two pillars—the clergy and the army. The king, in addition to proclaiming himself god

or the son of a god, was the army chief and often took the field as the actual commander of the army. This tradition of close association between rulers and the army persisted down through the centuries under Arab and Ottoman rule. So closely connected were the army chiefs with the caliphs and sultans that often the viziers and grand viziers were chosen from among the army officers who served in the royal courts. Not infrequently they established matrimonial relationships with the reigning dynasties. The Arab and Ottoman armies, at times when the army chiefs had become more powerful than their masters, often deposed one ruler after another at their pleasure. Just as the Praetorian guard dethroned one emperor after another, so the Arab legions and Ottoman janissaries put to death one sovereign after another, replacing them by their own nominees. The struggle between army officers and sovereigns degenerated to the throat-cutting level, so that either the army or the dynasty had to be liquidated. When society was subjected to this kind of internal struggle, the very foundation of its political organization reached a breaking point and a radical change in the regime became inevitable. This significant feature in the history of Eastern societies, which often recurred (it is not suggested that it is inherently cyclic in nature), indicates that recent events in the modern Middle East should not be surprising.

In the modern Middle East, following the old established military tradition, keen interest has been shown in organizing well-disciplined national armies along European lines. Even such new countries as Iraq and Syria, when they were under a Mandate and there was no real need for armed forces, aspired to organize small national armies for future enlargement. When Iraq and Syria had attained independence, special care was given to reorganize and enlarge the national forces, which were deemed necessary to act as guardians of the newly won independence. In countries which had an earlier independent status, the army figured even more largely in national life; in the case of Turkey and Iran, the Kemalist and Pahlevi regimes probably

[171]

owed their establishment to the army as much as to the strength of character and the statesmanship of their founders. In Egypt, from the time of Muhammad Ali, the army proved to be the chief personal preoccupation of the viceroys, who spent on it lavishly for the consolidation of their power. From the British occupation (1882), however, to the declaration of independence (1922), the army was reduced almost to a police force. But the interest in reorganizing a national army was revived, especially after the signing of the Anglo-Egyptian Treaty of 1936, not only to repel foreign aggression, but also to enable the army to become the symbol of the new national life.

Most of the Middle East army officers are drawn from the middle class or the ruling oligarchy: very few have come from the poorer classes. And most of them have been recruited on the basis of a national conscription. A majority of the soldiers are illiterate, but many of them who have remained in the service long enough have received elementary education in addition to military training. It is the officers, rather than the soldiers, who have been instrumental in involving the army in politics. Elementary and high-school education carries with it indoctrination with a spirit of intense nationalism. Moved by patriotism as well as by personal ambition, many high-school graduates enter the law colleges or military academies with the idea that a career in law or military service is a steppingstone to high government position. Not infrequently high-school teachers and lawyers, dissatisfied with their professions or believing their ambitions can better be attained in the army, enter military schools and resume their public careers in the military service. General Nagib is not the only officer who had a background in law before he entered military training, and those who for a short time served as teachers or civil servants may be counted in the hundreds.

Even in military training, where discipline and the military profession require the isolation of the army from politics, nationalist indoctrination is continued. Army officers often play

an active part in the decision of national issues. A case in point is the Assyrian uprising in Iraq. The army officers moved to suppress the uprising not only because they were bound to do so by military order, but also because they had their own views on the matter and decided to solve the problem in a manner satisfactory to their own national consciousness. This explains why certain excesses were committed by the Iraqi army officers in handling this problem.

The Palestine war, by far the most important issue and one which had a far-reaching effect on almost all the Arab countries, may be cited as another case in point. The views of the army officers, it is now known, differed on many points from those of the politicians in power. Not only was the advice of the military regarding purely technical matters (such as the general command and the supply of weapons) not heeded by the politicians, but also the military had disagreed with their governments regarding the conduct and the prosecution of the war. In this, it is true, the army was under the influence of opposition parties (such as the Muslim Brotherhood), but the army officers also had their own political ideas, which differed from those of their governments.

Thus it is clear why, after the Arabs lost the war, the Arab army officers and the politicians in power blamed each other for the blunders committed, and when the army felt it had unjustifiably been selected as the scapegoat, the officers reacted (to mention only one specific reason) by overthrowing the politicians and punishing them for their mistakes. The recent military intervention in Lebanon has been temporary because of the relatively minor military role played by this country in the war. In Iraq, however, the army has already staged seven military *coups*, and its recent invitation to carry on the administration is so tempting that it may once again dominate the political scene. The Jordanian army has long been under rigid British tutelage and therefore no move could be expected. But in the case of the Syrian and Egyptian armies, which were seri-

ously beaten and had a great deal to suffer on account of their governments' failure to supply weapons (in the case of Egypt the government supplied defective weapons), the army's intervention in politics may be regarded as a vindication of the army's role in the Palestine war and the failure of the politicians to support the military.

Occupying such a high position in the national life of the Middle Eastern countries, the army officers have been approached by various ideological and political groups (except perhaps the Communists, who were severely punished if they did so) trying to win them to their side. Because of the conservative and intensely nationalistic background of most of the army officers, it is not surprising that in the Iraqi and Egyptian armies the ultranationalistic and religious movements were the most influential, especially the Pan-Arab groups in Iraq and the Muslim Brotherhood in Egypt. The Syrian army, emphasizing liberalism before anything else, has paid only lip service to religion and proved to be lukewarm to conservative and religious groups.

The elements which showed intense interest in political activities were the younger rather than the older army officers. Older men occupying high military positions and winning the favors of the heads of states and governments were likely to be more concerned with their own interests than with national reform. Some of these older officers held their positions not because of personal merit but for the purpose of ensuring that the army would remain loyal to those in authority. Not infrequently some of them were related to the king or cabinet ministers, and their interests thus became identified with those of the ruling oligarchy. As a result, the younger army officers often organized themselves into small groups (either at informal friendly gatherings or in secret meetings) to discuss national issues. Not infrequently they broached the idea of the necessity of the army's intervention in order to overhaul the political machine, if not to establish a military dictatorship. The young

army officers always chose their leaders from among the older army officers whom they could trust and whose records were clean. Such leaders were often chosen on the basis of seniority in military service, provided that their military integrity was beyond reproach and that they were not self-seeking. Thus Bakr Sidqi rose in Iraq, Husni al-Zayim, Hinnawi, Shishakli, and others in Syria, and Muhammad Nagib and Nasir in Egypt. Their leadership and able command, recognized by all, had been tested in war: Bakr Sidqi in his operations against the Assyrian and Middle Euphrates tribal revolts; al-Zayim, Shishakli, Nagib, and Nasir in the Palestine war.

The underlying motive which prompted the army officers to engage actively in politics was, of course, the need for a social revolution which it was not possible to achieve by democratic procedures. The army seems to hold relatively moderate views acceptable to the majority of the people and is able to provide strong leadership capable of enforcing social reforms with celerity and a minimum of opposition. The people, ready to give the army officers an opportunity to try their approach to reform, have as a rule responded jubilantly to the change at first, though their enthusiasm soon cools off because of the ruthless methods and continual repression which are likely to follow when reform measures are carried out by force.

The Palestine war has been singled out as the principal reason for the sudden military *coups* in Syria and Egypt. A state of intense fermentation, however, had long been in existence. Criticism of existing conditions had frequently been voiced, but no better occasion than the defeat suffered in Palestine had yet presented itself. It gave the critics an opportunity to demonstrate their dissatisfaction and to pour out their angry criticism of everything they considered wrong. Books and pamphlets, as well as newspaper articles, were published in an ever-increasing number; some of them—as had rarely happened in the past—went into several editions and were widely read all over the Arabic-speaking countries. Such pam-

phleteering, a novelty in the Middle East, released many dynamic forces. In *Meaning of the Tragedy*, Costi Zurayk, then president of the Syrian University, was the first to discuss in a booklet the profound national frustration caused by the Palestine war.[6] He called upon the people to press their rulers for reform. This was followed by another booklet, *The Lesson of Palestine*, written by a Palestinian lawyer, offering a constructive plan of social reform, including a Fertile Crescent unity scheme, and calling for immediate action.[7]

Most devastating of all, perhaps, is the book written by an Egyptian religious teacher, Khalid's *From Here We Start*, in which the whole religious system, as interpreted and practiced by Muslims today, is shown to be incompatible with modern life.[8] Khalid rejected the restoration of a theocratic state and advocated the reinterpretation of Islam on a socialistic basis. In another book entitled *Citizens, Not Cattle*, Khalid attacked the oligarchic regime of Egypt and strongly defended the individual's rights to equality, liberty, education, and work.[9] His earlier book was at first suppressed by the government, but upon its release it went into several editions and was read all over the Arab world. Neither the government's opposition nor the severe and even vulgar criticism of his opponents could discourage Khalid from publishing his second book, which is even more trenchant than the first in its sweeping criticism of social conditions. These, as well as other less significant books, have been widely read and have had a far-reaching influence on public opinion.

The Palestine war brought matters to a head, since it directly involved the army in a struggle with the civilian politi-

[6] *Ma'na al-Nakbah* (Beirut, 1948).

[7] Musa al-Alami, *'Ibrat Falastin* (Beirut, 1949). This book has been summarized and translated in *The Middle East Journal*, III (October, 1949), 373–405.

[8] *Min Huna Nabda'* (Cairo, 1950). An English translation by Isma'il al-Farnqi was published by the American Council of Learned Societies (Washington, D.C., 1953).

[9] *Muwatinun La Ra'aya* (Cairo, 1951).

cians. The ruling oligarchy watched carefully lest it lose its hold over the army. When the Arab governments lost the war, the military, in spite of public statements that the war was satisfactorily conducted, were blamed for the defeat. This set in motion the movement, both in Syria and Egypt, to investigate the causes of defeat; but before investigations could reveal the malefactors, the politicians tried to influence the investigators. This aroused the army officers, who feared that the responsible politicians might escape punishment, and prompted them to act.

Four Middle Eastern countries may be specifically cited as having experienced military *coups d'état*: Turkey under late Ottoman rule, Iraq, Syria, and Egypt. Two military *coups* took place in Turkey (1908, 1909); seven in Iraq (1936–1941); five in Syria (1949–1954); and two in Egypt (1881, 1952). (In Iraq the army once more came into the picture in 1952, but this time by the invitation of the head of the state to maintain public order; in Lebanon the army acted only as a caretaker during the interim of a governmental change.) These sixteen military *coups* by no means exhaust the list. They have been selected as instances where the army has clearly taken control of the actual conduct of government, not merely where former army officers—as Kemal Atatürk and Shah Reza Pahlevi—played the role of the politician.[10]

All of these military *coups* took place either with the avowed purpose of re-establishing a constitutional regime (as in the case of Turkey) or of "cleansing" an already established democracy of evil influences which paralyzed its working. The military sought the active co-operation of nationalist elements, and

[10] It is not the writer's purpose in this article to give the history of the various Middle Eastern military *coups*, but rather to discuss the general character of military rule as well as its impact on politics. For the history of military rule, see Alford Carleton, "The Syrian Coups d'Etat," *The Middle East Journal*, IV (January, 1950), 1–12; Rashid al-Barrawi, *Haqiqat al-Inqilab al-Akhir Fi Misr* (Cairo, 1952); M. Khadduri, *Independent Iraq* (London, 1951).

at the outset their rule was conducted in close co-operation with and was supported by the liberals. Later on the military dominated the scene, and the liberals (if not the nationalists) were either pushed to the background or dropped from power. The religious groups have as a rule been reluctant to support military rule (although in Egypt the Muslim Brotherhood temporarily gave its blessing to General Nagib), either because they had come to terms with former regimes (as in Turkey) or because their ideas proved to be too reactionary to be tolerated by the army. In Syria the Muslim Brotherhood, even though it opposed the premilitary regime, failed to give support to the military because of their active co-operation with liberal elements.

The military pretended that they had assumed power either to prepare the way for liberal reforms or to carry out the reforms themselves. In reality they seized power without having been prepared for, or having had practical experience in, carrying out reforms. Their move to clean the Augean stables met universal approval, but this is a negative approach to reform. The Herculean task would be to carry out real social reform in a manner satisfactory to all. At best the reform program of the military was eclectic; it included various ideas and proposals that had become popular among the people, but these had rarely been integrated into a broad reform program, and plans for their implementation were lacking. A few liberal thinkers, such as Ziya Gökalp in Turkey and the Ahali group in Iraq, tried to formulate broad social programs for the movements they supported, but such philosophical apologias had little or no influence on the minds of the military.[11]

Probably more serious attempts at agrarian reform have been considered, though not actually undertaken, under the military regimes of Syria and Egypt (the distribution of state-owned

[11] For an evaluation of Ziya Gökalp's ideas and influence on the Committee of Union and Progress and the military, see Uriel Heyd, *Foundations of Turkish Nationalism* (London, 1950).

land among the peasants in Syria and the limitation of land ownership to a legal maximum of two hundred acres in Egypt).[12] But though these platforms have become popular among the masses, it would seem that the improvement of economic conditions depends primarily on finding new means of increasing agricultural production, not on merely distributing (as in the case of Syria) or redistributing (as in Egypt) the land among a large number of people. Syria needs both the capital and know-how—which she has refused to receive under the Point IV program—for the exploitation of its vast undeveloped territory, and Egypt, an already overpopulated country, needs new means for increasing production, agricultural or otherwise, to make possible the achievement of social reform.

The suspension of democratic life in favor of military rule, although greeted with almost universal approval, has its own weaknesses and evil influences. Most dangerous of all seems to be the difficulty in persuading the army, once the job of overhauling is done, to withdraw from politics or relinquish power. In spite of repeated assurances by leading army officers that their intervention was only temporary, the lessons of history are not reassuring. Military rule in Egypt (1881–1882), Turkey (1908–1918), and Iraq (1936–1941), showing no signs of withdrawal in favor of civil government, persisted until it was overthrown, in all the foregoing instances, as a result of war with foreign countries.

In Syria the military have survived a period of five years, and no indication has yet been given as to when military rule will end since the new civil government has been brought to power by still another army *coup*. They have avoided fighting with a neighboring country, which is still technically at war with Syria. Such a contest would test their strength and ability to survive. Their silence about war with Israel, a war which originally had

[12] See texts of the Syrian land decrees and the Egyptian Land Reform Law in *The Middle East Journal*, VII (Winter, 1953), 69–81. See also Doreen Warriner, "Land Reform in Egypt and Its Repercussions," *International Affairs*, XXIX (January, 1953), 1–10.

given them an excuse to overthrow civilian rule, as well as their alignment with one Arab country against another, reflects their apprehension lest the military regime collapse from within or be overthrown by an attack from without. In the circumstances, military rule is likely to continue for an indefinite period in Syria as well as in other Arab countries, so long as public opinion remains dissatisfied with the civilian politicians and the army officers can maintain their reputation as the guardians of national interests. If, on the other hand, the army leaders should engage in an internecine struggle for power, as has happened in the past, there is a possibility that the military regime might eventually collapse from within.

Nor is the effect of politics on the military a happy one. "A general has only one aim," said Müffling, "a general who is also a sovereign must have two; his actions as a soldier will always be subordinate to politics." [13] Politics imposes restraints upon sovereigns who, in their careers as generals, should not submit to political forces in order to achieve the highest military success. If the general ever proved to be a successful sovereign, he must have submitted to restraints which no successful general would tolerate. Sudden rise to power seldom permits its victims, except perhaps in exceptional cases, to adjust themselves to the new positions they occupy. The all-powerful leader is tempted to assume a charismatic character, which often alienates his supporters and admirers. The Middle East experience with army rule demonstrates again the truth of Lord Acton's saying, "Power tends to corrupt, and absolute power corrupts absolutely." New leaders who swept to power to rid their people of arbitrary rule and corruption often could not avoid developing in themselves what they hated in their enemies. And this seems to have been true of Husni al-Zayim and Shishakli in Syria no less than of Bakr Sidqi in Iraq. It is to be hoped that Colonel Nasir will be an exception to the rule.

[13] Müffling, *Die Feldzüge der Schlesischen Armee*, p. 52, cited by Yorck von Wartenburg, *Napoleon as a General*, ed. W. G. James (London, 1902), I, 151.

Finally, a word may be said about the opinion prevalent among the Arabs, both military and civilians—comparing the progress made under the Kemalist regime with the state of anarchy and confusion in their countries—that each Arab country needs its own Kemal Atatürk to carry out reform with a strong hand. They often quote with approval the saying of Sayyid Jamal-al-Din al-Afghani, a Muslim leader who advocated Pan-Islamism during the latter part of the nineteenth century, that the East cannot possibly be reformed save by a benevolent despot. When the Kemalist regime, after Atatürk's death, was transformed into a working democracy, it bolstered the army's argument that a great deal of spade work had to be done in the way of "cleansing" before the civilian politicians could be permitted to govern along democratic lines. The military, however, failed to understand that the Kemalist regime was not established overnight by entrusting power to the military, but that Kemal from the beginning made it clear to his fellow army officers that they had to choose between the army and politics. He launched his social reforms in the formative period by democratic methods, spending endless hours in trying to persuade his opponents, displaying patience and tolerance rarely to be found among statesmen with a military background. It was not until the Kurdish rebellion of 1925, when Kemal's prestige and power had already been established, that certain repressive measures were employed. The so-called loyalty trials, purging the regime of obstinate opponents, represented the only purge in the history of modern Turkey.

Atatürk's imitators in the neighboring Arab countries, misunderstanding the nature of Kemalism, tried at first to influence political decisions from behind the scenes only to discover (facing nonco-operation or opposition from civilian politicians) that they had to take over the control of government themselves. In so doing, under the pretext of purging the regime of dangerous or corrupt personalities, they inaugurated a regime of repression which aroused anxiety and fear instead of inspiring

order and security. General Bakr Sidqi not only exiled the leading ministers of the cabinet he overthrew but also ordered the assassination of General Jafar al-Askari and persecuted a dozen others; Colonels al-Zayim and Shishakli arrested and exiled honest as well as corrupt people; and General Nagib, following the same pattern, after forcing King Faruq to abdicate, arrested the king's entourage as well as other politicians on the grounds of corruption. There can hardly be an end to repression once it starts, and it soon involves persons of integrity. The control of government by the military, ruling according to their light with no direct public restraint, creates a governmental problem no less difficult than the problem which prompted the army to seize power.

The basic factor underlying the passing of authority from civilian to military hands is the assumption that democracy has "failed." The people of the Middle East, without handing over authority to either right or left (the religious or the communistic) elements—though both of them came very near to seizing power—resorted to an old trick, which has now become fashionable, of removing the undesirable sovereign by turning his own Praetorian guard against him. While the military has reduced the danger of right or left rule, a greater difficulty has arisen. Once the army officers were firmly installed in the saddle, how could they be removed from their newly won positions? This seems to be the greatest of the dangers of military rule; even if you concede the valuable contribution of the army in carrying out certain reform measures quickly, the experiment may not be worth trying at the expense of suspending for an indefinite period the democratic processes of government. It is true that the operation of democracy has met with dissatisfaction in almost all Middle Eastern countries. This does not necessarily negate the generally accepted principle that government belongs to the people and, therefore, must be controlled by the people. If democracy has failed in the Middle East, it has

failed only because it was transplanted into a social milieu unprepared for it.

The return to democracy, whatever the means to be employed for its restoration, seems to be the safest way toward ultimate stability and progress. In countries where the force of the old local traditions is still strong, it is not to be expected that the working of democratic institutions would admit of comparison with their operation in Western countries accustomed to democratic traditions. As Aristotle often affirms in the *Politics*, the citizen must be educated in the spirit of the constitution under which he lives. At present, the value of democracy must be regarded as mainly educational: that is, it must help to develop democratic habits and traditions necessary for the functioning of democratic machinery.

If democracy has "failed" at all, it has failed because in a shrinking world the Middle Eastern people have become aware of their backwardness in comparison with the West; but it is not the fault of democracy that they did not catch up with the West. The fault lies with the people themselves. Not until the people are cured from within, socially and economically no less than politically, can they live a salutary democratic way of life. And this approach is not new to the Middle East. The Prophet Muhammad, in a Qur'anic injunction, reminded his people, "Verily Allah changeth not that which is in a people until they change that which is in themselves." This change from within can be achieved only by sound education—which is lacking among the great majority of the people—an education (in addition to the social-economic reforms already stressed) which will provide them with the spirit of the constitution under which they live.

(X) S. R. SHAFAQ

The Clergy in Islam

IN A CONSIDERATION of the clergy in Islam, the first problem is to find a corresponding Islamic term for the word "clergy," but that is not possible. The Greek word *kleros* and the Latin *clericus* are not in complete accord with the present meaning, i.e., a group of men set apart by ordination to serve God and conduct worship in the Christian church. The word does not have an analogous concept in Islamic terminology. Even the word "church" in the sense of ecclesiastical government or of the whole body of Christian believers has no corresponding term in the Islamic languages and the Persian word *Kelisia* (*Ecclesia*) or Arabic *Kanissah* does not indicate the meaning of the word "church" as a body of believers.

Although it usually is best to avoid raising matters of semantics simply because some old authors may have used terms in a certain way, in this case it is apparent that Islam in its origin did not institute any clergy. This seems equally true of early Christianity. A ministry of the church, in the sense of a definite cadre of offices, and a crystallization of the doctrine of apostolic succession, as a principle of the continuity of authority and divine right, did not exist during the early days of Christianity.

An organized priesthood seems to have been born out of need during the later periods.

Islam advocated absolute surrender or abandonment of one's self to Allah. For the blood kinship of the Arabs, it substituted the community of faith. Islam has no church, no priests, no sacraments. A real Muslim is alone in the presence of Allah; in life and in death, he may always address Him directly without any need of mediators. There is no interference between man and his Creator. This attitude goes even beyond the most absolute Protestantism.

Evidently, during the rise of Islam and the lifetime of the Prophet, a faithful Muslim believed he was under the direct rule of Allah; he almost instinctively lived in the Kingdom of Allah. This government of Allah was ruled by the divine law, the *Shari'ah*. The will of Allah and the juridical order and religion, i.e., law and morals, are two aspects of the same divine will.

The basic principle in the life of a Muslim is individual liberty. But this liberty, *hurriyyah*, has its limit, and that limit is precisely what is called law, which concerns both body and soul.

In the orthodox view the Prophet did not organize any ruling body to succeed him. When he passed away, the need was felt for a successor to the great teacher. There came into existence the institution of successorship, the Caliphate. The speedy spread of Islam beyond the boundaries of Arabia necessitated more co-ordinated administration and also the codification of the laws.

Four sources of the law were discerned:

1. The *Qur'an*, the holy book as revealed to the Prophet.
2. Tradition (*hadith*), originating from the Prophet's original statements.
3. *Sunnah*, usages and customs of the Prophet, mainly, but also of the community, which came down by oral transmission, sanctified by the Prophet.

4. *Ijma*, consensus of the representative people.

As a matter of fact, the second and third elements could be considered together as one source, for both originate in the first place from the Prophet through his sayings or deeds. Some schools like the Hanafi add another source, i.e., opinion of a religious leader obtained by a sort of analogical reasoning. Accepting this explanation, the four sources could be restated as: (1) *Qur'an*; (2) tradition and *sunnah*; (3) consensus; and (4) reason.

By necessity the first attention of the early leaders was directed to the study and interpretation of the *Qur'an*. Among the notable people of Medina were some who were found to read and recite the *Qur'an* correctly; they were the reciters (*kurra*). Others who interpreted were called the commentators (*mufassirun*).

Individuals distinguished themselves in collecting and reciting the *hadith* or tradition, and they were called the reciters of tradition, the traditionalists (*muhaddithun*). Gradually offices of *qadi*, or judge, were created, and religious courts were formed where important cases were submitted to a qualified jurist, who was called *mufti*, a consultant in law, whose *fatwa*, or statement of legal issues, was needed. This process led to the emergence of special scientists of the law and theology, i.e., the jurists (*fuqaha*). *Fiqh* (jurisprudence) is the science of law. Thus as early as the second and third century of Islam prominent *Qur'an* commentators, jurists, traditionalists, and legal consultants began to make their appearance. It was then that the founders of the four legal schools, i.e., Hanafi, Maliki, Shafi'i, and Hanbali, established their teachings. In the essentials of faith all of the four schools were in agreement, though they differed in some legal interpretations and methods.

Thus Islam, as far as the social administration was concerned, was organized into a system, and, in fact, a class which acquired religious authority similar to the clergy was produced. This was the class of *'ulama'*, or the learned leaders. The word, as used

in the *Qur'an*, meant merely the learned, but in later stages it also denoted a special class of religious doctors. These *'ulama'* could continue in their studies in order to attain the stage of *ijtihad* and be a *mujtahid*.

Ijtihad literally means to exert one's self to reach the highest stage of religious learning in order to have the privilege of forming an opinion and passing independent judgment in religious matters. In its earliest usage it was equated with reasoning. Every *mujtahid* could have his judgment on the cardinal religious questions. But he was not considered as infallible because he was free to use his opinion (*dhann*). But *ijtihad* combined with the *ijma*, or consensus, would ordinarily be considered unerring. This broad application of the *ijtihad* passed later into special *ijtihad*.

A few prominent *'ulama'* could be called *mujtahids* when they were followed by *muqallids*, imitators, who did not exercise their independent reasoning powers. Because of this, some proposed to restrict the word *mujtahid* to the founders of the four schools. The other *mujtahids* were to be considered as secondary ones who could pass judgment on minor matters. Gradually, therefore, many great Muslim doctors held that no scholar besides the four leaders, however eminent, could qualify as a *mujtahid*. But some other leaders, like Ibn Taymiyah and al-Suyuti contested this and claimed for themselves the right to form their own opinions.

According to the Shi'ah sect, the right of *ijtihad*, or the discovery and authoritative enunciation of fresh religious truths, is allowed to all those who by reason of their learning and the grace of Allah can attain it. A Shi'ite *mujtahid* is believed to be a *locum tenens* of the hidden Imam, or the divine leader, till the latter appears and rules *de jure divino*, bringing peace and equity on earth. Thus together, the doctrine of *ijtihad*, i.e., the right of intelligent reasoning on important matters of the faith, and the principle of *ijma*, or consensus, i.e., the right of the Muslim people to govern itself, could make a solid basis for

[187]

a liberal and democratic development of the Islamic peoples, as Western scholars like Goldziher, Arnold, Gibb, and others have maintained.

The title *mullah* is also worth consideration in this connection. Apparently, it came into usage mainly in Iran with the Safavi period in the sixteenth century and spread over all the Islamic world, especially in India. The derivation of the word is somewhat doubtful. Some think it is a corruption of the word *mawla*, in Arabic, meaning the Lord, the Great Friend. For example, it is written in the *Qur'an* that Allah is your Friend, *Wallahu Mawlakum.*

A *mullah* means a learned man in religion. The word *'ulama'* is, of course, more general, for it could be applied to all learned men, lay or religious, whereas *mullah* denotes learned in religion just as *mujtahid* does. But a *mullah* is not necessarily a *mujtahid.* All *mujtahids* can be called *mullahs,* or *'ulama',* but not everyone of the *mullah* class, nor everyone of the *'ulama'* could be considered a *mujtahid.*

Today many questions arise concerning the present function of the clergy in the Middle East. It should be remembered that as a result of the origin and development of Islam their activities are almost everywhere tied somehow to law. One of the great roles opening up before the clergy is the opportunity, by using the doctrine of *ijma* and relevant *hadiths,* to bring about a compromise between the religious and secular laws.

Many have questioned whether or not this is possible. In Islam religious and secular laws are inseparable. Secular law must remain unto itself until a compromise can be effected between contemporary secular problems and basic Islamic precepts. Moreover, secularization of law reflects a Western point of view; any attempt at separation of religion and law would basically change Islam. Is not the idea that there is a true separation of law and religion in the West essentially false? Christianity and Judaism are interwoven with the Greek con-

cept of justice. In Islam it is also impossible to separate justice and law.

In the Middle East there is a real undercurrent of thought in terms of conscience and the needs of society. In spite of some reactionary clergymen, there are many who are loud in their cries demanding social justice. In the past there have been many Islamic societies with extensive secular legislation, *qanun*, which did not impinge on the law of religion.

One cannot re-emphasize too often the potential flexibility of Islamic law. *Ijma, ijtihad,* and *hadith* in themselves recognize and accept a certain secularizing philosophy. There is the *hadith,* "The laws change according to the times."

The Intellectuals in
the Modern Development
of the Islamic World

A SOCIOLOGICAL study of the intelligentsia in the modern Near East would be of value: a study assessing its size, composition, political behavior, economic weight, and the like—its "behavior patterns." Such a description would be welcome; here, however, is offered an essay of a different sort. The endeavor is rather to analyse and interpret; and concern is with the function in society not of a class of people so much as of the ideas that they hold and purvey. For the essential behavior of an intellectual is that he thinks. The relevant questions would appear to be: What does he think, and how, and why? How effectively does he communicate? How is his vision related to the historical processes in which his society is involved?

Geographically, it seems proper in this case to change the coverage from the Near East to the Islamic world. Israel is not here discussed; for its intellectuals do not participate in a common universe of discourse with the intellectuals of their neighbors, the Arabs. They live in juxtaposition, but do not read each other's books. On the other hand, extending consideration as

far east as Pakistan and Muslim India (the omission of Indonesia is recognized) is justified in that the Islamic world so conceived constitutes an intelligible whole for certain intellectualist purposes. For instance, the thinkers of Lahore and Aligarh are concerned, as it were professionally, with the ideas and behavior of their fellow Muslims in Cairo and Istanbul. This has been less true vice versa, but is currently becoming more so (for instance, Iqbal is being increasingly read in Iran, and has recently been translated and commented on in Arabic and Turkish).

Economically, this area has little integration. Ideologically, however, it has a fair amount (along with differentiation). Moreover, the very questions of its having ideological, and indeed of its having economic or political, integration or differentiation are important matters for the intellectuals.

The proposed use of the term "intellectual," also, must be clarified. Indeed, on the meaning ascribed to it much of the argument turns. For those who must have an operational definition, one might proffer the following: an intellectual is someone who would be recognized as such in an Oxford senior common room. Such a definition postulates that the intellectualist tradition exists in western Europe and suggests that its existence elsewhere can be correlated therewith. The contention will be here advanced that something similar exists in today's Islamic world. However, the significance of this remains inert unless one adds a descriptive account, and elaborates in universal terms what one believes to be implicated. An analytical definition, then, is presented.

Aristotle discriminated between the yogi and the commissar within each of us by stating that man has two intellects, the theoretical and the practical. The practical intellect deals with the manipulation of things and the adaptation of means to ends—with "know-how," if you will. The theoretical or speculative intellect has as its function the apprehension of ideal ends, the recognition and contemplation of truth itself. To transpose

[191]

the point that he was making into more modern terminology, it may be said that the word "intellect," as indeed the word "reason," has two meanings: one referring to technical rationality (as in such phrases as "the production belt rationalizes manufacturing"), one to transcendent rationality (as in "the production belt derationalizes man"). In the classical world it was felt that the thinker, insofar as he was thinking correctly, was thereby participating in the transcendent structure of the universe; was lifting his mind into contact with something not only permanent, but more real and more valuable than anything offered among the changeful phenomena of the work-a-day world. The modern age is inclined to prefer the view that to think correctly is definable in terms of ability to participate efficaciously in the flux of those phenomena; to control their change. The intellect's function here is to serve as an instrument for the satisfaction of the body's wants, and the expediting of mundane activities. This stands over against the earlier persuasion that the function of the intellect, or anyway of this intellect, is to know the truth—and thus incidentally to give man serenity and supreme contentment even when his wants are not satisfied and his activities are frustrated.

It is not that intellectualism can be correlated with inaction. This part of the intellect is a spectator; yet the whole man can and should act. His action should, however, be the servant of his mind; not vice versa.

Without wishing to commit oneself to Aristotle's particular formulation, which as a matter of fact seems inadequate in the twentieth century, one may yet admit that in general he had something of a point. The present writer suggests that the term "truth," and the human mind, both have a transcendent, even divine, reference. It is important to note that this is implicitly or explicitly rejected by a good deal of Western modernity. The moderns do not use Aristotle's terms; but if they did many would simply aver, virtually as a dogma, that the practical in-

tellect alone exists. They hold that man's theoretical intellect, along with the absolute reason lying behind the phenomenal world, with which it claims to be in touch, is sheer fiction; they just are not there.

For the purposes of the present study—to detect and analyse the role of the intellectuals in today's development of the Muslim world—it is important to note that the present writer, at least, believes that they are there. Indeed, it is proposed to define the term "intellectual" in relation to the theoretical intellect. The later Aristotelians wrote that the theoretical intellect is potential in every human being, is actual only in a few. Those few would be the intellectuals. In other words, the term may be correlated with "know-what" rather than "know-how." Be he never so brilliant, the mere technician, whether in physics or philosophy, in production or in politics, is not what is meant here by an intellectual. *The intellectual is the man who makes a habit of using his mind to see the world as it metaphysically is.*

Not that it is contended that an intellectual must by definition agree with any particular metaphysics; or even be interested in or tolerant of any metaphysical theories. Also, to adopt a certain interpretation of the universe and of man does not *ipso facto* make one an intellectual. Many have accepted the classical view of a rational universe because they have been taught it—that is, they have used their practical intellect to arrive at this view. Others have used their own brilliant speculations (*sic*) to arrive at a contrary doctrine. John Dewey and Karl Marx were certainly both intellectuals, though both claimed to reject a transcendent universe. Indeed, anyone who believes that pragmatism is *true*, or that a communist society would be *good*, could qualify under our definition. The believer in God does not claim that atheists do not exist; he merely opines that they, like others, exist by the grace of God. Similarly, it is not here suggested that materialists or positivists or behaviorists are

not intellectuals. The contention is simply that if they are intellectuals it is because, despite themselves, their intellects are free.

Whether a man is an intellectual or not does not depend on what views he holds, but on how he arrives at them.

Whether a society, on the other hand, produces intellectuals or not, and sustains them as a class, does depend *inter alia* on what views it holds. The writer can clearly remember in his own youth when he genuinely thought that the noun "intellectual" was a term of abuse ("a person who merely thinks"). If some cultures, such as those of Greece and China, have been such as to encourage (sociologically and otherwise) the lover-of-wisdom class, this is discouraged by the development of some other cultures, such as those of modern America (where, for instance, the universities are less and less geared to produce the intellectualist type) and the Soviet Union. Intelligent men are to be found everywhere; intellectuals are historically circumscribed.

How does all this relate to the situation in the modern Islamic world? It has been necessary to introduce this preliminary material in order to establish or clarify some of the propositions which follow.

The first of these is that in modern Muslim society intellectuals, so conceived, exist. This is fundamental. It is also, at least on the modern scale, new. Recently the area celebrated in Baghdad the millenary of Ibn Sina. Insofar as this was sincere— insofar as the Arabs were really concerned to honor that thinker and what he stood for, and not merely to honor themselves through a figure whom outsiders admired—it might be taken as a symbol of the rebirth of the intellectual in Islam. One cannot say that he re-emerges after a thousand years; and indeed perhaps for Turkey he never lapsed. Yet in the Arab world, and probably in Iran, the modern upsurge of the intellectual as he has been here defined follows a period of some centuries—the period which may be called the Arabs' Middle Ages, that began not long before Europe's Middle Ages ended, and is only

now coming to a close. In Muslim India the intellectual as a class is something quite new; the only conspicuous medieval instance that comes to mind is the emperor Akbar, and it is not clear whether he may well be called a Muslim. In those intervening centuries there were plenty of intelligent men— men who used their intellects to *reason about* the *Qur'an* and the whole cultural heritage, but not to judge them. It is only in recent times that once again persons are behaving on the assumption, whether explicit or unconscious, that the human reason is not only a process to be applied to truth, but a source of it—a critic of premises as well as of the arguments built thereon.

Even in classical Islam the Greek view that the universal *logos* is immanent in the human *logos* was never quite integrated into the civilization. It was not quite clear, again, whether Ibn Sina himself was a Muslim or not—that is, whether he is to be counted a member of the community. Admittedly, *"Huwa al-Haqq"* has throughout been essential to Islam; and one possible translation of it is, God is the truth. Few, however, seem to have interpreted this in the sense that man through exercising his reason participates in the divine.

The official view, reflecting the general Semitic concern with the will rather than with the mind, has been rather that man comes into touch with God through behavior, through righteousness; men participate in the eternal scheme of things when their lives conform to a pattern of goodness, rather than when their ideas conform to a pattern of truth. This seems to the present writer the substance of the *Shari'ah*. Moreover, the Sufi alternative, or supplement, stresses feeling rather than, or as well as, will; conducing to a direct awareness which transcends mind along with phenomena. Although there is still room for debate, it is not unfeasible to regard the *Mu'tazilah* of the ninth and tenth centuries as an intellectualist movement as here conceived, and to interpret their subsequent and definite rejection by the Muslim world as representing a classical Islamic repudi-

[195]

ation of the independent speculative intellect. Indeed, this general thesis would seem corroborated by the long struggle which even the Asha'irah, eventually orthodox, had in winning acceptance for their, or indeed for any, systematic theology. This reflects the general distrust in which theology had been held in Islam; even though for theology reason is the servant, not the source, of faith. In the historical Islamic tradition, then, the intellectual has been peripheral and precarious.

This situation became the more marked in the later centuries, down to the nineteenth; during which the intellectual almost disappeared. Today, however, he is conspicuous and important. This, then, is the first great change.

Further, it is not merely that the intellectuals themselves exist. There is today, throughout the Islamic world, a very considerable body of persons, not themselves intellectuals, who recognize the intellectuals and respect them; and look to them for leadership. Where a century or more ago it was the 'ulama' or the pir, the traditional religious leaders, who had prestige and whose pronouncements carried weight, nowadays there has developed in some quarters a quite remarkable disdain for these men—a feeling, almost a tacit assumption, that they are passés, old fogies who of course do not understand the world in which they live, and who of course cannot solve its problems.

Even religious leadership is in process of passing from them to university graduates; there are believing Muslims who more and more feel that it is the intellectual who will clarify their faith. The lack of an ordained clergy facilitates this process. The establishment of the new Faculty of Theology at Ankara University, and of Departments of Islamics (Islamiyat—a new word) in all the universities of Pakistan, illustrates it (and is designed to promote it). The title of Iqbal's major work, The Reconstruction of Religious Thought in Islam, is itself eloquent. In the Arab world the growing sense that something should be done about the Azhar is a straw in the same wind.

And if all this is true in the religious field, how much more in other matters. Of considerable sociological importance is this fact that a large body of people respect the contribution which reason can make to a proper understanding of the world, and look increasingly to the intellectual to tell them what is what, and to define social goals. The immense influence of Ziya Gökalp and of Iqbal are worth pondering.

In this connection one may press a point about communism. It is trite to say that communism owes its strength in Asia to the workers and peasants in all their crushing poverty—trite, but not true. The workers and peasants supply the motive force and content of the movement, but the ranks of the intelligentsia provide the organization and direction. Leave the proletariat such of its own leaders as regard Marxist theory and practice as merely an instrument for satisfying their class's worldly wants; but take away those leaders—including many sons of the well-to-do with sensitive conscience and nimble mind—who believe the theory to be approximative to Truth and the practice to be conducive to Justice; and one might wager that the whole movement would collapse within six months. The strength of Marxism lies in its appeal not to the stomach but to the intellect.

To return to our modified Aristotle, it is the theoretical intellect that is meant here, not the practical. The point is that Marxism appeals to a sense of values.

One more comparable point on this matter of leadership concerns the University of Ankara and its role in the Turkish transformation. That university, now an intellectualist center of some import, grew out of a series of training schools—that is, of institutions for the practical intellect. First came the Law School, set up to train Turks to administer the new European codes. Next came the Pedagogical Institute, to produce teachers to impart the new education (advised by Dewey, by the way, but never really freed from Paris intellectualism). And so on. All had practical objects. Yet the training somehow included

an awakening also of the theoretical intellect. For the spirit of the whole movement has throughout been permeated with a new idealism. The strength of Atatürk's dream, too, lay in its appeal to the intellect. The role of the intelligentsia in Turkey has been to effect the revolution.

Perhaps part of the basic significance of the recent introduction of true elections in Turkey is that the determination of the country's policy—though not yet its administration—is in process of shifting from the intelligentsia to the people as a whole.

It is not only in Europe, or even America, that there has been on occasion a *trahison des clercs*. The great betrayal of the intellectuals is when they abandon their role of criticism *sub specie aeternitatis:* when they use their intellect for some ulterior purpose and make it the servant, not the master, of life. One has seen this happen in our day in the West with Marxism on the one hand and with industrial technology on the other. (May one even detect perhaps in the universities of the United States some beginnings of a trend toward knowledge *ad majorem Americae gloriam?*) The process begins with honest confusion and may end with intellectual dishonesty.

In the Islamic world, it has taken the form chiefly of apologetics. In Turkey the temptation has been toward a Turkish apologetics; though to a significant extent it is being resisted or overcome. The Turkish Historical Society at Ankara was formed to write history with a purpose, a history that would glorify the Turks; fairly quickly, however, it has reverted to trying to write history that will be true. In other countries, especially in the Arab world and Muslim India, the chief aberration has been the endeavor to use the intellect to glorify Islam. (Among the Arabs it has been also to glorify the Arabs, though the Arab's religion is sufficiently ethnocentric that he can readily intertwine the two.)

A great deal of what passes for liberalism has been less a sincere admiration of its ideal than a desperate search for its applause. To take one example, the intellect has often been

called upon to prove that Muslim or Arab society does, or in the roseate past did, embody the liberal values—rather than the will being called upon to see to it that it embody them, once the theoretical intellect has (if it has) seen those values to be sound and the practical intellect elucidated how they may be implemented. Again, the historian has tended to use his prowess to demonstrate, for example, the scientific development in classical Islamic civilization, rather than to explain it; to champion, rather than to understand.

As regards religious affairs, a similar attitude is marked. Perhaps little evinces so poignantly the contemporary plight of Islam among its modernists, as the vast amount of intellectual effort that has been poured into proving it admirable. For many, Islam would seem to have become something to be proud of, rather than something to be lived.

There is a connection between this "defense of Islam" (al-difa' 'an al-Islam) and the traditional function of reason in classical Islamic theology. In both, the intellect is subservient. In the latter case, however, to faith; in the other, to pride. And faith, after all, is another, a nonintellectual, form of apprehending the truth. The orthodox, therefore, may still have integrity. The modernist, often lacking faith, yet uses reason to prove that Islam is a good thing; the orthodox knows it is a good thing, and uses reason to work out its implication and its implementation. Or he uses it to convince others; the modernist, to convince himself. The true Muslim and the true intellectual would perhaps be synthesized in liberalism, or maybe in something yet to be born. The modern apologist, on the other hand, tends to be neither a good Muslim nor a good intellectual and to eventuate, therefore, in insincerity.

It was stated above that the characteristic—if you like, the true—behavior of the intellectual is to think, to be a spectator of the truth. What has been described is a kind of misbehavior. Indeed, it might be permissible to indulge the extravagance of calling it, metaphorically, a kind of shirk—an allegiance of the

[199]

mind to something other than *al-haqq*, the truth. It is, of course, an aberration. If it was somewhat prevalent in Muslim India before 1947 and if to some extent still in postpartition India there is more than a little weakness in the Muslim's determination to see himself and his situation at all costs as they in bald fact are, yet in Pakistan the establishment of the new dominion has presented its Muslim leadership with a challenging responsibility to which on the whole it seemed at first remarkably to be rising. The dreamy wish-fulfillment romanticizing of previous days was disciplined by the restive reality of concrete tasks demanding attention; and the exhilaration of independence worked toward replacing irresponsibility with self-criticism.

In Iran the intellectual has apparently still not on any scale settled down to his task as the responsible analyst and critic of life. In Egypt, on the other hand, development seems to be rapid, after a long period of confusion. From the recent tendency (begun even before the army *coup*) of the Arab intellectuals to move into the *Ikhwan* camp, two possibilities would seem to emerge. One, presumably, is the possibility of, in the end, the disaster of an almost Hitler-Rosenberger reactionary-ism, with the intellectuals' intellect quite sold out to the blind emotional fury of a nostalgic mob. The other possibility, and the one which on balance appears perhaps somewhat more likely, or at least for which one may hope, is that of a movement toward a synthesis, at last, of the Islamic religious tradition with an intellectualist perspicacity of modernity—a synthesis which, with due regard to Point IV, seems the area's most fundamental need.

In Turkey the intellectuals have, on the whole, behaved with a unique self-critical realism. One receives the impression that what most distinguishes the Turks in the Islamic world of the twentieth century is intellectual honesty. Nor does Turkey's dynamic advance leave undemonstrated the practical value of theoretical insight; since they constitute the only people in

contemporary Islam who have really known what it is that they want.

One final point—one more generalization about the manner of the modern Muslim world's intellectualist behavior. It is obvious enough, once it is made. Yet the ramifications are large, and the point deserves and would repay considerably more study than the brief mention given it here. It rests on the observation (to which Turkey is an interesting partial exception) that today's Muslim intellectual is everywhere not merely bilingual, but linguistically bicultural. The intelligentsia of Muslim India and Pakistan speak, read, and write English; they are at home in that tongue. In Iran, the Arab world, and Turkey, the situation is similar as regards French (occasionally, in Turkey, German) or again English, or both. This phenomenon, one may suggest, is quite different from and fundamentally much more important than any intracultural bilingualism—by which the same Muslim may know Persian in addition to Urdu or Turkish, or a Westerner may know French or German in addition to English. (One wonders how many Westerners know any Oriental language so effectively that their theoretical intellect can and does operate in it.) To be cross-culturally bilingual—not superficially but thoroughly—is a matter of no mean import.

In order to suggest of how great import it may be, attention may be drawn, let one hope not irresponsibly, to one other conspicuous instance in Near Eastern history when a comparable cross-cultural situation arose: the Hellenistic period. In ancient Alexandria, for instance, the intellectuals were men who spoke Semitic at home but Greek at the university. The fermentation resulting produced, in Philo's mind, what Wolfson's exaggerated but significant thesis regards as the basic structure of the philosophy that dominated Jewish, Christian, and Muslim thought for the next sixteen centuries. Out of the interaction of this period arose also the historical forms of Christianity (in-

cluding the till now permanent form of basic Christian dogma); and early science (experimental science is in some senses an offspring of the marriage of Semitic activism with Greek rationality). It is doubtful that St. Paul is understood until he is seen as one of the *'ulama'* who received also a Western education.

The bicultural language situation today is complex, for it is not symmetrical. It is not simply a matter of one's being an intellectual in two different languages, even two different cultures. Rather, it is a matter of thinking in two languages while being an intellectual in only one of them. This is truest in Pakistan and India, where virtually all higher education has been in English. It happens there that a man and his own father talking together will discuss the arrangements for dinner in Panjabi, the arts in Urdu, and anything philosophic in English.

The situation is less extreme in the Islamic world further west; and when Turkey was held up as somewhat of an exception to the generalization that the intellectuals of Islam are linguistically bicultural, it did not mean that in that country fewer intellectuals are at home in a Western language. This may or may not statistically be true, but the question is rather of what goes on within the mind. The point of significance is that probably only in Turkey is it possible to be an intellectual entirely in one's own tongue. The Turkish intellectual probably knows French and regularly reads it; he may speak it fluently and may hold a Sorbonne degree. Yet he thinks and writes in Turkish, even intellectualist books. And another Turk who knows no French can follow what he has to say.

The Indo-Pakistan intellectual writes in English, and a knowledge of English extends considerably further down in society than does an ability to follow his ideas. Arab intellectuals write their books in Arabic, but it is a question how much of them another Arab can understand who does not have a Western-language education. Gibb has stated, "It is at the present time impossible to produce an adequate Arabic translation of any

advanced work of modern science or philosophy. Even if the effort were made, the result would be unintelligible except to those readers who could mentally retranslate it into the Western terms." [1] The situation is in process of evolving. In the recent past, certainly, the Arab's mind which climbed into the rarefied atmosphere of speculative and independent intellectuality used a ladder of foreign terms for at least the top stages of its ascent. Today the educated generation which is growing up is still on the whole familiar, even intimate, with European languages, and fairly dependent on them as a source for ideas of the intellectualist type. Yet this is not entirely so, and this generation finds that it does have some access to those same ideas and, more important, the same process of thinking, without straying out of the language which also embodies its tradition.

For Persian a tentative judgment, rather hesitatingly advanced, would be that this process is also in evidence and has developed further than with Urdu, considerably less far than with Arabic.

Being an intellectual is, then, also linguistically circumscribed. It is not possible here to pursue the many ramifications of the situation; in questions of communication, of the synthesis of diversely perceived truths, and many more. One may sum up thus: the confluence of intellectuality and tradition has taken place within many individual minds; but for the social mind which is language, an integration has as yet hardly been achieved.

To conclude. The intellectual is one who uses his mind to see the world as it truly is. He is not actionless; and even more, the society which honors and follows him is far from quiescent. Only, action is subordinate to truth as best one sees it. His role in the contemporary Near East is surely crucial. In that region today what is there more important than to see things clearly, and to know what the problems and the goals really are? The ability and the will to do are essential, but first is to

[1] H. A. R. Gibb, *Modern Trends in Islam* (Chicago, 1947), p. 48.

know what should be done. Karl Marx said: "The philosophers have tried to understand the world; our task is to change it." Noting with sadness that man's changing of it may, after all, be for the worse, one may well recognize that the endeavor to understand remains important.

The Minorities in the

Political Process

NEAR EAST society is segmental, not unitary. The number of minorities varies with the yardstick. Measured by ethnic, linguistic, and religious standards, the diverse communities in the area which embraces the independent Arab states (exclusive of Libya), Iran, Israel, and Turkey probably exceed twoscore. Some groups may be characterized by the special garb, barb, and craft of their members. But the sartorial, tonsorial, and occupational features symbolize no more than externalities. Many of the minorities such as the Druzes, the Kurds, the Lurs, the Bakhtiyaris, and the Qashqais are concentrated in certain districts. Others, notably the Armenians, the Greeks, and the Jews, are scattered. Though thrust one upon the other and interacting in the daily pursuits of life and livelihood, the several social bodies for centuries have successfully resisted cultural assimilation to the dominant units in each land. The Samaritan remnant presents the most uncommon case of group survival. It consists of less than three hundred individuals who live for the most part in the vicinity of Nablus—now located in Jordan—where the sect originated more than two thousand

years ago. Lebanon best illustrates the land without a numerically dominant community, for none of its ten Christian or three Muslim sects constitutes an absolute majority of the total population.

A description of the Near East cultural mosaic is one thing. An explanation of its origins and evolution is quite another. Suffice it to say that many forces operating over several millennia have contributed to the fragmentation of Near East society. Successive migrations from outside the region and from within have introduced new ethnic strains and diffused the old. The traditions of inclusive religious organization and decentralized administration have kept alive differing languages, legal institutions, political forms, and social customs. Tribalism and parochialism have thrived in wide districts where villages are still isolated from one another because of undeveloped means of communication. These factors and many others have not yet been fully examined. Indeed, it may be said without exaggeration that the pluralistic aspect of Near East society has hardly begun to be studied.

The present essay attempts no more than to probe suggestively into one small aspect of the contemporary phase of the question—the minorities in the political process of Near East countries. This exploratory survey of the majority-minority political relationship is limited to the independent states which in the past half-century have instituted parliamentary forms. Four—Turkey, Lebanon, Syria, and Israel—emerged as republics and four others—Iran, Egypt, Iraq, and Jordan—originally as constitutional monarchies. Parliamentary government in half of these countries has broken down in the past six years, either to military dictatorships—Syria and Egypt—or to temporary rule by civilian decree—Iran and Lebanon. The restoration of the elective legislatures and their constitutional prerogatives in Iran, Lebanon, and Syria does not necessarily clarify, as of the time of writing, the future political course of these three Near East lands. In the circumstances, this study will deal largely

with the period preceding the several parliamentary crises.

It might be well to begin with a summary of facts and figures. Accurate population statistics are, in most cases, unavailable even to the governments concerned. The demographic data which follow should therefore be regarded, at best, as reasonable approximations.

Six of the eight states are predominantly Muslim, ranging in percentage from nearly 85 in Syria,[1] 90 in Jordan, 92.5 in Egypt, and 96 in Iraq to roughly 98 in Iran and Turkey. But Sunnite Egypt and Jordan apart, the Muslim communities are not uniform, for they are further divided along linguistic, ethnic, and sectarian lines. Probably as many as 15 to 20 percent of the Muslims in Turkey are Shi'ites and about 8 percent more are Kurds who, though Sunnites, speak their private language, which is related to the Iranian group. Some 19 percent of the Syrian Muslims belong to schismatic sects, primarily 'Alawis, Druzes, and Isma'ilis in descending numerical order; an added 8 percent are Kurds. For every Sunnite in Iraq there is one Shi'ite; yet more than one-third of the Sunnites are Kurds, while less than 2 percent of the Shi'ites are Iranians. At the most only two out of every three Muslims in Shi'ite Iran speak Persian; every fifth Iranian uses a Turkish dialect; every fourteenth Muslim is a Sunnite Kurd; in the western tribal districts, Lurs and Bakhtiyaris speak Persian dialects; and concentrated further south, in Khuzistan and along the Persian Gulf littoral, there are Arab tribes, who form about 3 percent of Iran's total population. The political separatism to which the differences give rise has tended to disunite the dominant religious communities in countries where the political gulf between Muslims and non-Muslims—chiefly Oriental Christians and Jews, who themselves constitute a variety of incompatible factions—has generally widened in the last three decades.

Regionwise, Lebanon and Israel are minority states in the

---

[1] Excluding beduins, variously estimated between 300,000 and 400,000, who in any case do not participate in Syrian national politics.

preponderantly Muslim Near East. While departing from the norm, the religious structure of the two countries, nevertheless, goes far to explain intercommunity political relations in each. The Christians are officially held to constitute a slight majority in Lebanon, according to 1944 estimates, nearly 53 percent of the total. In the absence of a reliable census, Muslims have disputed the official contention. The 1944 statistics indicated that the Maronites, an autonomous uniate church which has accepted Papal supremacy, formed the largest single community; yet its membership did not surpass 29 percent of the country's population. The next communities in order of size included the Sunnites with 22 percent, the Shi'ites 18.5, the Greek Orthodox 9.7, the Druzes 6.6, the Greek Catholics (whose uniate church is known also as Melkite, a Roman Catholic affiliate employing Greek liturgy) 5.7, and the Armenian Orthodox (Gregorians) 5.2. The adherents of the remaining six Christian sects and of the diminutive Jewish community numbered less than 5 percent each.

Approximately 89 percent of the population of Israel at the end of 1953 were Jews, 7.6 Muslims (Sunnites), 2.4 Christians (chiefly members of the Greek Catholic and Greek Orthodox churches) and 1 percent Druzes. The ritual differences among the Jews are politically less significant than the division between those who emigrated from Europe and those from the Muslim countries of Asia and North Africa. The European majority, in the first six years of the fledgling state, was whittled down from more than 75 percent to perhaps less than 60 percent.

Seven of the states adopted written constitutions; and the Israel *Kneset* (legislature) enacted a bill on June 13, 1950, directing its Committee on the Constitution, Legislation, and Justice to frame a written constitution. No time limit was set, but the committee was instructed to draft a series of fundamental laws, each to be presented to "the *Kneset* as the committee completes its work and all . . . [the fundamental laws] together shall comprise the state constitution." The constitu-

tions of Egypt (Article 149, Constitution of April 19, 1923),[2] Iran (Article 1, Supplementary Fundamental Laws of October 7, 1907), Iraq (Article 13, Constitution of March 21, 1925), and Jordan (Article 2, Constitution of January 1, 1952) declare Islam the official religion of the state. The preamble of the 1950 Syrian Constitution noted that Islam is the religion of the majority of the people and—retaining the formula of the 1930 Constitution—of the president of the republic and stipulated (Article 3) that Islamic law shall be the main source of legislation.[3]

The governments of Lebanon, Turkey, and Israel are secular. Yet by convention the president of Lebanon is invariably a Christian (Maronite). In Turkey, where the formal separation of religion and state was consummated by amendment of the Constitution on April 10, 1928, only a Muslim Turk can hope to become president. The Transition Law of February 16, 1949, and the State President (Tenure) Law of December 3, 1951, which define the procedure for electing the president of Israel, make no mention whatsoever of religion. Still it is clear that no one but a Jewish citizen may aspire to the office.

If it is argued that these usages do not differ substantially from those in the United States or France, where only Protestants and Catholics, respectively, have been elected president, other practices should be considered. The Constitution of Iran (Article 58, Supplementary Fundamental Laws of October 7, 1907) explicitly lays down that only Muslims born in the country may attain the rank of minister. (Membership in the cabinet has been largely confined in practice to those who, in addition to the qualifications listed, are also Persian in speech.) No other Near East constitution has a similar provision. Nevertheless, Christians and Jews since the mid-1920's have been excluded from cabinet posts in Iraq, where the governments have generally been controlled by the Sunnite Arabs, a minor-

[2] The 1923 Egyptian Constitution was abolished on December 10, 1952.

[3] The 1953 Syrian Constitution deleted the reference to Islam as the religion of the majority but retained the other stipulations (Article 3, paragraphs 1 and 2). The 1950 Constitution was reinstated on March 1, 1954.

ity community. Shi'ites and Kurds are always appointed to the short-lived cabinets, but only three Shi'ites have ever served as prime minister: Salih Jabr (March 29, 1947—January 29, 1948), Muhammad al-Sadr (January 29—June 6, 1948), and Fadhil al-Jamali (September 17, 1953—April 21, 1954). The Copts in Egypt, an indigenous Christian community which traces its antecedents back to the pre-Islamic period, constitute about 6 percent of the country's population. Under the 1923 Constitution Copts have occupied ministerial posts in virtually every government, a distinction not shared by other non-Muslims since the 1920's; but all governments have been dominated by Muslim Arabs. Since April, 1950, at least one Christian (Palestine Arab) has been named to every cabinet in Jordan; but the governments are still run by the small circle of Sunnite Arab politicians—a few of them Jordanized Palestinians—who received their original experience in the earlier Transjordan regime and who consistently acquire a majority of the seats. From the outset, Sunnite Arabs have also controlled the Syrian governments, despite occasional Christian premiers, while the cabinets in Turkey have been exclusively Muslim and in Israel exclusively Jewish. In Lebanon the procedure of selecting a Sunnite Arab as premier and apportioning the other ministries among other numerically important sects has remained essentially unchanged.

If the minorities thus have been either severely limited or wholly excluded from participation in the executive branch of government in the Near East lands, they nevertheless have been represented in the legislatures. The electoral laws of five of the states contained explicit provisions for the election of minority deputies. The Iranian law of August 1, 1909 (Article 36), laid down that the Armenians, the Chaldeans (adherents of a uniate affiliate of Roman Catholicism, using Syriac liturgy), the Parsis (Zoroastrians), and the Jews were each to have one deputy in the *Majlis*. The Iraqi law of May 27, 1946 (Article 9), augmented the number of Christian and Jewish deputies

from four to six for each community. Additionally, the two groups were represented in the appointive upper chamber by one senator each. The Jewish community shriveled in size from about 135,000 in 1949 to less than 15,000 in 1952. Accordingly, when Jewish Senator Ezra Menahem Daniel died in March, 1952, no successor was named. The six Jewish deputies later resigned, and in June the legislature approved an amendment to the 1946 statute, striking out the stipulation regarding Jewish representation in the lower chamber. The non-Muslim communities in Syria (Article 3, Electoral Law of September 10, 1949) and all communities—Muslim as well as non-Muslim—in Lebanon (Annex, Table 2, Electoral Law of August 10, 1950) were assured proportional representation in the respective unicameral legislatures.

In Jordan the king appointed the upper chamber or Council of Notables (Article 36, Constitution of 1952). The latest Electoral Law (enacted on April 5, 1947), which thus related only to the Chamber of Representatives, specified (Article 18) the number of Muslims—Arabs and Circassians separately —and Christians who were to be returned in each district. In preparation for the election of April, 1950, when Palestine Arabs participated for the first time, a supplementary law was adopted on December 13, 1949, applying the same principle to the new electoral districts on the west bank. The provision of the 1946 Constitution (Article 33), which declared that "due regard has to be given [in the Electoral Law] to the fair representation of minorities," did not appear in the 1952 instrument. Still there was little reason to assume that minority representation would not be explicitly guaranteed in any fresh electoral law, more especially since the number of Christian citizens had more than tripled (from 30,000 to about 100,000) with the annexation of Arab Palestine.

The 1923 Constitution (Article 78) and the 1935 Electoral Law (Article 55) of Egypt listed, among those eligible for the senate, the principal religious leaders of the non-Muslim com-

munities, and on occasion the crown appointed such individuals. Otherwise, neither the Electoral Law of Egypt nor those of Turkey and Israel made any special provision for minority representation. Still, Christians and Jews (other than clerics) were returned to both houses of the Egyptian legislature. Non-Muslims have sat in the unicameral Turkish *Meclis* since 1934, and in the elections of 1950 and 1954 all the major parties ran minority candidates. About 83 percent of the Arab segment of the Israel electorate—a somewhat higher percentage than in the Jewish community—took part in the election of July, 1951. Arab candidates appeared not only on three of their own tickets but on those of the Communist and Mapam (pro-Soviet) parties. The number of Arab deputies more than doubled, from three in the first *Kneset* to eight in the second.

From this brief factual summary, it might be inferred that the guarantees to the minorities—indeed, the assurances to all citizens of political and civil liberties, representative government, and equality of political, social, and legal rights—adequately meet the needs and that the governments concerned have effectively upheld these guarantees and have executed fairly the political arrangements as formulated in the several organic laws. Such inferences, however, are totally unwarranted.

All of the Near East countries under review have sought to establish nation-states on the Western pattern. But nation-states have emerged in the West only where earlier local community or district loyalties have given way to a larger common allegiance. Such a condition has never existed in the Near East. For this reason, a single community in each state has come to dominate the others—Turkish-speaking Sunnite Muslims in Turkey, Persian-speaking Shi'ite Muslims in Iran, Hebrew-speaking European Jews in Israel, and Sunnite Arabs in Egypt, Iraq, Jordan, and Syria. In Lebanon, the only exception, Maronite Christians and Sunnite Muslims have shared the favors between them. The state has, in the circumstances, become essentially the private agency of the privileged com-

munity. To its special interests the values and welfare of the minorities have been subordinated. The minorities have had either to conform to the nationalism of the dominant community—and thereby lose their group identities—or acquiesce in the status of second-class citizens or emigrate. If liberty and equality have not in fact been realized, it is clearly because there has been no real fraternity, no real community of interest.

The time-hardened pluralistic society of the Near East, it is clear, has provided uncongenial soil for transplanting Western political institutions. The separation of church and state in the Western democracies, the belief that religion is the personal concern of the individual, and the theory that the religious group is nothing more than a nonpolitical association are alien concepts to all Near Easterners, whether Muslim or non-Muslim, majority or minority. Near Easterners are captives of what would be regarded in the West as a conceptual ambiguity. They do not, and in fact within the region's social system cannot, distinguish between religion and nationality. It would be helpful to examine this question in its historical setting.

The Ottoman empire, as a Muslim state, adapted prevailing Islamic administrative practices to its purposes. The *Shari'ah*, or Muslim canon law, is inclusive, regulating political and social as well as religious matters, and is applicable to Muslims alone. The protected peoples or *ahl al-dhimmah* (the people of the covenant) who were also *ahl al-kitab* (the people of the Bible)—that is, Christians and Jews—were allowed from the very inception of Islam to manage their own internal community affairs. Islam accepted usages that had become firmly established in the ancient Near East, where differing ethnic groups, each with its private religion and often private language as well, were generally allowed full cultural freedom by whatever imperial regime governed the districts concerned. The practices survived in all the Islamic successor states of the 'Abbasid Caliphate. As the expanding Ottoman state annexed districts with non-Muslim population, the Christian and Jew-

ish communities were permitted to retain their traditional rights of confessional and cultural autonomy. Following the conquest of Constantinople in 1453, Sultan Mehmed II confirmed the autonomy of the Greek Orthodox, the Armenian Gregorian, and the Jewish communities throughout the realm. The very term *millet*, which was applied later to the recognized empire-wide Christian and Jewish communities, was the Turkish form of the Arabic *millah*, which meant "creed" and/or "people" (in the sense of a distinct ethnic group) and also, by the nineteenth century, came to mean "nation" and "nationality."

Until the second third of the nineteenth century, only three *millets* received formal recognition. By 1914 the number had multiplied to seventeen, among them all the principal Christian denominations in the empire. The *millet başı*, the chief of the community who was officially accredited to the Ottoman imperial government, maintained his residence in Istanbul and served as liaison between the community and the government. Each community was authorized to use its own language, to establish religious, cultural, and educational institutions, and to collect from its members the taxes levied by the imperial government. The juridical autonomy of the *millets* was substantial in disputes affecting members of the same community. The religious tribunals were at first competent to try all except cases relating to crime and public security; even these matters became the responsibility of the *millets*, as the imperial government weakened at the center in the seventeenth and eighteenth centuries. The jurisdiction of the religious courts, however, was restricted after 1856 to questions of personal status such as marriage, divorce, and inheritance. All other legal disputes had to be referred to the Ottoman mixed courts, which had come into being a few years earlier.

The autonomous administrations of the Christian and Jewish *millets*, like the Islamic government to which they owed their existence, thus exercised civil and religious authority. Or, to phrase it somewhat differently, if Islam was not only a religion

but a way of life, so too were Orthodox Judaism and the several branches of Oriental Christianity. Even the Protestant churches, whose membership comprised a handful of converts, chiefly from the Oriental Christian sects, were collectively recognized as a separate *millet* in 1850. Significantly, the Protestant *millet* itself was forced in a limited way to conform to the pattern of political and social organization that prevailed in the Ottoman empire. It might be added parenthetically that the laity acquired a voice in the administration of fiscal and civil affairs of almost all the *millets* from the mid-nineteenth century on, when the imperial government progressively authorized the formation of representative councils.

The partial secularization of the *millet* administrations reflected the growing influence of the European powers, which exploited, for their own political ends, the several *millets*. Each of the great powers, primarily motivated by the desire to establish claims to spheres of influence in anticipation of the ultimate partition of the Ottoman empire, placed one or more *millets* under its custody. Meanwhile many individual non-Muslim Ottoman subjects, particularly in the eighteenth century, had obtained for themselves and their heirs the same extraterritorial privileges accorded to foreign residents. While the further extension of these abuses was largely checked in the nineteenth century, European ideas of nationalism and the demand for full independence gained wide currency in the *millets*, especially those with main centers in southeastern Europe. The Asiatic provinces, however, were not entirely immune, as attested by the rise of the Armenian nationalist movement in Anatolia in the half-century preceding 1914. In the circumstances, the relationship between the dominant and the minority communities in the Ottoman empire gradually deteriorated.

Christians, Jews, and Parsis in Shi'ite Iran enjoyed religious autonomy comparable to, though not so clearly defined as, that of the *millets* in the Ottoman empire. The principles were not altered after World War I, although during the dictatorship

of Reza Shah the autonomy of the non-Muslim communities was as subject to arbitrary suspension as were the civil and political liberties of the favored community.

The *millet* system was retained in all the Ottoman successor states except Turkey. The United Kingdom in the period of the protectorate in Egypt (1914–1922) did not alter the established precedents, which were later guaranteed in the 1923 Constitution (Article 13). The continuance of the *millet* regime in Iraq was assured not only in the 1925 Constitution (Articles 13 and 16) but in special laws for each of the non-Muslim communities and in the declaration of May 30, 1932, to the League of Nations, which demanded a formal pledge for the protection of the minorities as one of the conditions for terminating the Mandate. Similar obligations were written into the Mandatory instruments for Syria (and Lebanon) and Palestine (and Transjordan). In Palestine and Lebanon, moreover, the Muslim communities acquired the status of *millets* in the Mandatory period.

Turkey officially dissolved the *millets* soon after the creation of the republic. Yet the *millet* mentality continued to control the relations between Muslims and non-Muslims. Despite the secularization of the government, Turkish-speaking Muslims remained the only citizens who, in practice, possessed full civil and political liberties. Non-Muslims were gradually weeded out of government service and, while conscripted into the army, were rarely issued arms or allowed to become commissioned officers. Such restrictions have been removed with the emergence of democracy in postwar Turkey. Yet the progressive restoration of religious freedom has been accompanied by the revival of an attenuated form of the *millet* system. Religious instruction was reintroduced in 1949 into all schools, including those of the minorities, in which the government pays the salaries of teachers of the Turkish language and culture. The non-Muslim communities were also permitted at that time to administer once again their public properties and to create for

the purpose lay councils, each authorized, with government approval, to select its principal clerical spokesman.

The Israel government, for its part, left unaltered the Mandatory regulations regarding the corporate rights of the Christian, Druze, and Sunnite communities. In the case of the last the government was at first handicapped by the almost total absence of *qadis, muftis,* and other religious functionaries who had fled Israel-held territory during the Palestine war. The training of new ecclesiastic officials has proceeded at snail's pace, despite the government's persistent efforts to fill the vacancies. For reasons of security, the exclusion of Christian and Sunnite Arabs from military service is likely to continue, at least until a formal Arab-Israel peace settlement is reached. But the Druze and Circassian units, which fought with Israel against the Arabs in 1948, still form part of the army. Thus Israel, which has achieved a greater degree of Westernization than Turkey and whose democratic institutions are more firmly implanted, conforms nevertheless to the Near East norm. Besides, Israel nationalism is Jewish nationalism, and though the dominant political parties are secular, as is the governmental machinery, Judaism permeates the national way of life. Unless Israel's Arabs are prepared to accept this way of life in full, they are destined to remain second-class citizens, as are the other minorities, for comparable reasons, in the nearby countries. But as a state with a highly developed sense of social responsibility, Israel has done, and will probably continue to do, much more than any of her Near East neighbors for all her citizens—whether non-Jews or Jews—in the realm of public health, social welfare, labor standards, and education. Yet even such a progressive social program in no way alters the fundamental fact that few, if any, of Israel's Arabs can identify themselves with the central function of the state as the instrument of Jewish national renaissance.

Insofar as the minorities are concerned, it is evident that the political concepts and conventions of Western democracy

have not yet been applied effectively in any of the Near East countries, not even in Turkey and Israel, where parliamentary government has become most securely rooted. The emergence of Israel was a special case, for its political dynamics derived largely from outside the Near East. But in all other states of the region, individuals from the minority communities played an important role in the movements that led to parliamentary government. At the planning stage democratic slogans were taken literally. The promise of representative institutions aroused for all people, majority and minority alike, the hope for an end to autocracy and for a voice in the determination of governmental policy. But no sooner were the constitutions written and the parliaments formed than the minorities were squeezed out and the governments transformed into the private agencies of the elite communities. To this development, the persistence of the *millet* mentality and traditions contributed substantially.

Here are a few illustrations. An Armenian, Malkom Khan, quondam Iranian minister to the United Kingdom, began publishing in London in 1890 a Persian-language periodical, *Qanun*, which was strongly Islamic in tone and advocated representative government for his native land. Malkom Khan was closely associated in the enterprise with Jamal-al-Din al-Afghani, who indefatigably pleaded the same cause for all Muslim lands. Also allied with al-Afghani and his Egyptian disciple, Muhammad 'Abduh, was an Egyptian Jew, Ya'qub Sanu'a, who established himself in Paris in 1877. Exiled from his native land by Khedive Isma'il for outspoken criticism of the regime, Sanu'a was barred from returning after the British occupation because of his endorsement of 'Arabi and the Egyptian nationalists. Arab army officers participated in the secret Committee of Union and Progress prior to its bloodless *coup d'état* of 1908. Yusuf Pasha Qattawi, an Egyptian Jew, became Minister of Finance and later of Communications in 1924–1925. Sasun Hisqayl, an Iraqi Jew, held the finance post at Baghdad several times in the mid-1920's. In fact, King Faysal

in 1921 had named Hisqayl to a committee of three which negotiated with the British in the drafting of the Iraqi constitution.

Soon after the Committee of Union and Progress came to power, non-Turks were prevented from enjoying the fruits of office. Even in the period of the republic, Armenians who became Turkish-speaking Muslims were not admitted to full-fledged membership in the dominant community. Long before independence was won in Iraq and Egypt and, in fact, before the Zionist question became a general Arab issue, Jews were debarred from cabinet posts. Kurds who accepted ministerial appointments in Iraqi governments were often mistrusted by their own community, where the spirit of nationalism and the hope of eventual independence have not flagged since the end of World War I. The Coptic community in Egypt never developed a movement for political separatism, although it has remained as jealous of its statutory and traditional prerogatives as of its religious identity. Although Copts, under the monarchy, sat in every cabinet, they hardly spoke for their fellow Copts. Makram 'Ubayd and Wasif Butrus Ghali, among the most successful Coptic politicians, were inclined in their political behavior to act more Muslim than their Muslim colleagues. Indeed, as a rule, minority deputies in the legislatures of most Near East countries have rarely represented the interests of their respective communities. In Lebanon, it might be added, the mixed membership of the political parties had little practical significance, since all the religious communities were guaranteed proportional representation.

The successful operation "of representative government requires that the population concerned should be sufficiently homogeneous," noted the Palestine Royal Commission in 1937. "Unless there is common ground enough between . . . [the] different groups or classes to enable the minority to acquiesce in the rule of the majority and to make it possible for the balance of power to readjust itself from time to time, the work-

[219]

ing basis of parliamentary government or democracy as we understand it is not there." Admittedly, Palestine presented an extreme case. Yet, the commission's observation might have been made with almost equal relevance on the Near East as a whole. In a *millet*-ridden society there is little or no mobility on the political plane not only between privileged and subordinated groups but even between one subordinated religious community and the next.

The *millet* mentality does not explain all aspects of the problem of the majority-minority political relationship in the Near East. Economic factors have conduced to the disabilities imposed on the minorities. In the past, Christians and Jews often constituted virtually the entire middle class of Muslim countries. In such cases as Egypt or the Mandated territories, where Britain and France governed for varying periods, the European powers tended to employ the minorities in numbers far larger than their relative proportion of the total population, primarily because they were literate, knew or could easily learn French or English, and possessed the necessary skills. Lebanese and Syrian Christians fell into this category in the opening years of the British occupation of Egypt. Though Arabs, they are still heartily disliked as a class by the Egyptian Muslims. Once independent, the governments, giving vent to a dual resentment, tended to root the minorities out of civil service posts and, as in Turkey, to eliminate them from commerce as well. As regards the Jewish communities in the Arab East, the question of Zionism and, later, Israel merely added another complicating and virulent irritant.

Many other subjects, relevant to the problem under review, would have to be taken into account in any exhaustive analysis. It would be useful, for example, to know to what extent the development in the Near East is unique and to what extent it resembles developments in other areas. A comparative evaluation of the parliamentary experiments in the Near East with those in the pre-Sovietized Balkans or in Latin America, or in

both, would therefore be enlightening. Moreover, even as regards the Near East, the legislation on citizenship, nationality, and—where it exists—the status and rights of the minority communities would have to be as thoroughly canvassed as the constitutions and electoral laws. So, too, would the application of the laws have to be examined. The political relations between the elite community and the minorities differ from land to land considerably more than it has been possible to indicate in so brief a study, and the particular manifestations in any country at any given time have resulted in no small measure from economic, social, political, and security conditions peculiar to that country. Besides, the subject matter is highly diffuse and does not lend itself to easy organization in a summary review. These facts are mentioned merely to stress the exploratory character of the present essay.

The Immigrant in Israel

THE Near East in general has been an area of emigration, directed almost exclusively to overseas countries, mostly to the American continent. Immigration to the Near East, on the other hand, has been confined, with the exception of a few overseas arrivals and a certain number of returning re-immigrants (from America to the Lebanon [1] and from the East Indies to southern Arabia), to the absorption of refugees from nearby countries and territories.

After the Greco-Turkish war of 1918–1922 an agreement was entered into by the two countries with regard to exchange of populations. By 1928, 1,220,000 Greeks from Turkey were resettled in Greece, and by 1946 Turkey had absorbed 860,000 Turks from Greece and other Balkan countries.[2] The immigration of Turks from Bulgaria has continued through subsequent years. In 1950 about 53,000 Turks entered Turkey from Bulgaria, and by mid-January, 1951, 58,000 more had immigration visas.[3] Between 1933 and 1936 some 12,000 Assyrians, mainly

---

[1] Averaging annually 2,700 from 1931 to 1933 (S. B. Himadeh, ed., *Economic Organization of Syria* [Beirut, 1936], pp. 13–20).

[2] *Greek Census of 1928* and *Nufus Hareketleri* (Ankara, 1948).

[3] *New York Times*, April 15, 1951; United Nations, *Migration Bulletin* No. 23, p. 55.

refugees from Turkey, were settled in the Jezira district of Syria under a League of Nations scheme. In earlier years several thousands of Assyrian refugees entered Iraq.

All of these immigrants had one major characteristic in common: they were Near Eastern peoples sharing largely the religions, languages, or cultures of the countries which admitted them. Their arrival, therefore, did not bring an ethnically or culturally new and alien element into the area. They were, of course, inevitably faced with economic difficulties and hardships of adjustment, but their settlement did not create any appreciable cultural tension in the immediate neighborhood where they settled, nor was their presence felt as a new cultural factor in the area as a whole. As far as cultural effects are concerned, the recent appearance and temporary or permanent sojourn of Arab refugees from Palestine in the neighboring countries, fall into the same category.

The Jewish immigration to Palestine and Israel is of a completely different character. From its very onset, in the year 1882, it brought into the Ottoman empire a population element with a European cultural and social equipment and nationalistic ideas. Within half a century the European Jewish immigrants built in Palestine a socioeconomic structure of their own, as well as a cultural edifice, both of which were largely European in character. This is one of the basic factors of which due account must be taken when an attempt is made to discern the major trends in the recent sociocultural situation in Israel.

During the sixty-five years of the Zionist movement preceding the establishment of Israel, almost nine-tenths of the immigrants to Palestine came from Europe, mainly from eastern and central Europe. The remainder came mostly from the countries of the Near East and North Africa. After the independence of Israel the ethnic composition of the immigration changed considerably.

It will be more convenient, for analytical purposes, to deal with the Jewish immigration to Palestine first and then to

turn our attention to the immigration to Israel. The first two immigratory waves (from 1882 to 1903 and from 1904 to 1913, respectively) can be disregarded here because they were small numerically (only 65,000 in the course of thirty-two years), because they absorbed relatively much from the traditional Oriental culture of Palestine and imparted to it little, and because much of what they succeeded in establishing in Palestine was lost in the years of World War I, when the Turkish authorities exiled to Damascus and other places a major part of the Jewish inhabitants.

From the end of World War I to the end of World War II, a total of 395,683 Jewish immigrants came to Palestine. Of these, 377,535 were immigrants registered with the British Mandatory authorities, and 18,148 were illegal immigrants. Of the former, 335,066 were registered also by the offices of the Jewish Agency for Palestine in Jerusalem, and consequently more particulars are known about them. Of these, 86 percent were Ashkenazi Jews from Europe, 6.5 percent were Sephardi Jews from Italy, the Balkans and Turkey, and 6.4 percent were Oriental Jews from the Near East and North Africa, mainly from the Yemen (4.4 percent of the total).

Again, of the total number of immigrants—taking earners and dependents together—almost 23 percent were "capitalists," people with limited but sufficient means to establish business enterprises in the country. For a number of years the minimum amount required from an immigrant family to qualify for a special immigration visa as a capitalist was one thousand Palestinian pounds. Most of these so-called capitalists invested their limited capital in small business enterprises in which they were able to make a living only because they invested in them their own labor as well. More than 47 percent of the total were laborers, and almost 19 percent were dependents of residents in Palestine.

It was the very high percentage of capitalists and laborers together which determined the socioeconomic structure of Jew-

ish Palestine. The numerical relationship between the two groups was fortunate: for every two laborers one capitalist immigrated, thus creating a steady demand for working hands. One of the most significant differences between the traditional Near Eastern social structure and that of the modern West is the absence in the Near East of anything comparable to the solidly entrenched and numerically significant middle class which is characteristic of advanced Western countries. With the immigration of about 84,000 small capitalists (including their dependents) a middle class on the European model came into being in Jewish Palestine, sharply differentiating the entire social structure of the Jewish sector of the country from that of the Arab sector, as well as from that of other Arab states.

The influx of capital, together with the immigration of large numbers of mostly young working people, tended to induce the developing economy of Jewish Palestine to base itself on industry on a scale approximating that of western Europe. Taking the total number of earners (125,000) who immigrated from 1919 to 1945 as a basis, one finds that according to their occupations abroad prior to immigration, 33.4 percent were workers in industry and handicrafts, 13.6 percent were unskilled laborers, 6.6 percent worked in building and construction, and 1.2 percent in transport and communications. The occupational structure of the immigrants thus closely resembled that which characterizes western Europe and the United States and differed widely from the typical Near Eastern occupational pattern.

A comparison with a small west European country and the only two Near Eastern countries (Turkey and Egypt) from which commensurate data are available points up the pronouncedly Western character of the occupational structure of this immigrant group. Additional data referring to the occupational structure of the three major religious communities in Palestine in 1931—the very middle of the 1919–1945 period —show that, while the Palestinian Muslims closely approximated the Turkish and Egyptian figures, the Palestinian Chris-

tians and the Palestinian Jews manifested an occupational structure similar to that of the Jewish immigrant pattern. As could be expected, an immigrant population with such an occupational structure tended to settle in towns rather than in rural areas. This resulted in a duplication of Western settlement pattern in Jewish Palestine. In a typical Western country the majority of the population lives in cities and towns; in a typical Near Eastern country the majority is rural.

Occupational structure and a settlement pattern gravitating toward the towns were, of course, not the only characteristics brought along by the immigrants from Europe to Palestine. They brought along, in addition, something which was less amenable to change: a set of demographical traits which testified to the extent of their assimilation, country by country, to the east and central European urban middle-class population of which they had formed an integral part for two or three generations.

The typical Near Eastern demographical traits have been in the main a very high birth rate (between 40 and 45 births annually per thousand of population), a very high death rate (30 to 35), and a very high infant mortality rate (100 to 350 per thousand of live births within one year).[4] Up to about 1930, the Palestinian Muslim population conformed to this general pattern. From that year on significant changes set in. Its birth rate, always higher than the Near Eastern average, increased and became one of the highest in the world, averaging 54 in 1944 and 1945; its death rate showed a marked decrease, reaching 17 in 1944 and 1945; and its infant mortality rate, too, was considerably reduced, to less than 100 in 1944–1945. Natural increase rose correspondingly from 23.27 in 1922–1925 to 37.88 in 1945. These improvements were largely due to the health

---

[4] United Nations, Department of Social Affairs, *World Population Trends 1920–1947* (December, 1949); United Nations, *Demographic Yearbook 1949–50* (New York, 1950); Royal Institute of International Affairs, *The Middle East* (London, 1950); *United Nations Social Welfare Seminar* (Cairo, 1950).

services established and maintained by the British Mandatory government of Palestine.

Into the still typically Near Eastern demographic pattern of Muslim Palestine of the 1920's and early 1930's, the Jewish immigrants brought their European low birth rate (averaging about twenty-eight from 1922 to 1945), their low European death rate (which continued to decrease in Palestine from an average of thirteen in 1922–1929 to an average of less than seven in 1943–1947, in part undoubtedly as a result of the younger age of the average immigrant), and their low European infant mortality rate (also decreasing from one hundred forty-four in 1922 to about thirty in 1946–1947). The maintenance and trend of this demographic record, in a country where health conditions were far from satisfactory, demanded a great and sustained effort manifested in the establishment of hospitals, maternity and other clinics, health services, and above all a form of semisocialized medicine, the Sick Fund (*Quppat Holim*) of the General Federation of Jewish Labor in Palestine, to which in the later years about half of the total Jewish population belonged.

The Western character of the society built by the Jewish immigrants in Palestine in the Mandatory period could further be demonstrated by adducing data as to expectation of life, marriage and divorce rates, income level, food consumption, clothing and housing standards, newsprint consumption, communication, social services, and the several forms of cultural production and cultural consumption. Such a detailed analysis of various aspects of the life form created by the Jewish immigrants in Palestine would, however, be too lengthy and it would not materially add to the conclusions deducible from the foregoing brief analysis of occupational structure, rural-urban distribution, and basic demographical data. These conclusions can best be summed up by stating that the Jewish immigrants to Palestine established there a life form which in its technological and organizational aspects was a transplant from Europe.

The new elements which gave Palestinian Jewish life its spe-cific flavor as compared with Jewish life in Europe lay in the ideological and intellectual fields, which, in their turn, could not fail to influence occupational structure and social forms. Thus agricultural labor was upheld as an ideal, and this resulted in the development of several new forms of collective and co-operative villages. The insistence on making Hebrew the lan-guage of the Jews of Palestine resulted in the creation of a new literature and the specific development of all those aspects of culture of which language is the vehicle. However, what mostly distinguished the Jewish immigrant in Palestine from his Arab neighbor were not these factors, but the differences in standard of living, in economic and social structuring, and other traits and complexes which were transplanted in almost unchanged form from Europe. The maintenance of these differ-ences in the years following the transplanting was partly the result of the continual inflowing of capital and of the institu-tionalized aid of world Jewry. The difference between the life, the culture, and the society of the Arab and the Jewish sectors in Palestine was, therefore, essentially the same as the difference between the life, culture, and society of any traditional Near Eastern country and those of any modern Western country.

The entrenchment of this Western-type society and culture in Palestine had been largely achieved when independence was gained in 1948. Following the oft-voiced demand for the open-ing of the gates of Palestine to all Jews, the Israeli government announced an open-door policy for all Jewish immigrants. Had the immigrants, who thereupon began to arrive in unprece-dented numbers, been of the same or similar character as those who had come up to 1947, the hardships of the first few years of Israel's existence might have been considerably mitigated. The Western-type life established in the country by the im-migrants who had come from the West might then have con-tinued to receive reinforcements from the same quarters.

But the postindependence immigration was profoundly dif-

ferent in many respects. First of all, the ethnic composition of the immigrants changed rapidly. Up to 1947 (inclusive), only a small proportion of the immigrants came from the Near East and North Africa. Out of a total of 434,992 immigrants from 1919 to 1947, the countries of birth of 358,641 were known. Of these, 312,306, or 84.4 percent, were of Ashkenazi origin, while only 46,335, or 15.6 percent, came from the Near East, North Africa, the Balkans, and Italy and were of Sephardi or Oriental Jewish origin.

After the establishment of Israel, when the gates of the new state were thrown open to immigration, the east European Jewish population was found to be closed in behind the iron curtain; the central European Jewish remnant turned out to be insignificant numerically; and the Jewish communities of western Europe, the Anglo-Saxon countries, and other overseas lands showed no inclination to immigrate to Israel in considerable numbers. The position of the one million or so Jews in the Muslim world had deteriorated in the meantime. Especially in the Arab countries, every Jew was suspected of Zionist sympathies. In view of the state of belligerency existing between these countries and Israel, to have Zionist leanings meant high treason. Therefore, the Jewish population of countries such as Syria, Iraq, the Yemen, and Egypt were natural candidates for immigration to Israel. Their mass transfer to Israel, either directly and openly, or in a roundabout and covert way, was agreed upon by the aforementioned countries one after the other.

The political leadership of Israel, however, felt that the country needed more man power than was forthcoming from all these reservoirs of immigration. Only a small amount of persuasion was required to set into motion a powerful immigratory current from Libya, Tunisia, Algeria, and Morocco, as well as from Iran and Turkey, since the news of the re-establishment of an independent Israel was received by the Jews of these countries in the nature of messianic tidings. At the same time, the Sephardi Jews of the Balkan states were also enabled to emi-

grate, so that practically the entire Jewish population of Greece, Yugoslavia, Bulgaria, and Albania moved to Israel. All this meant a rapid and very considerable increase in the Oriental and semi-Oriental (Sephardi) element among the Jewish immigrants to Israel.

In the four years 1948–1951, more than 700,000 Jewish immigrants came to Israel. Of these, the countries of birth of about 680,000 are known: 375,000, or 55 percent, were Sephardi and Oriental Jews, and 305,000, or about 45 percent, were Ashkenazi Jews. The proportion of the Sephardi and Oriental element among the immigrants increased sharply in the course of these four years from 32.8 percent in 1948 to 71 percent in 1951.

As a result of this increase in the proportion of Sephardi and Oriental Jews among the immigrants, the total number of this population element in relation to the entire Jewish population of Israel showed a marked rise. From 1936 to 1947 the Sephardi and Oriental Jews constituted from 20 to 23 percent of the Jewish population of Palestine. By 1951 this figure climbed up to 40 percent, and it still continues to rise.

The numerical ascendance of the Sephardi and Oriental Jewish element in the Jewish population of Israel is due not only to its increased share in the immigration, but also to another circumstance which in the long run will have a more lasting effect. The Oriental Jews have shared with the other Near Eastern peoples the demographical traits of high birth rate and high death rate. After their immigration to Israel, however, the medical and health services put at their disposal cut down immediately their death rate, and within a year also their infant mortality rate, without a corresponding decrease in the birth rate. The result of this demographical imbalance was a sharp upward climb in the rate of natural increase among the Oriental Jews in Israel. It can be foreseen that it will take at least one generation until such ideas as family planning can be inculcated in these communities and that in the meantime they will continue to evince an extraordinarily high rate of

natural increase. This prediction can be based, among other things, on experience with the Palestinian Muslim population during the last years of the British Mandatory regime. It can also be substantiated by a reference to a study, carried out among the Jews of Jerusalem, which demonstrated the pronounced tendency of each immigrant group to retain, for many years after its immigration to Palestine, the birth rate which characterized it in the country from which it came.

It can therefore be foreseen that, even though the large-scale immigration to Israel and the influx of Oriental Jews seemed to have come to an end by 1952, the latter will continue to gain numerically out of sheer demographic inertia and will constitute a significant majority in the country before a diminishing birth rate levels off their natural increase.

The occupational structure of the immigrants who have come to Israel since the independence shows considerable disparity with that of the immigrants during the Mandatory period. The most significant difference between the two immigrations is the marked decrease in the percentage of the gainfully occupied (or economically active) population in relation to the total number of immigrants. In the 1919–1945 period, of a total of 394,683 immigrants, 125,019, or 31.6 percent, were economically active abroad prior to their immigration, which means that the number of dependents per earner was somewhat more than two. In the years 1949 to 1951, of a total of 582,447 immigrants to Israel, only 138,223, or 23.7 percent, were economically active prior to their immigration—that is, each earner had an average of more than three dependents.

Significant changes can be observed also in the percentages of the various occupations among those gainfully employed prior to their immigration. Compared with the corresponding figures in Mandatory times, one notes first of all a decrease in those engaged in agricultural pursuits by more than two-thirds. The average of those engaged in industry and construction in the three years 1949–1951 is somewhat lower than the 1919–1945

figure, and, in addition, one suspects that the proportion of unskilled laborers must have been considerably higher in 1949–1951. The increase in transport and communications workers is due to the fact that many Oriental Jewish immigrants gave porterage as their occupation abroad, which was included under this heading. Persons engaged in public administration and professions also show a decrease, which, coupled with the generally much lower percentage of the economically active sector, was sufficient to create an acute shortage in professionally skilled people, such as doctors, teachers, and technicians. The increase in the category of domestic and personal service and clerical work was due to the relatively large number of people who returned clerical work as their occupation.

The sudden influx of such a great number of immigrants in itself, quite apart from their social and cultural characteristics, has resulted in a number of very significant changes in the ethos of the population as a whole. Coupled with the achievement of independence, it brought about a shift in the focal orientations as compared with the Mandatory period. Agriculture had occupied a focal position in the culture of the Jewish community in Mandatory Palestine. To be a pioneer, a member of a group setting up a new agricultural settlement, and to live and work in such a settlement, especially in one of the collective or co-operative types, were high social ideals. In Israel, in the turmoil of the Arab-Jewish war and its aftermath, amidst the economic difficulties of absorbing hundreds of thousands of immigrants and more than doubling within four short years the total population of the country, this ideal was lost. Agriculture for the average Israeli today, whether of old vintage in the country or a new immigrant, means a toilsome necessity, into which the new immigrants have to be channeled by means of direct economic and administrative pressure.

Yet with all the means at the disposal of the government of Israel to exert such a pressure, the percentage of those taking up agriculture has been smaller since the establishment of the

state than it had been during the Mandatory period when it was a matter of voluntary decision. The great majority of the new agricultural settlements—no longer of the radical collective type but rather based on a limited co-operation—has been established during the last four years by new immigrants from the Oriental countries, first of all from the Yemen and in the second place from North Africa. Since agriculture has lost the idealistic status and prestige it had in Mandatory days, a certain danger is present that the increasing percentage of Oriental Jews in the agricultural sector will come to be regarded by the urban population with something resembling the well-known contempt Near Eastern townspeople generally harbor for the fellaheen.

The place of agriculture as a national ideal is taken by the new ideal of statehood. The emphasis on statehood and independence is paramount, and no sacrifice is deemed too great if it serves the purpose of strengthening the state. Therefore, in spite of the sharp disagreements among the political parties with their differential orientations toward the extreme right, moderate right, secular or religious center, moderate left, and extreme left, there was never anything but complete harmony on the basic issue of immigration. The great economic hardship to the country brought about by the multitudes of penniless and destitute immigrants was clear, or has rapidly become so, to the electorate, which twice since the independence has gone to the polls to send its 120 representatives to the Kneset. Yet the question of limitation on immigration has never even arisen.

Similarly, despite the acute food shortage, there has been little grumbling over the government's policy of expending the major part of its unearned dollar income (such as loans from the United States and especially the considerable sums put at its disposal by the United Jewish Appeal in America) not on food supplies which could momentarily alleviate the situation, but on capital investment, machinery, and other equipment

[233]

which was more important from the point of view of national economy but the effect of which would be felt only in the long run. The conviction that the needs of the state as a whole come before the requirements of its individual citizens, even before the combined individual interests of the great majority of its citizens, is to this day the motive force behind much that is happening in Israel.

It is to this kind of somewhat rugged existence, in which life has been stripped of much that is additional to the barest necessities and which is actuated by an idea not yet wholly comprehensible to him, that the new immigrant must make his adjustment. In the case of the immigrants coming from Europe the change required to make a successful adjustment is merely social; in the case of the Oriental immigrant it is cultural as well. The European immigrant is faced with the necessity of learning a new language, Hebrew. He also must learn a new trade in order to be able to make a living, and in most cases a trade which by the old European scale of values is of a lower type than the one in which he or his father before him was engaged. In his business dealings he has to adjust to a special type of economy which is essentially a combination of socialistic and capitalistic practices. However, while the precise form that the way of life takes in Israel is new to him, he is familiar with each of its elements from his European background, and thus he soon recognizes Israeli culture as merely a new mutation of several of the factors which formed his old social and technological environment in Europe.

Difficult as it is to weather the stress of this *social change* required from the immigrant from Europe, the strain under which the Oriental Jewish immigrant labors until he accomplishes the *cultural change* demanded from him is greater still. He, too, has to undergo social changes which frequently are even farther-reaching than those faced by his European co-immigrant. But, in addition, he has to find his place in a culture many of whose main features were completely unknown to him before

his arrival in Israel. For a group of immigrants like the Moroccan and Iraqi Jews, and even more so for the Yemenite Jews, to adjust to Israeli life means to enter, and to learn to participate in, a culture different from the one in which they were brought up and in which they had learned to move.

The cultural changes, to the stresses of which the Oriental Jewish immigrants become exposed as soon as they land in Israel, extend into practically all aspects of life. They have to familiarize themselves with a new technology; circumstances often force them to abandon their old accustomed forms of social organization, such as the extended family and the religious community, and to pattern their social life after the dominant European model. The value of highly prized old cultural specializations such as arts and crafts, folk music, religious vocations, and the like are suddenly questioned. Cherished personality traits such as religious faith, contentment, and detachment become discolored when viewed in the new Israeli frame of reference and often appear instead as superstition, indolence, and apathy. As in other countries of the Near East and North Africa where certain groups of the indigenous population have been exposed too suddenly and too intensely to culture contact with Europeans, so in Israel many of the Oriental Jewish immigrants, especially the younger people, are ready to discard their old cultural content long before they are able to absorb anything but the outermost shell of the European forms of civilization. In such cases, the possibility of superficial and culturally pernicious Levantinization becomes an acute danger.

Thus the road the immigrant has to travel in Israel is by no means an easy one. Nor is it easy for the young state to absorb economically, socially, and culturally an immigrant mass which is more numerous than the older inhabitants, who themselves consist of an immigrant majority of but a little older standing. Nevertheless, there are signs that the venture is succeeding. The first signs of certain economic and technological improvements in the circumstances of the immigrants are already visible. The

[235]

reception camps have been emptied; housing conditions in the Work Villages, Transit Villages, and other settlements hastily constructed for the absorption of immigrants are being improved. With the increase of acreage under cultivation and the regulation of food imports, the nutritional situation, too, shows promise of betterment. The schools, attendance in which is compulsory for eight years, and the army, in which every person has to serve upon reaching his eighteenth year (men for 30 months, women for 24), are potent factors in the cultural absorption of the younger element among the immigrants and in welding them together into one people. The social and health services and recreational facilities of the widely ramified institutional network of the *Histadruth*, the Israel Labor Federation, are available to every member, and for the last few years over two-thirds of Israel's wage earners have been members. The increasing participation of the immigrants in these and other institutions, whether compulsory like the schools and the army or voluntary like the *Histadruth*, has created a growing community of interests and a feeling of belonging together which is the basis of national unity.

In the wider cultural context of Near Eastern developments, the successful absorption of Oriental Jewish immigrants into the Western-type cultural edifice of Israel will be of particular interest and significance. If the experiment succeeds in Israel, and especially if certain cultural traits brought along by the Oriental Jews from their traditional environments are retained while they assimilate Western cultural values, then the peoples of the Near East will be able to regard this as a small-scale demonstration of the compatability of the two cultural archetypes of the East and the West and will be more confident in the practicability of both retaining their highly treasured cultural values and absorbing the achievements of the modern West.

The Palestine Arab Refugee

THERE is no need to restate the importance of the Arab refugee problem in the Middle East. It has become one of the most persistently handicapping features of the region. Woven into it are almost all of the social forces that retard the establishment of peace and progress there. It threatens to become a permanent feature of the political landscape. It is imperative that strong efforts now be directed toward a study of it which aims at its solution. The purpose of such a study is to uncover whatever factors may be found which might lead to a successful attack upon it. No purpose could be filled by debating why the problem arose, nor the rights and wrongs involved. All situations which produce refugees, and there have been refugees since the beginning of history, inevitably include wrongs and tragedies which all men of good will deplore. As has often been said, the only "solution" for a refugee problem is to prevent it from arising.

Thus the concern here is with the future, and with the hope that by studying this great human tragedy a way toward a lasting settlement may be found—a settlement that will bring satisfaction to the hundreds of thousands of unhappy people in the refugee camps of the Middle East. It may be surmised

that, if and when a solution is found for this problem, it will contain ingredients helpful to the solution of many other problems, social and political, in the Middle East.

A note of caution should be sounded. To list the serious handicaps which prevent a complete presentation of all relevant data would require a book. However, some of the more important should be mentioned. Although official United Nations figures are used in this paper, they cannot be wholly relied upon since accurate statistics in regard to the refugees do not exist. Generalizations concerning attitudes and opinions, even though based upon personal observations or press reports, cannot claim accuracy. There has been no *The Governing of Men* written about the Arab refugee. As any community disintegrates, opinions and values change. The stresses placed upon individuals in the refugee camps and on systems of belief and social organizations have not yet taken their final tolls. Official sources of information are suspect to the objective observer. Field experience if it is recent provides a point of view of great value, but even it cannot claim to give a complete picture. Accordingly, all that follows must be viewed as the statement of only one observer whose claims fall far short of omniscience.

A brief outline of the efforts of the United Nations on behalf of the refugees is in order. Starting in September, 1948, the international organization created a short-lived Disaster Relief Operation dedicated to the immediate relief of the estimated 200,000 refugees who had, it was then believed, temporarily fled from their homes. As the numbers of homeless swelled by the hundreds of thousands, the United Nations established the United Nations Relief for Palestine Refugees (U.N.R.P.R.) for a period of nine months, or until the next harvest. U.N.R.P.R. began its work on January 1, 1949, and, with two extensions, continued until May 1, 1950. An interesting feature of this organization was its use of three nongovernmental relief agencies as its operating arms. These three agencies, the International Committee of the Red Cross, the League of Red

Cross Societies, and the American Friends Service Committee (Quakers), spending governmental funds, had practical field autonomy in their distinct geographical areas. The policy which guided the United Nations in these first stages was one which viewed the refugee problem as a temporary one awaiting only the early solution of military or political issues.

As the unfolding years proved this to be wishful thinking and experience emphasized the sterility of a program of direct relief, U.N.R.P.R. was terminated and a new agency was created, the United Nations Relief and Works Agency for Palestine Refugees in the Near East (U.N.R.W.A.). Under this agency, which is the one currently (April, 1955) administering the program, emphasis was to be switched from direct relief to work relief schemes which, in turn, were to be superseded by reintegration projects. The latter projects were to be designed to take people off the relief rolls and enable the refugee to establish himself and support his family. It may be said that "reintegration" was used, rather than the word "resettlement," because of the emotional and political handicaps inherent in the second word! Attempting to avoid all political connotations of what is actually its major assignment, the agency is still engaged in efforts which it hopes will lead to the decline of its relief rolls and a corresponding increase of families settled in new locations in the host countries and with new means of earning livings.

From the very beginning the official policy of the Arab governments has been to insist on both the right and necessity of repatriation for the refugees. Toward this goal, they have succeeded in having the General Assembly of the United Nations pass resolutions which place that organization on record as favoring the return of the refugees to their lands and homes, occupied by Israel since 1948. To the Arab governments, the "fact" of Israel must yet be proved. They allege it to be a totally artificial community kept alive in an oxygen tent since birth. They will not admit that it exists. They cannot admit this since

DISTRIBUTION OF ARAB REFUGEES—DECEMBER, 1953 *

Country & Area	No. of Camps	In Tents	In Barracks	Outside Camps	Total
Lebanon					
Beirut	1	401	—	15,543	15,944
Mountain	5	6,648	673	11,312	18,633
Sidon	2	10,315	—	13,880	24,195
Tyre	2	2,045	2,744	17,201	21,990
Tripoli	2	6,246	531	4,512	11,289
Biqa'	3	—	7,159	1,732	8,891
Total	15	25,655	11,107	64,180	100,942
Syria					
Damascus	3	1,145	5,774	40,315	47,234
North	4	24	5,700	4,093	9,817
Homs & Hama	2	—	3,850	3,538	7,388
'South	2	1,279	568	18,896	20,743
Total	11	2,448	15,892	66,842	85,182
Jordan					
Amman	2	8,149	5,558	61,988	75,695
Irbid	1	3,431	—	29,666	33,097
Nablus	7	18,344	10,549	90,711	119,604
Jericho	5	16,044	57,976	8,647	82,667
Jerusalem	4	5,449	5,350	49,160	59,959
Hebron	2	10,574	—	44,242	54,816
Ramallah	4	8,640	2,135	42,630	53,405
Total	25	70,631	81,568	327,044	479,243
Gaza					
Deir el Balah	2	—	10,395	14,376	24,771
Khan Yunis village ..	1	—	12,099	14,930	27,029
Nuseirat	2	—	25,250	643	25,893
Rafah	1	—	25,220	1,561	26,781
Rimal	2	3,597	13,533	16,846	33,976
Khan Yunis beduins .	—	—	—	32,971	32,971
Zaitun	1	—	3,390	34,418	37,808
Total	9	3,597	89,887	115,745	209,229
Grand total	60	102,331	198,454	573,811	874,596

* These figures were charted especially for this article by the U.N.R.W.A. office at Headquarters, Beirut, Lebanon.

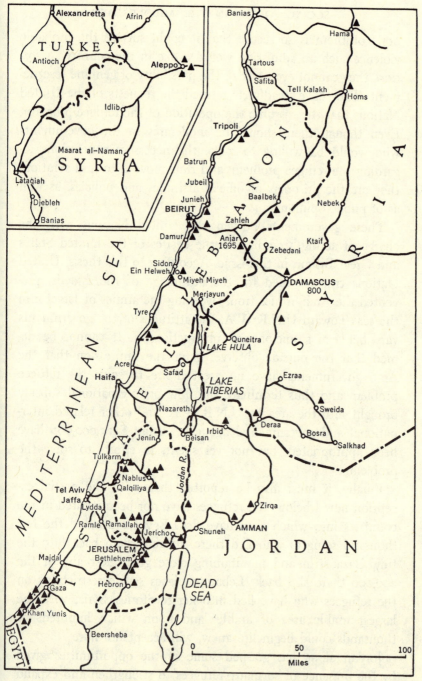

Map IV. Location of Arab Refugee Camps

none of them is so secure that it could survive the probable violence such an admission would evoke in the country. A *fortiori*, they cannot even talk of the possibility of genuine resettlement. They have steadfastly refused the requests of the United Nations that they assume the operation of the refugee program. Even though there should be moderates in the governments who would be willing to make the necessary concessions regarding the refugee problem, and thus move it toward solution, they are the prisoners of official attitudes and policies, as well as of public opinion.

These governments burden the United Nations with the charge of acting according to the desires of the United States and Great Britain in this issue. According to this thesis, United Nations truces, timed for the advantage of the Israelis, prevented the Arab armies from sweeping the armies of Israel into the sea. Toward U.N.R.W.A. the attitudes of the governments vary between suspicion and obstructionism. It cannot be denied that the outside observer gains the impression that the Arab governments have no great desire to solve the refugee problem and thus terminate the flow of international subsidy brought into the area by U.N.R.W.A. and other related international and governmental agencies. About $425,000,000 have been appropriated, but not yet spent, in efforts to solve the problem.

Finally, it must also be reported that, with the partial exception noted below, the refugees have not been wanted in the countries into which they have fled. Egypt evacuated the few thousand refugees who fled there, turning them back into the tiny Gaza strip and maintaining close guard lest any of the 200,000 there slip back. Lebanon places severe restrictions on the refugees who have fled into her territories. Syria, with the largest usable area of arable land upon which hundreds of thousands could begin life anew, will accept no more.

Jordan alone has grasped some of the opportunities given by the presence of so many refugees to strengthen and expand

her national life. While still holding to the official policy of the Arab states regarding repatriation back into Israel, this tiny desert kingdom, nevertheless, has granted citizenship (reluctantly accepted in many cases) to her 480,000 refugees and thus doubled her population. She has also evidenced a willingness to explore ways and means of establishing resettlement projects, which no other Arab state has yet done. Even where Jordan's attitude has been uniquely co-operative, her many difficulties, however, illustrate the problems which must be solved throughout the Middle East if the refugee issue is ever to be settled.

Jordan is plagued by lack of administrative strength and experience in her governmental organization as well as by the highly personalized nature of her politics. Her economic position is thoroughly dependent upon British annual subsidy and the United Nations imports for relief to the refugees. She insists, rightly, upon proof that a refugee family is self-supporting before it is taken off the rolls of international relief. But to make refugee families self-supporting by any minimal standard, when most of the indigenous population is so far from this goal, would mean a total economic revolution in the country. Yet another obstacle is the fact that although central governmental officials may be found most co-operative while discussing a scheme, the reverse may be true of local officials on the spot.

Where this government has allowed private schemes aimed at settling refugees in new agricultural settlements to get started, other familiar Middle Eastern problems have frequently arisen. The landlord may demand too high a price for the use of his land. Sometimes this amounts to four-fifths of the year's crops— paid to him in return for having supplied seeds and tools. Or he may expect the United Nations to terrace his lands for him, with all future returns going to him. Or, again, water may be found at a depth which makes its cost too high. Or it may be found in unusable quality, or not at all! Lands offered by the government in some cases have been found to be incapable of supporting crops; or capable of supporting crops for which there

is no accessible market. Thus even though a government may be co-operative, the difficulties involve may make inevitable a long-range international or governmental subsidy. These difficulties explain but partially why so few refugees have found new homes and work.

The policy of the government of Israel with regard to the refugees has been, and is, that Israel cannot agree to repatriation not only because this would create a military threat from within the country but also because lands and housing to take care of such numbers no longer exist. Of the 170,000 Arabs remaining in Israel, some 18,000 are classified as refugees. Most of these are the usual "hard-core" cases—people too old, too sick, or too ill equipped to learn new ways or to become economic assets to their families or villages. Many have been cut off from their relatives. Citizenship has been extended to all Arabs within Israel, and these unfortunate groups of the "hard core" are under the care of the Ministry of Social Welfare.

Among all the discussions about governments and international organizations, sight is often lost of the refugee himself and his attitudes. He and his ideas are the centers of the problem. Misled during the fateful year of 1948, if not before, he has since reaped an increasingly bitter harvest of hates and fears. The leadership of the Palestine Arab community failed him during 1948 and is still offering him short-sighted and negative policies. To undertake some risky generalizations, it might be said that the typical refugee (if such there be) would proportion his bitterness something as follows. First, he would say that the Arab states lost the war, that they encouraged him to leave his home promising his prompt return with their soon-victorious armies, and that they have given him only token friendship in his misery. Next, he would probably blame the United States for his plight since, in his mind, she made Israel possible, aided her, recognized her, and continues to subsidize her. Then the United Nations would come in for its share of antipathy for its early meddling in the war, for the partition-

ing of the Mandate, and for its wretched relief grants. These, by sustaining him in misery away from his home, forcing him to wear cast-off Western clothes, appear to the refugee to place the stamp of international approval on what has happened to him.

The British are hated. Here, the reason is apparent, because they allowed the Jews during Mandate days to gain the strength which they displayed during early May, 1948. The refugee believes that only British orders to halt prevented the British-officered and British-trained Arab Legion of King Abdallah from defeating the Israelis. He feels that if the Western big powers wished, he could return to his home tomorrow. It should be added, however, that absence is making the heart grow fonder, and in some instances the British and their Mandate administration are held in fairly high regard. As a matter of fact, in private conversation one can find refugees whose attitude toward even the Jews reflects the thought, "At least they hired us and brought us business." However, the sum total of official, group, and individual attitude is almost wholly one of dislike.

The fellah, who makes up perhaps 80 percent of the total refugee population, cannot think beyond the negative and unproductive lines indicated above. His formerly secure world of face-to-face relationships with a few well-known persons has vanished. This small world, peopled by relatives and fellow villagers, was small in a geographic sense and small in a psychological sense. Where he still knows *mukhtars*, or former landowners, or shaykhs in the case of the beduins, he still follows their leadership and will do so tomorrow. But in many cases this leadership is no longer available. Accordingly, it is not surprising to find that the fellah is now fairly disorganized and leaderless—an easy prey to all the troubles which feed upon social disorganization. Visited today by an official commission, his confusion may lead him to state a seemingly firm agreement with its suggestions. Another visiting commission tomorrow may find equally firm agreement with a contrary suggestion. Or one

may be met with an emotional aggressiveness wholly inappropriate to the circumstances.

Security now consists of the camp and its rations. The outside world becomes increasingly uninviting. Among the 60 percent of the refugees who live outside camps, crowded into villages, but receiving camp rations, there is a pronounced movement toward the static stability of the organized camps. This may well swell camp enrollments in the near future. With more camps, and thus better medical controls, the annual net increase of births, now about 30,000 annually, would grow. The refugee population is already a remarkably young one. One-half of the total number is under fifteen years of age! This fact may have a bearing on future acceptance of some compromise solution to the over-all problem. Such research as is available shows that the younger age groups produce more individuals willing to find permanent settlement in the host countries than middle or older age groups. Education also appears to lead toward this acceptance, and the 40 percent of children of school age now in UNESCO or other schools will probably increase. But, as of now, schemes for reintegration are minutely scrutinized for the profit which must surely go to the initiators. For example, the few families now engaged in building permanent houses for themselves would not believe that they really were for them. The refugee's age-old suspicion of any official, his psychological and economic insecurity, and his fear of Western colonialism and meddling combine to produce a negative reaction to any proposal. He is not capable of advancing constructive suggestions of his own.

Much has often been said about the possibility of the refugee embracing communism. Insofar as the average fellah is concerned, he probably knows nothing about it or, if he has heard of it, understands it not at all. Among the educated groups of refugees, it is doubtful that communism has made much headway. Rather, with that political know-how which characterizes so much Arab attitude, it is probable that they realize the

strength of their bargaining position vis-à-vis the United Nations and the United States, just as do the Arab governments. Both have learned that they can increase their benefits with no commitments if they just threaten to turn Communist. The use of this tempting position probably accounts for most of the so-called communism which the anxious press reports from time to time. It does not necessarily indicate that the refugees are embracing communism. However, it cannot be denied that Communists have attempted to gain footholds in several areas and camps. Issues are at hand in Israel, the Gaza strip, Lebanon, and West Jordan which can be made to serve their purposes. They will no doubt continue to fish in the troubled waters of the refugee camps, which have for them so many attractions.

In the refugees' world of uprooted families and disturbed emotions, apathy and boredom are frequently marked by violence. Red Cross officials have had their cars burned with no apparent reason except that they were new and shiny and thus probably represented proper targets for the release of tensions. New, permanent-type housing has been torn down by the refugees in some places. Retreat back to the filthy tents of the camps was probably to impress the outside world with their plight. Strikes and work stoppages are almost monthly problems for United Nations administrators. Shootings and threats of shootings often appear to be directed toward the nearest bystander or fellow refugees. Demonstrations are "spontaneously" organized in rapid fashion for visitors. Indeed, irrational violence, one of the inevitable products of individuals living under the strain of being unwanted and of being injured, is a feature of refugee conduct. Finally, the future political allegiance of the refugees vis-à-vis their host governments remains a matter of some doubt. This does nothing to diminish the already too-high emotional content of man and groups.

On the affirmative side, attention must be drawn to the fact that many refugees have wanted and found employment of a sort. Although statistics are lacking, it may be hazarded that

most young, ambitious, and educated refugees have found positions. Of this group many were officials of the former Mandate, teachers, or businessmen. The crying need for trained personnel in the Middle East has aided this movement. Yet it is often said that lawyers and doctors among the refugees have found the fewest opportunities for work which they are willing to accept and are, therefore, among the bitterest groups of all.

It has been estimated that 60 percent of the 85,000 refugees in Syria have found some kind of employment from time to time, even though that country has by no means shown herself to be willing to open her vast, unused tracts of arable land to them. U.N.R.W.A. itself employs close to 6,000 refugees. Possibly 12 percent of the refugees in Jordan have found employment, mostly of short-term varieties. The situation in West Jordan regarding employment is bad. With unemployment among the local population in Lebanon and laws designed to prevent refugees from working there, the situation is also tight in that state. The refugees in the Gaza strip are in the worst possible situation with regard to work. For a time a subsidized weaving project employed 1,800 people out of the 200,000 refugees, but it had to be abandoned. No amount of study has as yet uncovered any viable economic activity in that isolated, poverty-stricken, crowded area.

In all areas, should jobs become available, the refugee can afford to work for lower wages because his minimal wants are supplied by U.N.R.W.A. This "unfair competition" against local inhabitants does not help make the refugee a welcome addition in the host countries and tends to depress prevailing (and already too-low) wage rates. Should training schemes on a mass level be instituted among the refugees and give them skills not enjoyed by local populations, another source of friction may well be created. Further, before this program is instituted, the complicated organizational pluralism from which the Middle East suffers, with competing and overlapping governmental, international, and private agencies, should be tidied up.

The net result of these conditions and attitudes is the growth of the "refugee mentality" which observers can always detect in any similar situation, be it a displaced person camp in Germany or a refugee camp in Lebanon. The feeling of being unwanted has not been lessened by flight into lands of similar culture. Everyone else is blamed for the disaster which has come upon the refugees. Rational criticism is not applied to their own society's ills. No really close ties exist between the different scattered groups in five countries. Apathy becomes compounded with fear, hate, and lack of hope. The desire to return to their own homes, constantly reiterated and always close to the emotional surface, can easily and artificially be stimulated at any time by those wishing to lead them or to divert their thoughts from acceptance of resettlement. As wholesale schemes come and go, the refugee is neither asked what he will give nor what he will accept. The cycle of defeat, failure, mistrust, and ignorance goes on and on with no evident way of breaking it. Further disintegration can be expected. If an effective appeal is ever to be made to the refugee, it will be based on belief and feeling and appreciation for the values of Arab society, not on Western rational thought.

As of now it can be said that, omitting the possibility of repatriation, neither the Arab governments nor the refugees themselves desire to accept what the West would call "the realities of the situation." The emotional, political, and capital investment in the *status quo* is too high. The task is to find *incentives* for a change in these attitudes. The governments must be given proof that this situation is an opportunity for them to lead and direct their countries into eras of greater prosperity and political stability. They must be convinced that it is in their own self-interest to put the wrongs of the past out of their minds and to play a creative role in guiding the forces which will move the Middle East toward a better future. They should note well that they are not in control of those social forces which make political success in the region such a fleeting joy. Time is

not on their side. They must in all fairness be told firmly the limits to which the United States and other Western powers are willing to go in pouring financial and technical aid into the region.

Once this basic change in governmental attitudes has come about, the second step may be taken. This is the effort to change the attitudes of the refugees themselves. Again, *incentives* sufficiently strong must be found. Recent steps toward the release of the refugees' bank accounts, now blocked in Israel, and toward compensating them for property owned in their former villages will encourage the fraction of the refugees now inclined to strike out for a new life. Outside settlement possibilities must be made more attractive than the security and ease of camp rations. The path of economic and social betterment must be discussed openly and frankly in the camps and attached to specific projects. The movement out of camps in whole family or village groups must be ensured, rather than the selection of unrelated individuals for a given project. Progressive landlords in all the areas must be given encouragement, and not labeled Communist.

When the attitudes of the two paramount groups, the governments and the refugees, have changed, the West and the Middle East together must employ all their social inventiveness in an attack on the more technical problems of administration, finance, and natural resources. Since the refugee problem is closely woven into every one of the region's major social facts, this means in essence a guided social and economic revolution. Policy and field co-ordination among the agencies of the United Nations, United States, and others must be realized rapidly. The pioneering roles of nongovernmental organizations which dare to explore projects forbidden to the United Nations and governments must be used to the fullest possible degree. It seems possible that among these experienced, nonofficial private agencies may well be found the key to breaking the existing stalemate. Their programs should, while remaining wholly

independent, receive encouragement. New land, power, and water resources can be discovered and brought into use on terms which serve the many and not the few. Training schemes should be broadened to include both refugee and local populations.

As these, and as yet undiscovered, projects are undertaken, the memory of past sufferings and wrongs may be lessened with the passage of time. The tragedy of 1948 may be turned into profit for the refugee and the country into which he has fled much as Greece profited in the early 1920's from the uprooted Greeks from Asia Minor. The wrongs of the past must not be allowed to dominate the future. Only such a solution as this can change the refugee problem from a self-defeating social problem in the Middle East into a vehicle of progress.

The Crisis in the Near East

For many Americans, crisis in the Near East means oil and the strategic power it represents in the cold war—to be denied to the Soviet Union, secured for the West. In this context, Iran's nationalization of her oil industry has been critical, not only for what it has meant for the British and their largest overseas industrial enterprise, but for its effect upon the stability of the industry in nearby countries, much of it in the hands of Americans. The successful settlement of this dispute by the negotiating of an agreement between Iran and an international oil consortium, together with renegotiated agreements in nearby countries, all of which adhere roughly to the 50-50 sharing principle between owning governments and operating companies, has done much to stabilize this huge Near Eastern industry, at least for the immediate future. The longer future will depend upon the implementation of these agreements and the general political climate of the area. Important as this power resource is in itself, and for its effect upon the economic co-operation of the Near East and the West, nonetheless in total perspective it is of relatively secondary importance.*

* This essay is in part based on the Baker Lecture given by the author in Dallas, Texas, in March, 1954.

Indeed, economically more critical than oil as power and problem is water. One of the paramount changes in the area is the conviction of the masses that an economy of scarcity and their own poverty are no longer necessary nor inevitable, but rather it is possible—and their right—to share in the world's plenty. Americans are as responsible for this growing impression as are the Russians, if not more so. The basic economy of the area is and must continue to be agricultural; and for its development water is essential. Oil revenues may be important to prime the pump of economic development in the area, but if water does not flow on millions of more acres, with all land better tilled and more productive for the masses, the oil may turn out to be a curse instead of a blessing.

The really critical economic problem of the area is whether, by new techniques of irrigation and cultivation and by more socially just distribution of the land and its produce to the masses, the newly awakened hopes of the people for better living can be realized. Both tasks are stupendous, affecting and affected by those many political, social, and cultural problems which force all concerned deeper into the Near East crisis.

The immediate form in which Near Eastern economic problems present themselves is political. Rightly or wrongly, the people of the area believe these problems are primarily political, that political changes and solutions—at both domestic and international levels—must come before economic improvement can be expected.

From the point of view of the United States, absorbed in the cold war and seeing everything in relation to the stark facts of power polarization on this globe, it is only natural that the central political problem and crisis should appear to be in the field of international relations. It shocks Americans to find others who do not feel as they do about Russia and communism; and the very fact that these others do not indicates the modification of such polarization of power now developing. In this respect the Near East is no exception to the rest of Asia. Turkey

[253]

excepted, and to a degree Iran because of her 1,200-mile border with Russia and her plateau as the only barrier between the USSR and Persian Gulf warm-water ports and fabulous oil, the rest of the Near East is really not much alarmed by the Soviet threat. Those responsible for government and policy generally know the issues and danger, but their public is neither so much aware nor concerned.

Everybody, however, from ruler to peasant, is aware of the "Western Problem," which to them is essentially "imperialism" and "colonialism." The drive against Britain for them is basic and to it they can give all zeal and enthusiasm, with the cold war involvement primarily fortunate as a bargaining lever. For them the potential Soviet threat must take second place to the present varied limitations on sovereignty exercised by Britain; they fear the Western emphasis on the Soviet danger is much motivated by the desire to hang on to these privileges and that with the passing of the danger Western privileges may be more difficult to eliminate. One may quarrel with the validity of this judgment, but not with the fact that it is held widely in the Near East; and it is not eliminated, though mitigated, by the Iranian oil and Suez agreements of 1954.

Traditionally a sphere of British influence, the Near East has been primarily Britain's responsibility and problem, but in this clear position other Western powers have been unwilling to leave the British. World War I was concerned with Germany's challenge to this position and was followed by France's, then Italy's, demand to share it. Since World War II the United States has become increasingly involved, whatever be her motivation or conditioning. Pushing both the Near Eastern states and Britain toward an understanding, the United States has attempted to determine a solution for the Palestine problem, to create a Middle East Defense Organization, to effect a compromise on Iranian oil, and to negotiate a Suez settlement. Only the latter half of this program has been successful, but that success has helped to alleviate some of the suspicion and re-

sentment that have accrued to the United States in this middle-
man role. A decade ago American prestige was sky-high, based
as it was on a century of political unconcern, yet with many
cultural and philanthropic relations. Today this prestige is at
low ebb, for in the role of Western leadership the United
States must now share, if not indeed bear, the blame for Near
Eastern political frustration, especially because of previous
claims to philanthropy, Wilsonian self-determination, and the
Atlantic Charter.

To appreciate the liability of the Atlantic Alliance in most
of the Near East one must underscore how deeply, indeed
pathologically, these peoples feel about the British, and therefore to a degree about the West. Deplore it, demolish it ration-
ally though one may, only Westerners are affected, not Near
Easterners: the facts must be faced. In Iran, Americans are not
yet equated with the British, but many suspect them deeply.
In most Arab lands they are probably more distrusted than the
British—primarily because they bear the major responsibility for
the existence of Israel.

Wherever this responsibility is located or, rather, distributed
—for there are shares to go around to all concerned—the important fact to be noted is that there is no peace between Israel
and her neighbors and little prospect of it. An armistice may
be possible, and even enforced by mutual consent and self-
restraint or by a more powerful third party; but peace cannot
be enforced unless one of these powers is prepared to dictate
such enforcement. Each belligerent party to the armistice fears
and watches with suspicion every move of the other lest the
balance of power shift and make dictation by one possible. And
thus far the third power—the United Nations—has been unwilling to dictate beyond the present *status quo* in suspense,
presently becoming more and more acute.

When fear and suspicion stalk and stultify much Western
political life, reflecting the tension everywhere in the world,
the West can scarcely sit in judgment on Israelis and Arabs

[255]

for so regarding each other. The Israeli lives precariously in fear when he cannot trade with his natural environment, and one neighboring ruler announces that it would be worth the sacrifice of ten million Arabs to throw Israel into the sea. The Arab lives in the same atmosphere, convinced that extreme Israeli statements about recovering David's kingdom are real and that Israel is a bridgehead of Western domination of the area, if not politically, then economically. Nor is the situation much helped by American protestations of "impartial friendship," when grants of financial aid to date fail to accord with this profession. One may disagree with and deplore the points of view of both peoples; but they are there, hard up against each other, stubborn and dangerous components of the political crisis in the Near East.

The critical nature of international relations among the countries of the Near East, and between them and the West, arises from a deeper, more difficult and subtle crisis in Near Eastern society itself. The symptoms of this crisis are familiar enough: abolition of monarchy and outlawing of the Muslim Brotherhood in Egypt and the more recent shakeup in that country's leadership, the army *coup* in Syria demanding a return to a civilian rule, the oil nationalization movement and then the sudden overturn in Iran of Dr. Mosaddeq by the army and pro-Shah groups—to mention but a few. These events are impossible without pressure by substantial sections of the public, which is determined above all else to have change, a change that will bring to more of the people more of the benefits of the common life. The essence of the internal political crisis in the Near East is how to replace the poverty of the people by the plenty they are told exists elsewhere in the world, and how to give these same people more voice in the organization and benefits of the state. In all this there develops tension between the people and their governments and leaders when the latter fail to effect satisfactory change and progress. In short,

local Near Eastern politics is so chaotic and critical because it articulates the social revolution now in progress.

Accelerated trade, increased exploitation of resources, varying degrees of industrialization, more desire for and dependence upon manufactured imports, development of internal and external communications, widespread military service, burgeoning bureaucracies, the rapid spread of education, accelerated urbanization—these are but the outstanding phenomena attesting a shift of the center of gravity and power in Near Eastern society. The old dichotomous pattern is passing: no longer is power the monopoly of a small elite—royalty, the landed aristocracy, the men of the law, the pen, and the sword—with the masses on the land and a relatively small group of artisans in the towns depressed and inarticulate and the handful of urban merchants despised and insignificant. Today the middle class is growing rapidly, by economic pressures on both sides and from within. The emergent middle or third social force is demanding an increasing share in the benefits of the common life, and in political power which it believes can guarantee and guard them.

To most Americans and Westerners, this would normally seem well and good, to be viewed as natural and with sympathy, rather than with critical eyes. But in the Near East this change does not enjoy leisure for fulfillment as in Western society; rather it is accelerated by all kinds of complications. The most serious, contributing much to the current social crisis, is the demand that this middle-class revolution include the proletariat, both of the city and countryside. And this internal complicating pressure is compounded by its shrewd application and manipulation by sophisticated communistic groups allied with and orientated to the total impact of the Soviet Union on this area. Moreover, the West and the development of democratic social institutions are embarrassed by the fact that such institutions already borrowed from the West are not only unable in

this society to stand current social strains and to channel the people's deepest desires but seem best to lend themselves to manipulation by the oligarchical aristocracy, which desperately, all too often blindly, clings to its power and privileges.

This social crisis is partially compounded of the fact that Near Eastern peoples are possessed of the Western concept of nationalism and the nation-state but not yet possessed of its reality, which presupposes and demands a degree of social solidarity and homogeneity attained by no Near Eastern state except Turkey and possibly Lebanon and Israel. In others, the gulf between people and rulers, peasants and landlords, tribesmen and townsmen, minorities and Muslims, diverse ethnic and linguistic groups, precludes that degree of unity and stability any state must have to exercise its autonomous functions in the family of nations.

At the heart of this tension is the clash of family and national loyalties. The family or clan has been the basic unit of Near Eastern society for millennia; the ecumenical context in which these units have been more or less loosely welded together has been the religious commune to which they gave allegiance and in which they co-operated for larger ends. Yet today the nation-state and militant nationalism are thrust between these two, claiming to overarch, if not indeed to supersede them. There emerge tensions and fears, hesitation and irresolution on the part of individuals and groups who suspect, generally unconsciously, that ancient values are threatened, and therefore they draw back from wholehearted allegiance to the nation, at least to the state or incumbent government as the nation's claimant representative. Just when the state or government wishes and needs to present a strong front against some opposition or threat, so often a politician's or statesman's family and communal ties will interfere and hopelessly tangle the web of decision.

Part of this crisis in the Near East is that its people are fascinated by all the promises of modernization, including the

dissolute aspects of urbanization and the heady wine of nationalism; yet at the same time they are not sure, but only half-convinced, and deeply distrustful and fearful that down this path, as a price for all this, may lie nemesis and the loss of many values they have long cherished and may too late discover to be of the essence of their social and spiritual integrity.

This drives analysis of the crisis deeper: to the intellectual and spiritual level, where the problem is primarily the relation of Near Eastern and Western ideas of the nature of civilization. At the level of the material and physical, science and technology, the Near East welcomes Westernization, regards it as part of the universal human heritage. But when it comes to Western political, economic, and social ideas and ideals, mores and institutions, they now have second thoughts and doubts. Western nationalism, education and literature, law and secularism—these and other concepts have come to dominate much of the area. Many thoughtful Muslims have begun to wonder if they are not becoming entangled and compromised at the deepest level of philosophical belief and religious faith. Many more irrational, emotional believers, sensing intuitively the danger, flail and rail indiscriminately and intemperately against the West and its influence.

Indeed, lying back of so much politically expressed opposition to the West is the fear that the social penetration and cultural influence of the West may compromise and corrode the basic tenets of their faith, their ideal of the good life, and the traditional world view that undergirds it. It is unconscious and intuitive but nonetheless real. Were the West suddenly to solve the Palestine problem and Middle East defense, in addition to the Suez and Iranian oil, the West would likely soon find other difficulties in its relationships magnified to primary importance. It is the intuitive protest of the materially weaker and less dynamic culture raising warning signs of defense and self-preservation.

The sharp point of this crisis for Muslims is the position

of authority accorded their Holy Book and Law revealed by Allah through the Prophet Muhammad. There has always been substantial secularism in Islamic society and government, but Westernization has so vastly extended its sway that now the *Shari'ah* or Law, in most countries outside the Arabian Peninsula, is limited in authority to matters of personal status: marriage, divorce, inheritance, and the like. Society and culture are in transition, suddenly loosed from old moorings, and the Islamic corporate soul is troubled by the trend, appalled at so much disintegration of morals and mores, convulsed and irresolute as it faces basic decisions that will inevitably shape the future of the Near East, its culture and civilization.

If the impact of the mixed secular and religious culture of the West poses a critical problem in the soul of Islam, how much more the challenge of communism! The attraction of Islamic peoples to communism can be real; it is folly to rely on the current cliché that Islam is a sure bulwark against communism. There is enough in political and social theory and practice in Islam to make authoritarianism, messianic leadership, unified ideological theory and practice, the total and compact co-ordination of all society, attractive to Muslims. Many Soviet methods might be palatable to Muslims could they be sure all Communist promises of material plenty and physical power would be fulfilled. To Asiatics, Soviet attainment of extensive, powerful industrialization quickly is persuasive; and many ask if political and economic freedom, never a much-cherished value or experience of the ordinary Muslim, would not be a cheap enough price to pay for such a result, especially when with it cultural and even religious autonomy are promised.

This critical decision may depend upon how the issue finally confronts the Near East. If clear-cut, with the atheistic implications of dialectical materialism fully comprehended, the deeply rooted religious outlook of true Muslims may bring the rejection of communism. But the economic and social appeal of the new faith may so obscure the ultimate philosophical

basis of it that Muslims would never be presented with a clean decision. It is part of the West's responsibility to help the Near East see that the issue is clarified, not confused; to demonstrate to Muslims that more abiding and abundant rationalization of the economy and final attainment of real independence are only possible in co-operation with the West and the free world; and to prove that only in such co-operation can the abiding and indispensable values of Islam be re-interpreted and preserved for the good of humanity.

This then takes the West back unto itself in the West and the concluding observation that the crisis in the Near East does not belong peculiarly to that area but to all mankind in these days of decision. All those who trace their cultural origins across the millennia to the birth of civilization in the Fertile Crescent of the Ancient Near East have much in common and much at stake in these critical times. There is a sense in which all stand or fall together—or rather that only together can all go forward to a better and more abundant life for the whole man and the whole of humanity.

Westerners face, as do their brothers in the Near East, a theological and philosophical crisis not wholly unlike theirs. For the West the final pattern for the interaction of its highest faith and social institutions has not been found. Scarcely can the West be said to have attained complete and confident self-understanding: where is the West and whither does it go? Moreover, it can fairly be asked whether Americans have attained that serene and wise maturity of national life in which American loyalty patterns and political policies are most meaningful in terms of the full possibilities of human beings and humanity everywhere. In so many instances the political and economic decisions of the nations and peoples of the Near East are contingent upon the prior decisions of the more powerful and autonomous nations and peoples of the West. Americans share more mutuality than their provincialism and pride care to admit.

To meet this crisis, in the Near East and here in the West, there is need for much more understanding between the two areas and cultures at the deepest levels of thought and insight. Near Easterners know the West better than it knows Islam, but even their knowledge is superficial and lacks depth. Most of the Near East think of the West as materialistic, and many in the West return the compliment. A Near Easterner knows as little about what really "makes an American tick" as the American does of him. There has yet to be any creative interaction between Islamic and Western thought; and this must come if each is to attain to that self-knowledge and understanding which is the point of departure for any deeper understanding of the Universal Reality that is their mutual Destiny.

A unique creative contribution of the Near East to humanity is the concept of personal, ethical monotheism, symbolized by Jerusalem, a city holy to all three of the great monotheistic religions. Its history has been one of tragedy, howbeit from its tragedy have issued streams for the healing of the nations. Its faith in the unity of God, the Creator and Redeemer of all mankind, should be reflected in the reality of the unity of one humanity. Instead today the Holy City is rent in tragic twain: each part languishes economically for want of the other and its own fulfillment; each is poisoned politically as it eyes the other in suspicion, if not hatred; two apparently divergently patterned societies question the possibility of co-operation without vital compromise. Yet both claim the same general theology and philosophy, essentially the same basic view of the world and universe. Again in history Jerusalem, meeting place of East and West, symbolizes and epitomizes the crisis of the Near East, of humanity. Is the decision of the drama again to be tragedy? Only the Playwright knows. It is for all in humility and integrity to try to learn to play aright their given parts in mutual trust and co-operation.

Bibliography

MORE than forty thousand books in Western languages on subjects relating to the Near and Middle East have been published in the last century and a half. Many are mere travelogues; others are tracts of dubious value; and few touch upon the subjects presented in the essays of this volume. The literature in the serious and professional periodicals is probably more useful and enlightening with respect to the ideas contained in the present volume. Even in this medium, however, most of the articles, like the books, are concerned with general problems of the area as a whole, with general problems and development of a single country or political unit, or with a specific field or discipline related to one state or province.

A bibliography, therefore, limited to items which more or less parallel the essays of this volume would not be very extensive. An excellent point of departure for anyone wishing to pursue any of the topics of this volume would be *A Selected and Annotated Bibliography of Books and Periodicals in Western Languages Dealing with the Near and Middle East with Special Emphasis on Mediaeval and Modern Times* (Washington, D.C., 1952), *With Supplement* (1954), edited by Richard Ettinghausen. Forty-nine contributors (nine of whom

are contributors to this present volume) have brought together first-rate representative titles on every conceivable subject dealing with the Near and Middle East. Thus one can find listed books on law, religion, anthropology, politics, history, economics, art, geography, education, literature, language, and many other fields.

Some of the more recent books which cover in general the points of view of the several authors and the idea contained in the expression "social forces" are: Harold B. Allen, *Rural Reconstruction in Action: Experiences in the Near and Middle East* (Ithaca, N.Y., 1953); Eleanor Bisbee, *The New Turks* (Philadelphia, Penn., 1951); Alfred Bonné, *State and Economics in the Middle East: A Society in Transition* (London, 1948); W. B. Fisher, *The Middle East: A Physical, Social, and Regional Geography* (London, 1950); Halford S. Hoskins, *Middle East: Problem Area in World Politics* (New York, 1954); J. C. Hurewitz, *Middle East Dilemmas: The Background of United States Policy* (New York, 1953); Nejla Izzeddin, *The Arab World: Past, Present, and Future* (Chicago, 1953); George Kirk, *The Middle East in the War* (London, 1953); George Lenczowski, *The Middle East in World Affairs* (Ithaca, N.Y., 1952); and the Royal Institute of International Affairs, *The Middle East: A Political and Economic Survey* (London, 1954).

The thesis advanced by Professor Speiser in his essay, "Cultural Factors in Social Dynamics in the Near East," is quite original and recent. Other literature directly on this topic does not exist. Professor Speiser has written on several different subjects; perhaps a representative work is his *Mesopotamian Origins* (Philadelphia, 1930). Other works which may help one to fathom the Arab "ethneme" are: Philip K. Hitti, *History of the Arabs from the Earliest Times to the Present* (London, 1953); Bernard Lewis, *The Arabs in History* (London, 1950); Gustave E. von Grunebaum, *Medieval Islam: A Study in Cultural Orientation* (Chicago, 1946); and Nabih Amin Faris, ed., *The Arab Heritage* (Princeton, N.J., 1944). Many periodical arti-

cles are very helpful in understanding the problems involved in describing such an "ethneme." Its complexities may be seen in such articles as: Nabih Amin Faris, "The Arabs and Their History," *The Middle East Journal*, VIII (1954), No. 2, 155–162; Sa'id B. Himadeh, "Economic Factors Underlying Social Problems in the Arab Middle East," *ibid.*, V (1951), No. 3, 269–283; Arthur Jeffery, "The Political Importance of Islam," *Journal of Near Eastern Studies*, I (1942), 383 ff.; E. Shouby, "The Influence of the Arabic Language on the Psychology of the Arabs," *The Middle East Journal*, V (1951), No. 3, 284–302; John A. Wilson, "Islamic Culture and Archaeology," *ibid.*, VIII (1954), No. 1, 1–9; and Costi K. Zurayk, "The Essence of Arab Civilization," *ibid.*, III (1949), No. 2, 125–139.

Of all the topics in this volume, there probably is more literature on "The Nomads" than on any other, perhaps because the West has found them more romantic, more exotic, and more akin to their own prehistoric forebears. Most of the studies are limited to nomads of one particular area of the Middle East, such as H. R. P. Dickson, *The Arab of the Desert* (New York, 1949), and E. E. Evans-Pritchard, *The Sanusi of Cyrenaica* (London, 1949). The few general works on Middle East nomads from central Asia to the Atlantic are best represented by C. U. Ariens-Kappers, *An Introduction to the Anthropology of the Near East in Ancient and Recent Times* (Amsterdam, 1934), and above all by Professor Coon's *Caravan: The Story of the Middle East* (New York, 1951).

What book on the Middle East has not touched upon the village? But only recently have scholars of the West or of the Middle East become interested in the life of the Middle Eastern village. Today many governmental officials advocate land reform as one solution of some of the ills of the area; thus, "The Villager" of the Middle East has emerged as an important person and the serious literature about him and his society has begun to increase. Two very basic and competent studies are: B. A. Keen, *The Agricultural Development of the Middle East*

(London, 1946); and Doreen Warriner, *Land and Poverty in the Middle East* (London, 1948). Other studies of significance are: Carleton S. Coon, *The Impact of the West on Middle Eastern Social Institutions* (New York, 1952); Douglas D. Crary, "Geography and Politics in the Nile Valley," *The Middle East Journal*, III (1949), No. 3, 260–276; W. B. Fisher, "Unity and Diversity in the Middle East," *Geographical Review*, XXXVII (1947), No. 3, 414–435; John Gulick, "Conservatism and Change in a Lebanese Village," *The Middle East Journal*, VIII (1954), No. 3, 295–307; Henry Habib-Ayrout, *The Fellaheen* (Cairo, 1945); Gideon Hadary, "The Agrarian Reform Problem in Iran," *The Middle East Journal*, V (1951), No. 2, 181–196; Mahmut Makal, *A Village in Anatolia*, trans. from the Turkish by Sir Wyndham Deedes and ed. by Paul Stirling (London, 1954); Afif I. Tannous, "The Arab Village Community of the Middle East," in Board of Regents, Smithsonian Institution, *Annual Report, 1943* (Washington, 1944), pp. 523–543; "Land Reform: Key to the Development and Stability of the Arab World," *The Middle East Journal*, V (1951), No. 1, 1–20; and "The Village in the National Life of Lebanon," *ibid.*, III (1949), No. 2, 151–163.

"The Israeli Farmer" of Professor Weinryb's essay has been the subject of numerous articles, and no serious study of modern Palestine or the State of Israel can fail to mention him. R. R. Nathan, O. Gass, and D. Creamer, *Palestine, Problems and Promise: An Economic Study* (Washington, 1946), gives detailed information, without emotional predilections, of the economic and social situation in Palestine before the establishment of Israel. An earlier study of basic economic problems of the state can be found in David Horowitz and Rita Hinden, *Economic Survey of Palestine* (Tel Aviv, 1938). A description of the Seven-Year Plan with chapters devoted to agriculture can be found in the publication of the Ministry of Finance, Government of Israel, *Data and Plans Submitted to*

the Jerusalem Conference (Jerusalem, 1953). A. G. Black, Chief of the Foreign Agricultural Operations Mission in Israel, *Report to the Government of Israel on National Agricultural Plans and Programs* (Rome, 1953), gives a picture of agriculture in Israel with some information on settlement policies and the various types of settlers. Other studies touching upon the Israeli farmer are: S. Koenig, "The Crisis in Israel's Collective Settlements," *Jewish Social Studies*, XIV (1952), 145–167; Hal Lehrman, *Israel, the Beginning and Tomorrow* (New York, 1951); and Jenny Nasmyth, "Israel's Distorted Economy," *The Middle East Journal*, VIII (1954), No. 4, 391–402. Professor Weinryb has written many articles on this and related subjects, among which should be noted: "Economic and Social Forms in Palestine," *Jewish Review*, II (1944), 141–176; "The Lost Generation in Israel," *The Middle East Journal*, VII (1953), No. 4, 415–429; and "Middle Eastern Agriculture in the Inter-War Years," *Agricultural History*, XXVI (1952), 52–59.

"The Industrial Worker," as everyone readily understands, is a newcomer on the Middle Eastern scene, but in an industrial age such as ours he has already become the subject for serious study and consideration. Of interest is the volume of the International Labour Office, *Labour Conditions in the Oil Industry in Iran* (Geneva, 1950). With special reference to Palestine are: Gerhard Münzner, *Jewish Labour Economy in Palestine* (London, 1945); and *Labor Enterprise in Palestine* (New York, 1947). The latter of these describes the enterprises owned by *Histadruth*, the largest Israeli labor union. William J. Handley, "The Labor Movement in Egypt," *The Middle East Journal*, III (1949), No. 3, 277–292, discusses some of the topics mentioned by Mr. Stauffer in his essay in this volume. A study with special reference to rural aspects of this problem is Beatrice McC. Mattison, "Rural Social Centers in Egypt," *ibid.*, V (1951), No. 4, 461–480. An important study on similar industrial labor problems in India is Radhakamal Mukerjee,

The Indian Working Class (Bombay, 1945). Another contribution by Mr. Stauffer is his "Labor Unions in the Arab States," *The Middle East Journal*, VI (1952), No. 1, 83–88.

There is considerable literature on workers' problems in underdeveloped areas in general and the reader may find much pertinent information in Wilbert E. Moore, *Industrialization and Labor* (Ithaca, N.Y., 1951), Bert F. Hoselitz, *The Progress of Underdeveloped Areas* (Chicago, 1952), or H. W. Singer, "Economic Progress in Underdeveloped Countries," *Social Research*, XVI (March, 1949), 1–11. Of special interest is Simon Rottenberg, "Labor's Role in Industrialization," *Annals of the American Academy of Political and Social Science*, CCLXXXV (January, 1953), 85–90, and UNESCO, "Social Implications of Technological Change," *International Social Science Bulletin*, IV (Summer, 1952).

For the past several centuries the West has had considerable interest in commercial ventures in the Middle East, and in the present century industrial development in the area has attracted the West. Literature on "The Bazaar Merchant," as such, is negligible, and references to his attitudes and his role in society are scattered in works more generally appraising the economic and commercial affairs of the Middle East. Together with "The Entrepreneur Class" and "The Economic Planners," there can be considered a wide variety of studies on the economic phase of Middle Eastern social development. To view social forces at work on economic behavior it should be worth while to examine some universal problems as presented in Floyd H. Allport, *Institutional Behavior* (Chapel Hill, N.C., 1933); Nels Anderson, *Urban Sociology* (New York, 1935); and George C. Homans, *The Human Group* (London, 1951). Many references to the economic background of the Middle East are to be found in H. A. R. Gibb and Harold Bowen, *Islamic Society and the West: A Study of the Impact of Western Civilization on Moslem Culture in the Near East*, I, Part I (London, 1950).

To consider the area by countries, an excellent survey of all branches of the economy and the main social trends in Egypt is found in Charles Issawi, *Egypt at Mid-Century* (London, 1954). Another view is expressed in A. A. I. El-Gritly, "The Structure of Modern Industry in Egypt," *L'Egypte Contemporaine*, Nos. 341–342 (1947), pp. 363–582. Probably there are more studies of the economic development of Turkey than of any of the other states of the region. A beginning can be made with Donald E. Webster, *The Turkey of Atatürk: Social Process in the Turkish Reformation* (Philadelphia, 1939). Further surveys and analyses are: International Bank for Reconstruction and Development, *The Economy of Turkey: An Analysis and Recommendations for a Development Program* (Baltimore, 1951); Max Weston Thornburg, Graham Spry, and George Soule, *Turkey: An Economic Appraisal* (New York, 1949); and E. R. Lingeman, *Turkey: Economic and Commercial Conditions in Turkey* (London, 1948). Countless specialized articles have appeared recently. To mention only two: William Diamond, "The Industrial Development Bank of Turkey," *The Middle East Journal*, IV (1950), No. 3, 349–352; and Robert W. Kerwin, "Private Enterprise in Turkish Industrial Development," *ibid.*, V (1951), No. 1, 21–38. Likewise, a survey of the problems of the Syrian and Lebanese economies can be found in Sa'id B. Himadeh, *Economic Organization of Syria* (Beirut, 1936). Similarly, for Iraq one should read: F. H. Gamble, *Iraq: Economic and Commercial Conditions in Iraq* (London, 1949); International Bank for Reconstruction and Development, *The Economic Development of Iraq* (Baltimore, 1952); and Norman Burns and Brad Fisk, "Development Projects in Iraq," *The Middle East Journal*, V (1951), No. 3, 362–370. For Afghanistan, one should begin with Peter G. Franck, "Problems of Economic Development in Afghanistan," *ibid.*, III (1949), Nos. 3 and 4, 293–314, 421–440. Other valuable sources for economic affairs in Afghanistan are: V. Cervin, "Problems in the Integration of the Afghan Nation," *ibid.*, VI (1952),

No. 4, 400–416; S. N. Shah, *Trade with Afghanistan* (Kabul, 1946); A. C. Jewett, *An American Engineer in Afghanistan* (Minneapolis, 1948); Martin H. Ekker, *Economic Aspects of Development of Afghanistan*, Technical Assistance Administration, United Nations (New York, 1952); and U.S. Senate, 83d Congress, 2d Session, Committee on Banking and Currency, *Obtaining Financial Aid for a Development Plan* (Washington, D.C., 1954). S. Rezazadeh Shafaq and J. D. Lotz, "The Iranian Seven Year Development Plan," *The Middle East Journal*, IV (1950), No. 1, 100–105, gives an idea of economic planning and its problems in Iran. The works on this subject referring to Palestine and Israel are legion. Two of the standard works are: W. C. Lowdermilk, *Palestine, Land of Promise* (New York, 1944); and James Buchanan Hays and A. E. Barrekette, *T. V. A. on the Jordan: Proposals for Irrigation and Hydroelectric Development in Palestine* (Washington, 1948). An economic survey for the whole of the Middle East can be found in Hedley V. Cooke, *Challenge and Response in the Middle East: The Quest for Prosperity, 1919–1951* (New York, 1952). Another more specialized survey for the entire area is Feliks Bochenski and William Diamond, "TVA's in the Middle East," *The Middle East Journal*, IV (1950), No. 1, 58–82, which has been considered so significant that it has been translated into Arabic and published in Cairo.

"The Role of the Army Officer in Middle Eastern Politics" is a subject which can be treated easily if one is content with a superficial examination. Few critical studies have, as yet, appeared. For Egypt, considerable insight is revealed in Rashed el-Barawy, *The Military Coup in Egypt: An Analytic Study* (Cairo, 1952), and the power and role of the Muslim Brotherhood is presented in J. Heyworth-Dunne, *Religious and Political Trends in Modern Egypt* (Washington, 1950). The episodes in Syria are treated in: Alford Carleton, "The Syrian Coups d'Etat of 1949," *The Middle East Journal*, IV (1950), No. 1,

1–11; and Majid Khadduri, "Constitutional Development in Syria," *ibid.*, V (1951), No. 2, 137–160.

Religion is fundamental to the Middle East, and "The Clergy in Islam" has always been an interesting subject for the West, perhaps because the West was never sure whether or not Islam had a clergy. Certainly books and articles on Islam and its position in the modern world are being published almost every month. Two well worth considering are: H. A. R. Gibb, ed., *Whither Islam?* (London, 1932); and H. A. R. Gibb, *Modern Trends in Islam* (Chicago, 1947). Reaction of leaders of Islam to modern developments and to Western thought are well presented by Eastern writers in Sir Muhammad Iqbal, *The Reconstruction of Religious Thought in Islam* (Lahore, 1944); and Sayed Kotb, *Social Justice in Islam*, trans. by J. B. Hardie (Washington, 1953). The attitudes of Islamic leaders to Western secularism, democracy, and communism are voiced in Dorothea Seelye Franck, ed., *Islam in the Modern World* (Washington, 1951). The needs for an Islamic "Reformation" to meet the challenge of the Western world are outlined by John S. Badeau, "Evolution in Religion," in Sydney Nettleton Fisher, ed., *Evolution in the Middle East: Reform, Revolt and Change* (Washington, 1953), pp. 13–22.

"The Intellectual in the Modern Development of the Islamic World" can be seen in Sir Muhammad Iqbal, *The Reconstruction of Religious Thought in Islam* (Lahore, 1944), for, without doubt, Iqbal is one of the great intellectuals of the Middle East in recent years. An interesting viewpoint on this subject is given in Kenneth Cragg, "The Intellectual Impact of Communism upon Contemporary Islam," *The Middle East Journal*, VIII (1954), No. 2, 127–138. Pertinent material on this subject may also be found in T. Cuyler Young, ed., *Near Eastern Culture and Society: A Symposium on the Meeting of East and West* (Princeton, N.J., 1951).

Supporting evidence on the role of "The Minorities" in the

political process of the Middle East is widely scattered and often elusive. Helen Miller Davis has assembled many, though not all, of the relevant organic and electoral instruments in *Constitutions, Electoral Laws, Treaties of States in the Near and Middle East* (Durham, 1953). Readers interested in the Ottoman background will profit from the general treatments in Arnold J. Toynbee and Kenneth P. Kirkwood, *Turkey* (New York, 1927); and Sir Harry Luke, *The Making of Modern Turkey* (London, 1936). A. H. Hourani provides illuminating descriptive data on the situation in the Arab East at the close of World War II in *Minorities in the Arab World* (London, 1947). Recent information on all of the countries covered in the present essay may be gleaned from *The Middle East: A Political and Economic Survey* (London, 1954), prepared by the information department of the Royal Institute of International Affairs. More specialized works are: Siegfried Landshut, *Jewish Communities in the Muslim Countries of the Middle East* (London, 1950); Clyde G. Hess, Jr., and Herbert L. Bodman, Jr., "Confessionalism and Feudality in Lebanese Politics," *The Middle East Journal*, VIII (1954), No. 1, 10–26; and Don Peretz, "The Arab Minority of Israel," *ibid.*, VIII (1954), No. 2, 139–154.

A study valuable as background information for an understanding of the political, military, and constitutional problems facing "The Immigrant in Israel" is David Ben-Gurion, *Rebirth and Destiny of Israel* (New York, 1954). Factual summaries of the progress made in the absorption of immigrants are contained in the annual *Government Yearbook*, published in Jerusalem by the State of Israel. The different cultural backgrounds of the immigrants and their adjustment to life in Israel are discussed in Raphael Patai, *Israel between East and West: A Study in Human Relations* (Philadelphia, 1953). Educational work and settlement problems of the Oriental Jewish immigrants are reviewed in Carl Frankenstein, ed., *Between Past and Future: Essays and Studies on Aspects of Immigrant Absorp-*

tion in Israel (Jerusalem, 1953). Special studies on limited aspects of the problem of health, agriculture, public institutions, etc., are found in: Abraham A. Weinberg, "Acculturation and Integration of Migrants in Israel," *International Social Science Bulletin*, V (1953), No. 4, 702–710; Zena Harman, "The Assimilation of Immigrants into Israel," *The Middle East Journal*, V (1951), No. 3, 303–318; and Raphael Patai, "Jewish 'Refugees' in the Middle East," *Journal of International Affairs*, VII (1953), No. 1, 51–56.

As for "The Palestine Arab Refugee," there is as yet no adequate study of the personal attitudes and reactions of the refugee himself. Objective studies of the Arab refugee problem as a whole are few. Valuable information is contained in the *Annual Reports*, issued since 1951, by the Director of the U.N.R.W.A., and in the *Reports* of the United Nations Mediator and of the United Nations Conciliation Commission. Another document with much interesting material is *Palestine Refugee Program*, Hearings before a subcommittee of the Senate Foreign Relations Committee, 83d Congress, 1st Session (Washington, 1953). The best review of the resettlement question is contained in S. G. Thicknesse, *Arab Refugees: A Survey of Resettlement Possibilities* (London, 1949). Joseph B. Schechtman, *The Arab Refugee Problem* (New York, 1952), is not objective in its point of view. There are many articles on the subject. Among the better are: W. de St. Aubin, "Peace and Refugees in the Middle East," *The Middle East Journal*, III (1949), No. 3, 249–259; Channing B. Richardson, "United Nations Relief for Palestine Refugees," *International Organization*, IV (1950), No. 1; "The Refugee Problem," *Proceedings of the Academy of Political Science*, XXIV (1952), No. 4; Georgiana G. Stevens, "Arab Refugees: 1948–1952," *The Middle East Journal*, VI (1952), No. 3, 281–298; James Baster, "Economic Aspects of the Settlement of the Palestine Refugees," *ibid.*, VIII (1954), No. 1, 54–68; Don Peretz, "The Arab Refugee Dilemma," *Foreign Affairs*, XXXIII (1954), No. 1;

and "Problems of Arab Refugee Compensation," *The Middle East Journal*, VIII (1954), No. 4, 403-416. Another refugee article discussing the enigma of the attitudes of the refugee is Fred C. Bruhns, "A Study of Arab Refugee Attitudes," *ibid.*, IX (1955), No. 2, 130–138. A slightly different refugee problem of the Middle East is presented in Huey Louis Kostanick, "Turkish Resettlement of Refugees from Bulgaria, 1950–1953," *ibid.*, IX (1955), No. 1, 41–52.

There are a number of books and articles paralleling the essay by Professor Young. Many of those cited in the third paragraph above touch upon a number of his points. One of the better articles presenting many of the problems outlined, or at least suggested in this volume, may be found in Farid Hanania, "Political Evolution," in Sydney Nettleton Fisher, ed., *Evolution in the Middle East: Reform, Revolt and Change* (Washington, 1953), pp. 31–41. Westernization problems are presented in Raphael Patai, "The Dynamics of Westernization in the Middle East," *The Middle East Journal*, IX (1955), No. 1, 1–16. The reaction of Middle Easterners to communism is discussed in Walter Z. Laqueur, "The Appeal of Communism in the Middle East," *ibid.*, IX (1955), No. 1, 17–27.

Index

[No reference in this index is made to Arab, Islam, Muslim, Middle East, and Near East. Because of the variety of the topics discussed, only proper names have been indexed.]

Armenians, 37, 96, 124, 127, 128, 129, 130, 205, 208, 210, 214, 215, 218, 219
Arnold, T. W., 188
Ashkenazi Jews, 224, 229, 230
Asia Minor, 7, 16, 18, 118, 119, 215, 251
al-Askari, Jafar, 182
Assaili, 121
Assyrian, 173, 175, 222
Atatürk, Mustafa Kemal, 14, 15, 20, 21, 128, 171, 177, 181, 198
Atlantic Charter, 255
Atlantic Ocean, 34
Atrek, 41
Ait Attas, 34, 36, 37
Australia, 42, 120
Azhar University, 166, 169, 196
al-Azim, Khaled, 131

Babol, 41
Babylonia, 18
Badawi (Badu), 26, 29, 30, 31, 32, 33
Baghdad, 38, 100, 102, 103, 194, 218
Bakhtiyaris, 36, 37, 39, 205, 207
Balkans, 220, 222, 224, 229
Baluchis, 33, 34, 40, 41
Baluchistan, 33
al-Banna, Shaykh Hasan, 167
Banque Misr, 125, 126, 127, 134
Barzanis, 38
Basra, 117
Beirut, 89, 100, 103, 105, 106, 119, 120
Belgium (Belgian), 122, 123
Benhazera, 28
Berbers, 26, 34, 35
Biqa', 92, 103
Black Sea, 44, 118
Bokhara, 41, 87
Bonaparte, 118
Boston, 34
Brahuis, 33, 34
Brazil, 120
Britain (British), see Great Britain
Bulgaria, 222, 230
Bu Yahyi, beni, 28

Cairo, 118, 166, 191, 270
Caliphate, 185, 213
Capitulations, 118, 133
Carr, E. H., 136
Caspian Sea, 40, 44
Caucasus, 117
Central Bank of Afghanistan, 151
Central Bank of Turkey, 128
Chaldeans, 210
China, 117, 120, 194
Christians (Christian Churches), 2, 19, 44, 60, 96, 118, 119, 121, 122, 184, 188, 201, 202, 206, 207, 208, 209, 210, 211, 212, 213, 214, 215, 217, 220, 225, 226
Circassians, 211, 217
Committee of Union and Progress, 218, 219
Communist, 22, 36, 39, 78, 91, 96, 97, 163, 170, 174, 212, 247, 250, 260
Constantinople, see Istanbul
Copts, 127, 210, 219
Corsica, 36
Cromer, Lord, 124
Crusaders, 117
Cyprus, 92
Cyrenaica, 29
Czechs, 134

Damascus, 87, 88, 100, 103, 105, 106, 121, 122, 140, 224
Daniel, Ezra Menahem, 211
Dasht-i-Lut, 33
David, King, 256
Detroit, 84
Devotees, see Fida'iyan
Dewey, John, 193, 197
Dhahran, 32
Diaspora, 65
Dickson, 29
Dravidians, 33
Druzes, 205, 207, 208, 217
Dutch, 123
Duveyrier, 28

East Indies, 222
Egypt (Egyptians), 12, 13, 14, 18, 19, 21, 22, 26, 45, 47, 48, 50, 56, 85,